THEORIES OF ETHICS

Edited by
PHILIPPA FOOT

OXFORD UNIVERSITY PRESS

Oxford University Press

OXFORD LONDON NEW YORK

GLASGOW TORONTO MELBOURNE WELLINGTON

CAPE TOWN IBADAN NAIROBI DAR ES SALAAM LUSAKA ADDIS ABABA

DELHI BOMBAY CALCUTTA MADRAS KARACHI LAHORE DACCA

KUALA LUMPUR SINGAPORE HONG KONG TOKYO

ISBN 0 19 875005 6

First published 1967
Reprinted 1968, 1970, 1974

FILMSET BY ST PAUL'S PRESS, MALTA
PRINTED IN GREAT BRITAIN
AT THE UNIVERSITY PRESS, OXFORD
BY VIVIAN RIDLER
PRINTER TO THE UNIVERSITY

CONTENTS

INTRODUCTION

I

THE ARTICLES reprinted here centre round two topics lately much debated: firstly the nature of moral judgement, and secondly the part played by social utility in determining right and wrong. Both these debates go back to the eighteenth century, for at that time philosophers divided for and against the moral sense and intellectualist theories of moral judgement, and at the end of the century Bentham laid down that the principle of utility was the foundation of moral good.

The later articles in the volume (numbers IX–XII) are quite simply about utilitarianism, so their relation to the past is clear. Numbers I–VIII are less obviously related to the subject of eighteenth-century battles; but nevertheless the connexion is close. Like ourselves Hume and his contemporaries were concerned with the possible, or impossible, objectivity of moral judgements. In what, they asked, did the virtuousness of virtuous actions consist? How was it apprehended? Was it rather judged of or felt? Did we know what we ought to do by the intellect or by a moral sense? Was there, indeed, anything there to be known, or did moral discourse rather express our feelings than speak of our discoveries about virtue and vice? Hume himself decided that the search for objective moral properties was vain, and argued that in calling an action virtuous we say nothing but that we feel a pleasing sentiment of approbation in contemplating it, a theory that seemed to explain how moral judgements were linked to action. For we shall naturally be concerned to do, and to promote, what affects us in this pleasing way, whereas if the morality of actions were said to lie in something of which our reason tells us it would have to be shown why this discovery should have a necessary influence on the will.

One might say that the problems that trouble us at the present time are precisely Hume's problems. More directly, however, it has been Professor G. E. Moore who has set the stage for us, and the name of Hume does not even appear in the index of Moore's *Principia Ethica*. It is as if we have started with Moore and then worked back from him to Hume. Let us first then say something about the immensely influential arguments advanced by Moore in 1903.[1] Moore's central thesis was that goodness is a simple non-natural property discovered by intuition. The rest of his ethics was built on this foundation, since Moore believed that other moral judgements, for instance those about right action, were related to the basic intuitions of goodness, right action being action that produced the greatest possible amount of good. This last belief made Moore into a kind of utilitarian, but it is not this part of his theory that has interested people most. What seemed particularly important, at least in succeeding generations, was his idea about the judgement that got the whole thing going. Moore insisted that these judgements were objective, and he explained that they were made by intuition. He is therefore called an intuitionist, sharing this label with philosophers such as Prichard and Ross who agreed that moral intuition was the basis of moral judgement, even if they disagreed about where the intuitions came in. An intuitionist is one who believes that in the end we must 'see' that certain things are good, or right, or obligatory. Up to a certain point, they say, one may argue a question of morals, showing that individual cases fall under particular principles by the nature of the facts; but in the end one is driven back to a point at which one can say nothing but 'I see it to be so'.

The difficulties in this position are by now clear enough, and he would be a brave man who would assert, like Ross in the middle thirties, that 'every ethical system admits intuition at some point'. For moral intuition, unlike the ordinary kind of intuition that tells one what someone else is thinking or feeling, is supposed to be the 'apprehension' of a quality whose presence cannot be discovered in any other way. Now of course if one knows intuitively that, for instance, someone who is showing no obvious signs of it is angry, then one says 'I just know'. But one learns what it is to be angry from the other cases, and in principle one can put a check on one's intuitions by taking evidence that would settle the matter. Thus one discovers whether, or in which cases, one can trust one's intuitions, and some people's intuitions are demonstrably better than others because more closely correlated with the independently established facts. This independent check is just what is lacking for the supposed moral intuitions, and attempts to assimilate the two by talking, for instance, about intuitions that 'stand the test of time' or those of 'more highly

---

[1] G. E. Moore, *Principia Ethica*. (See Bibliography for all publications whose details are not given in the footnotes to this Introduction.)

developed peoples' are simply a cheat. For what tells us that the correct moral intuitions may not be those that we think of first but later abandon ('first thoughts are best')? What tells us that primitive peoples do not have a faculty of correct moral intuition that civilization tends to destroy?

It seems, then, that the intuitionist's talk about 'apprehension' and 'seeing' is unjustified given his own premises; so also his claim that the man who 'judges' on the basis of his 'moral intuition' is putting forward an opinion about an objective matter. For without any method that could, even in principle, decide between conflicting intuitions we seem to have 'the mere trappings of correction'. I say 'I am right and you are wrong' and 'I was wrong when I said . . .', but these sentences merely express a reaction. And if they merely express a reaction we are not far from the subjectivist theories that Moore and the other intuitionists rejected.

Why then, given the difficulties, did Moore support a theory of moral intuition against those who, like Hume, saw moral judgements as an expression of the speakers' feelings or attitudes? Moore's arguments against these theories are the subject that he and Professor C. L. Stevenson are debating in the first and second essays in this volume.

Moore had argued[1] that a man who says that a certain action is right or wrong cannot simply *mean* that he has a feeling of approval, or any other feeling or attitude, towards it. For, he says, that would imply that when one speaker says 'X is right' and another 'X is wrong' X would be both right and wrong; and when a man says at one time 'X is right' and at another 'X is wrong' that same individual action X would be at one time right and at another wrong. Stevenson counters by suggesting that 'X is right' means 'I now approve of X', arguing that if *consistently* applied this would have neither of the consequences suggested by Moore. Thus we cannot say, with Moore, that 'If "X is right" said by A is true, then *X is right*' and if ' "X is wrong" said by B is true *X is wrong*' for the conclusions, when translated, becomes '*I* approve (disapprove) of X' and I may be a different person from A or B. Moore has, however, a third argument which Stevenson is prepared to allow some plausibility. He says that a subjective 'attitude theory' fails to provide for the disagreement that clearly exists between two speakers who say 'X is right' and 'X is wrong' respectively. For if each is speaking only of his own feelings how will they contradict each other? Perhaps one has the feeling and one does not. Stevenson's

[1] *Ethics*, ch. iii.

reply is that there is indeed no logical incompatibility between the two statements: that the speakers do not necessarily hold contradictory *beliefs*. Nevertheless there is disagreement between them, since their attitudes are opposed. It is the expression of opposed attitudes that gives the opposition between A's 'X is right' and B's 'X is wrong', and it is in this way only that they need 'disagree'.

Stevenson is here drawing on the theory of the emotive meaning of ethical terms, which goes back to the discussions of the Vienna Circle in 1918–19, and was stated clearly by Ogden and Richards in 1923 when they wrote, in *The Meaning of Meaning*, that in moral language '. . . the word "good" serves only as an emotive sign expressing our attitude . . . and perhaps evoking similar attitudes in other persons or inciting them to actions of one kind or another'.[1] The theory had also been advanced by Professor A. J. Ayer in *Language, Truth and Logic*, but had nowhere been expounded in such detail as in Stevenson's articles in *Mind* for 1937 and 1938, and he was further to develop it in *Ethics and Language* published in 1945. There he says that a word's emotive meaning is what makes it suitable for such 'dynamic' purposes as expressing our own attitudes and changing those of other people, rather than the 'descriptive' purpose of communicating beliefs. The emotive meaning of a word is its tendency to produce *affective* responses in the hearer, and to be used as a result of *affective* states in the speaker.

Confronted by the suggestion that ethical disagreement might be merely disagreement in attitude, Moore, who characteristically said that this possibility had 'simply not occurred' to him, agreed that his arguments had been inconclusive. The cause of ethical objectivism now seemed in a bad way. As put forward by Moore it had involved the dubious notion of ethical intuition, and the arguments in its favour had collapsed. Meanwhile it was Moore himself who had attacked the other form of objectivism that might have held the field. For he had insisted that no definition of goodness could exist to link the property with provable matters of fact. Thus it was impossible to say, for instance, that 'good' just *meant* productive of happiness, when it might have been provable that certain things were good. Moore said that such theories committed the 'naturalistic fallacy', and this time he found the emotivists on his side.

That Moore's arguments against naturalism are inconclusive is the thesis of the third article in this volume, which is largely taken up with the discussion of what those arguments were. Moore thinks that no one has the right to put forward propositions such as 'pleasure

[1] p. 125.

and pleasure alone is good' on the basis of a definition: such state-ments must always be synthetic and never analytic. But what exactly is the 'fallacy' supposed to be? Professor Frankena considers three possible suggestions: (i) that the mistake is that of defining a non-natural property like goodness in terms of a natural one, (ii) that it is the mistake of defining one property in terms of *another*, and (iii) that it is an attempt to define the indefinable. Frankena argues that whichever version we take Moore has failed to show that any mistake is involved and has in fact simply begged the question. To establish (i) he would have to show that goodness *is* a non-natural property, which he simply states. For (ii) he would have to show, for each example, that goodness was 'some other thing' from the property with which it was being equated, and this he does not do. To establish (iii) he would have to prove that goodness is a simple and therefore indefinable property, which is something he asserts without proof.

Frankena says, and is surely right in saying, that Moore believed the naturalistic fallacy to be committed by any definition of good; but it is not this that later writers have in mind when they think of Moore as the great opponent of naturalistic ethics. They themselves are interested in ruling out a certain *type* of definition, and go back to what Moore said about the impossibility of identifying natural with non-natural properties. Unfortunately, however, Moore had never succeeded in explaining what he meant by a 'natural' property; the nearest he came to it was in saying that the goodness of a thing did not belong to its description as its natural properties did. So it did not seem clear what kind of definition was to be excluded. Stevenson, however, claimed that his theory of emotive meaning showed the truth for which Moore had been groping. The point was not that goodness was a special kind of property, for it was no property at all; rather there was a special kind of meaning belonging to ethical terms, and the defective definitions were those that omitted this emotive element in the meaning of 'good'. Thus Moore's non-naturalism could be defended while his intuitionism was undermined. We may notice that the emotivists and intuitionists are alike in one important way: both deny that moral propositions are open to ordinary kinds of proof. The intuitionist says that in the end one must say 'I just see that it is so', while the emotivist admits that he will be driven back to the expression of his fundamental attitudes. For both the argument will come to an end once all the facts have been exposed.

For a number of years it was emotivism, and theories related to

emotivism, that held the centre of the stage. Of related theories the
most influential was that developed by Professor Hare, which came
to be known under the label of 'prescriptivism'. Hare replaced
Stevenson's 'emotive meaning' with his own 'evaluative meaning',
explaining that words like 'good' and 'ought' were used 'evaluatively'
(to make 'value judgements') when they were used 'with commendatory force'. As so used they entailed imperatives, for Hare says that
he makes it a matter of definition that if someone is using the judgement 'I ought to do X' as a value judgement he must recognize that '. . .
if he assents to the judgement he must also assent to the command
"Let me do X"'.[1] Thus a man who uses the word 'good' evaluatively
must accept a first person imperative, and behind each particular
imperative will lie a general 'quasi-imperative' addressed, as it were,
to all persons at all times. Hare is not denying that words such as
'good' and 'ought' can be used 'non-evaluatively', but the definition
is supposed to have some rough correspondence with what we would
mean by a value judgement in everyday life. With evaluative meaning
Hare contrasts descriptive meaning, but like Stevenson gives no
account of this side of the dichotomy. To be descriptive a word must
be non-evaluative, so that he says there must be 'definite criteria for
its application which do not involve the making of a value judgement'.
A word may have both descriptive and evaluative meaning, but is
called a 'descriptive word' only if there is no evaluative element.

Thus equipped Hare proceeds to launch a full scale attack on ethical
naturalism, defining a naturalist as one who tries to equate value
words with those whose meaning is 'purely descriptive' and who
therefore believes he could deduce an ethical conclusion from
descriptive premises. The price of naturalism, says Hare, is the loss
of the commendatory or action-guiding force of the ethical terms,
and one of the great advantages that he claims for his own theory is
that it shows how moral judgement is necessarily connected with
choice. Indeed both Stevenson and Hare seemed to have provided for
the necessary connexion between morality and the will on which
Hume had insisted. In Stevenson the connexion between moral
judgement and action was built into the theory of emotive meaning:
an emotive word expresses the speaker's attitudes, which the listener
is thereby invited to share, and since an attitude is 'marked by
stimuli and responses which relate to hindering or assisting whatever
it is that is called the "object" of the attitude' this means that
the use of an emotive term tends to express the speaker's willingness

[1] R. M. Hare, *The Language of Morals*, p. 168.

to do certain things, and to influence the hearer in a similar direction. Hare, as we saw, had connected the evaluative use of language with the acceptance of first person imperatives, and quasi-imperatives addressed to the world at large. He could, therefore, claim that on his theory value judgements were essentially 'action guiding', bearing this relation both to the speaker's own actions and to those of other people. Picking up Hume's assertion that moral judgements are necessarily practical he connects this with Hume's famous dictum about the gap between 'is' and 'ought'. An 'ought' cannot be deduced from any descriptive statement, since 'oughts' have this special connexion with the direction of choices, and 'is' statements do not.

It is this position that Hare is defending against Professor Geach in the fifth article reprinted here. In his attack Geach had argued against Hare's explanation of the 'action-guiding' function of the word 'good', and so against his theory of evaluative meaning. Geach agrees with Hare that 'good' is an action-guiding word, for it belongs to the idea of *goodness* that normally and other things being equal people should choose things that they call good. But this does not mean that when used in its normal sense the word must be used 'for commending'. On any particular occasion the direction of choices may simply not be in question, and the word is not then used in any special way. Thus there is nothing to stop an expression of the 'good F' type from having a straightforward descriptive sense.

Geach does, however, see a difficulty in his own position. For suppose that the expression 'a good action' has a fixed descriptive meaning, and we can pass, say, from the fact that an action is an act of adultery to the fact that it is a bad human act. How are we to get from the supposedly descriptive sentence 'adultery is a bad human act' to the imperative 'you must not commit adultery'? Why should the thought that it is a bad action deter anyone from doing it? Geach replies that 'although calling a thing "a good A" or "a bad A" is not of itself something that touches the agent's desires, it may be expected to if the hearer happens to be choosing an A'.[1] And what a man cannot fail to be choosing is his manner of acting; so to call a manner of acting good or bad cannot but serve to guide action.

Not surprisingly Hare finds this reply quite unsatisfactory. He argues that if 'man' and 'action' are taken as functional words like 'knife' and 'soldier' then 'good knife' and 'good soldier' will of course have a 'fixed descriptive meaning'. But then it will no longer be true that what no one can fail to be choosing is his manner of

[1] See p. 71.

acting. For it could very well be that some individual had no interest in doing those things which make a man a good man, when he would choose his actions under some other heading and by other principles of choice. Geach has, therefore, failed to account for the fact that moral judgement, unlike some others of the 'good A' form, must be action guiding for *each* man whatever his particular desires. Hare himself had guaranteed this by insisting that 'good' when used evaluatively carries in its meaning a commitment to choice. Before a functional word such as 'soldier' it is not so used, or rather its evaluative import is neutralized by the word 'soldier'. For this word introduces a special point of view from which a choice would be made, so that it is as if one were saying '*if* trying to be a good soldier that is what I must do'. An expression which is, as a whole, evaluative, is one that carries an actual, not a hypothetical, rule of action, and this is what a moral judgement must surely be.

The problem that was vexing Geach was also troubling the present editor when she wrote the article 'Moral Beliefs', printed as number VI in this volume. In the first half of the article I had argued against the idea of an evaluative element in the meaning of the word 'good' which should be independent of its descriptive meaning, saying that we cannot make sense of the notion that a man is thinking 'this is a good action' if he brings the wrong sort of evidence to show that it *is* a good action. Nor will it necessarily help to appeal to feelings that he has, for there are some feelings that cannot be attributed to a man unless he has the right thoughts. This part of the article suggested that the expression 'a good action' had a fixed descriptive meaning, or at least that it was fixed within a certain range.

Now, this, though it has been in fact rejected by emotivists and prescriptivists, who think it a contingent matter if *our* evaluative terms possess a fixed descriptive meaning, is not right at the centre of the dispute between the two parties. For the anti-naturalist could agree that an expression such as 'good action' had a fixed descriptive meaning while still arguing for an extra 'volitional element' in value judgements. Perhaps a man who calls an action a good action must apply certain descriptions to it but *also* have certain feelings or attitudes, or accept particular rules of conduct? How else is the action-guiding force of the word to be maintained? In the second part of the article I suggested that it could perfectly well be given by the particular facts with which the goodness of a good action is connected. For some facts about a thing are such as to give *any* man a reason for choosing that thing. The difficulty was, of course, to show that the actions that we think of as good actions are actions of this kind. It can indeed be shown that any man is likely to need the virtues of courage, temperance and prudence, whatever his particular aims and desires. But what about justice? To be just is not obviously to one's own advantage, and may not happen to fit with one's affections and plans.

I was in this difficulty because I had supposed—with my opponents—that the thought of a good action must be related to the choices of each individual in a very special way. It had not occurred to me to question the often repeated dictum that moral judgements give reasons for acting to each and every man. This now seems to me to be a mistake. Quite generally the reason why someone choosing an A may 'be expected' to choose good A's rather than bad A's is that our criteria of goodness for any class of things are related to certain interests that someone or other has in those things. When someone shares these interests he will have reason to choose the good A's: otherwise not. Since, in the case of actions, we distinguish good and bad on account of the interest we take in the common good, someone who does not care a damn what happens to anyone but himself may truly say that he has no reason to be just. The rest of us, so long as we continue as we are, will try to impose good conduct upon such a man, saying 'you ought to be just', and there is this much truth in the idea that there are categorical imperatives in morals. There is also this much truth in the idea that the moral 'ought' has a special action-guiding force, for we should not say that a word in another language was a moral term unless it could be used to *urge* conduct in this way. But this is not to say that when used to do other things it has a different sense. After saying 'you ought to do X' one may without impropriety add 'but I hope to God you won't'; and one may say 'I ought to do it, so what?' without using the word 'ought' in a special 'inverted comma' sense; one means 'I ought to do it', not 'it's what you other chaps think I ought to do'. Of course such utterances must be an exception, since if people in general did not take an interest in the good of other people, and the establishment of rules of justice in their society, the moral use of 'ought' would not exist. But this gives one no reason to invent a special sense of 'ought'. One might as well say that there are *two* special senses, one for a man who in general takes account of moral considerations but is kicking over the traces just here and another for the amoral man who never takes any notice of what he ought to do.

It seems clear that anyone who rejects Hare's idea that words used to make an evaluation must entail imperatives, will also reject his particular arguments against the possibility of deducing 'ought' from 'is', and I assume that this is the real issue between him and Professor Searle in items numbers VII and VIII of this book. Searle argues that in at least one instance it is possible to deduce an 'ought' from an 'is'. For, he says, from certain premises telling us (1) that particular utterances made in particular circumstances count as promises, (2) that promises place the promiser under obligations, and (3) that Jones uttered these words in these circumstances, we can obtain, by deduction, the conclusion that, other things being equal, Jones ought to keep his promise. The *ceteris paribus* clause appearing in the conclusion is to take care of the fact that promises do not place the promiser under an absolute obligation, since the obligation may be overridden by other considerations, such as a prior obligation. Alternatively the clause can be put in the premises, after which a new premise is added to the effect that other things are equal, and a simple (non-conditional) conclusion drawn about what Jones ought to do. Many of the discussions of this article have centred round this *ceteris paribus* provision, but Hare's does not, and he seems right in thinking that this is not the central issue. Faced with any claim that an 'ought' has been derived from an 'is' via facts about an institution such as promising, Hare will reply as follows. Either, he will say 'I have obligation to keep my promise' is, or it is not, a prescriptive statement, that is, either it does or it does not entail a first person imperative. If it is not prescriptive it is not evaluative, and so there has been no deduction of an evaluative conclusion from premises that are purely factual. If, on the other hand, it is prescriptive it cannot be deduced from any descriptive statements of this kind, for the question is whether I, the speaker, do or do not subscribe to the rules of the 'game' of promising. Certainly the existence of the institution of promising requires that certain people do accept these rules, but that 'anthropological' fact does not bind my will, and from it I could deduce only another 'anthropological' fact.[1]

Searle would no doubt reply that the 'ought' that he is deducing is indeed not evaluative in Hare's sense, but then he denies that descriptive and evaluative statements can be distinguished as Hare supposes. He says that instead of looking for a special kind of meaning in 'evaluative utterances' we should look at all the many different things (evaluating among them) that we can do *in* using a particular form of words. Searle is here using Professor J. L. Austin's distinction

[1] See p. 120–121.

between the 'locutionary force' of an utterance, which is roughly equivalent to its meaning, and the 'illocutionary act' which the speaker may be performing in saying what he does.[1] Evaluating is just one of the many illocutionary acts that a given form of words may be used to perform.

Presumably Searle would make use of this same distinction between meaning and speech act in answering Hare's central challenge to his argument. According to Hare the crucial question is whether or not we can, with Searle, regard it as a tautology that 'Under certain conditions C anyone who utters the words (sentence) "I hereby promise to pay you, Smith, five dollars" places himself under (undertakes) an obligation to pay Smith five dollars'. (The question at issue is, roughly, whether it is a tautology that promises ought to be kept, which Searle had said that it was.) Hare says that if this were a tautology it could not state a rule of the 'game' of promising, since anything that does that must tell people *how to act*. In other words Hare is suggesting that there must be a prescriptive element in the words that state the rule. But Searle could reply that while the word 'ought' as used in certain circumstances does indeed have the illocutionary force of *enjoining* this does not mean that it has an extra *entailment* to get in the way of a deductive argument from 'is' to 'ought'.

I do not know whether I have diverged from Searle in inventing this reply for him, nor whether this would be exactly the right thing to say. In any case I agree with Hare in finding Searle's argument faulty, though my grounds are quite different from his. For it seems to me that while there is *in principle* no objection to the project of deriving 'ought' from 'is' Searle has tried to work from the wrong kind of premises, at least for a moral 'ought'. For he has tried to deduce an 'ought' statement from premises that are 'internal' to a particular institution, and this is not how 'ought' statements are used. To see this we have only to suppose that we have a thoroughly bad institution—say one connected with duelling—by the rules of which one has an obligation to shoot at another man once certain things have been said and done. We could then construct an argument parallel to Searle's which should lead to the conclusion that one ought to shoot at X. But in fact this is not what anyone who disapproved of the institution on moral grounds would say. He would deny that he had any obligation to shoot at his man, because of the evil social consequences of the institution, the point being not that

[1]Promising, advising, entreating, recommending, warning, reprimanding, are all examples of Austin's 'illocutionary acts'. See J. L. Austin, *How to do things with Words*.

he was not prepared to obey the rule (which might or might not be the case) but rather that he denied the *obligation* on account of his view of the institution. Thus one might say that while Searle was not wrong in principle in saying that 'ought' could be derived from 'is', he was inaccurate in thinking that it could be derived from these particular premises. For while some other words that might naturally be called 'evaluative' (e.g. 'owes') do seem to belong within an institution,[1] 'ought' could only be deduced from a set of premises which referred to such things as injury, freedom and happiness, i.e. to things that count in the scale of human good and harm. Thus one could indeed not deny that one owed a certain sum of money given certain institutions and certain institutional matters of fact of the kind that Searle is thinking of, but if one thought the whole institution harmful, and conceived it as a socially useful task to destroy it, one would say 'It is not true that one ought to pay what one owes'. 'One ought to keep one's promises' is thus not a tautological statement, and the most one can say is that promising presupposes the acceptance of an obligation on the part of a number of people. As to the deduction of 'ought' from 'is', we shall have to try the right kind of premises, and see how things turn out. Hare has not shown that there is in principle an objection to the project, but Searle has not shown that it can be done. Everything will depend on how the meaning of 'ought' in a moral judgement is related to such notions as those of injury and welfare, and this has yet to be worked out.

Looking back over the last twenty-five years one may be surprised, and a little sad, that this particular conflict, about 'fact and value', has occupied so much of our time. We seem to have rushed on to the field without waiting to map the territory supposedly in dispute, ready to die for some thesis about commendation or approval, about pro-attitudes or evaluation, before anyone had done much detailed work on the specific, and very different, concepts involved. In fact moral philosophy has benefited *relatively* little from the revolution which has elsewhere turned our attention to everyday language, and the more or less patient investigation of detail. It is strange, for instance, that as late as 1956 Geach should have had to argue that evaluation should not be represented by the, generally, senseless 'X is good'. And it is strange that more work has not been done on such concepts as that of an attitude, and on the small (or large?) differences between such things as approving, commending, recommending, advising,[2]

---

[1] See G. E. M. Anscombe, 'On Brute Facts', *Analysis* (January 1958).
[2] But see B. J. Diggs, 'A Technical Ought', *Mind* (1960).

praising, evaluating and the like. It will certainly be natural to turn to these topics now that Austin has shown us some ways in, and one feels that this part of moral philosophy will be bound to change, for the better, when his work has been more thoroughly absorbed. Austin himself says that 'the familiar contrast of "normative or evaluative" as opposed to the factual is in need, like so many dichotomies, of elimination',[1] and we are likely to find ourselves making many different contrasts where now we look for one.

II

In the articles printed as numbers IX to XII in this volume Mr Urmson, Mr Mabbott, Professor Smart, and Professor Rawls discuss a certain problem about the interpretation and defence of utilitarianism in ethics. They are, therefore, concerned with the thesis that actions are made right or wrong by their good or bad consequences, for we may take this as a general definition of utilitarianism, leaving open the question of whether good consequences are to be identified with the greatest happiness of the greatest number, as Bentham and Mill would have it, or whether with Moore we would believe other things besides happiness to be ultimate goods. Such distinctions are not discussed in these articles, which deal with an attempt to meet difficulties facing both kinds of utilitarian, who must try to reconcile the general principle of judging actions by their utility with the moral judgements that people actually make. Some of these are particularly troublesome. For instance, we normally think that there is some obligation to keep promises which does not depend on the utility of doing so. For although one may often be absolved from keeping a promise by the harm that would result from keeping it, we are not inclined to think ourselves absolved by the mere fact that keeping the promise would result in no good, or that breaking it would do more good than harm. Moreover it is reasonable to say that there are certain actions that no good consequences could justify, as e.g. torture, or judicial condemnation of the innocent, and even those who say that in some circumstances even these things would be justified usually jib at the idea that we would have the right secretly to fake up a trial, and then hang an innocent man, if by so doing we could save the lives of two. After all we do not regard even mental defectives as expendable in the interests of medical research.

[1]Austin, op.cit., p. 148.

To meet these difficulties it has been suggested that the utility test should be applied not to individual actions but rather to types of action, so that we should ask not 'will breaking this promise (framing this innocent man) have good consequences?' but rather 'would good or evil result from the rule that promises may be broken (innocent men framed)?' If the consequences of the rule would be bad then an individual action coming under the rule would be so, even though *its* consequences were good.

It is a version of this theory, sometimes called 'rule utilitarianism' as against 'act utilitarianism', and sometimes 'restricted utilitarianism' as against 'extreme utilitarianism' that Urmson is attributing to Mill. He does not suggest that he is a thoroughgoing rule utilitarian since Mill says that in certain cases the consequence test should be applied direct to individual actions, viz. when rules conflict, or when no rule applies. But Urmson thinks that Mill would want to answer some objections to the principle of utility by insisting that it is the tendency of a type of action that counts. Mabbott queries this interpretation of Mill, and himself raises difficulties about the rationality of looking to the rule. Smart goes further in declaring that it would be irrational to do anything which conflicted with the principle of utility as applied to individual cases. Why should we care about the results that our action would have elsewhere if it does not have them here? Smart declares himself an extreme utilitarian, and thinks that if our moral judgements conflict with the principle of utility so much the worse for them.

Rawls, on the other hand, thinks that the 'rule utilitarian' application of the principle of utility is right for certain cases, and believes that this helps to solve the difficulties of the utilitarian. Of the four articles his is the most complex and calls for special comment. In the first place it should be remarked that Rawls himself is not to be called a 'rule utilitarian' without much qualification. For he has made it clear in a later article[1] that he does not believe any version of utilitarianism to be compatible with all the principles of justice; he himself, therefore, does not subscribe to the principle of utility in any form. He does, however, believe that we should argue for and against some actions on utilitarian grounds, and for certain very special cases it is rule utilitarianism that should be applied. These special cases are ones in which there is an activity (as e.g. promising or punishing) which depends for its existence on rules of action which do not permit a man to decide what he will do simply by weighing consequences. Rawls

[1] J. Rawls, 'Justice as Fairness', *Philosophical Review*, (1958).

points out that there would be no such thing as promising or punishing in a world in which everyone did what he thought would bring the best consequences on each particular occasion, since a promise imposes other restrictions on what one is to do, and punishment must be according to certain rules about offences and penalties. Thus the institutions of punishing and promising presuppose behaviour which is in this sense non-utilitarian.

Rawls draws the conclusion that the justification of any action which presupposes such practices (e.g. breaking *a promise*) must be according to the rules of the institution, so that consequences can be considered only in so far as the rules allow for this.[1] It is the practice not the individual action that has to stand up to the utilitarian test. What is puzzling is why Rawls thinks that this conclusion can be drawn. Smart argues that an individual man who can break the rules without damaging the useful institution is irrational not to do so where the consequences would be good, and against this Rawls seems to have offered no defence. It is one thing to show that the rules governing a certain practice must be non-utilitarian, and another to show that an individual may not secretly appeal to the principle of utility against the rules.

Finally a word about the relation between the problems discussed in the two groups of articles, I–VIII and IX–XII. These are of different kinds, for Moore, Stevenson, Frankena, Geach, Hare, Foot, and Searle are talking about the logical character of moral judgement, whereas Urmson, Mabbott, Smart, and Rawls are considering the interpretation and adequacy of a suggested criterion of right and wrong. The latter are saying nothing about the status of the criterion, and are leaving it open whether the utilitarian (either act utilitarian or rule utilitarian) is to be thought of as an intuitionist, an emotivist, or a naturalist. He could be any one of the three since, given a certain version of the principle of utility, say 'actions are right in so far as they tend to produce the greatest happiness of the greatest number', this could be held to be either (a) a judgement made by intuition, (b) an expression of attitude, or (c) an analytic truth. So a decision for, or against, utilitarianism does not commit one to any particular position with regard to intuitionist, emotivist or naturalistic theories of ethics, and similarly intuitionists, emotivists and naturalists are equally free to accept or reject the principle of utility.

[1] See p. 165.

I

MOORE'S ARGUMENTS AGAINST CERTAIN FORMS OF ETHICAL NATURALISM

C. L. STEVENSON

IN THE THIRD CHAPTER of his *Ethics*,[1] Moore gave several arguments to show that 'right' and 'wrong' do not refer merely to the feelings or attitudes of the person who uses them. During the thirty years that have since elapsed, he has become more and more sensitive to the flexibilities of ordinary language, and I doubt whether he would still maintain that 'right' and 'wrong' are *never* so used. But perhaps he would still take seriously the view that *if* a man uses these terms in that way, he is not using them in any sense that is relevant to the issues with which moralists usually deal. Interpreting some of his arguments in a way that makes them support this latter contention, I wish to determine how much they prove.

The contention of the arguments, stated more formally, is that the definitions,

D1: 'X is right' has the same meaning as 'I approve of X', and

D2: 'X is wrong' has the same meaning as 'I disapprove of X',[2]

where 'I' in the definiens is to be taken to refer to whoever uses the terms defined, are definitions which distort or ignore the senses that are of most importance to normative ethics.

If Moore's arguments were successful in proving this contention, they would undoubtedly be of interest. There is presumably some roughly intelligible sense, or set of senses, in which not only pro-

---

From *The Philosophy of G. E. Moore,* ed. P. A. Schilpp, Vol. IV of the Library of Living Philosophers (Northwestern University Press, Evanston, Ill., 1942), pp. 71-90. (Future editions to be published by Open Court, La Salle, Ill. and by Cambridge University Press, London.) Reprinted by permission of the Library of Living Philosophers, Inc.

[1] Henry Holt and Co., N.Y., 1912.

[2] The words 'approve' and 'disapprove' may be taken to designate feelings which the speaker *tends* to have, thereby permitting him to speak truthfully about his present approval or disapproval even though he has no strong immediate feelings at the time. Moore has mentioned this in connexion with Westermarck, in *Philosophical Studies*, 332.

fessional writers on normative ethics, but also 'amateur moralists' of all sorts, are earnestly trying to decide what is right or wrong, and to argue such matters with others. These people would be helped by definitions which freed their usage of 'right' and 'wrong' from confusions. They would not be helped, however, by definitions which made these terms refer to something quite foreign to the issues which, confusedly envisaged though these may be, are troublesome to them. If D1 and D2, above, did this and if they were insistently introduced into any ordinary ethical argument, they might only lead people to 'change the subject' of their argument; and might do so in a way that would escape attention, because the old words would still be used. They might be 'issue-begging' definitions.

This consideration is not, of course, unanswerable. A theorist might reply that the way in which people usually use 'right' and 'wrong' is *totally* confused—that no clear issue could ever be salvaged from the ordinary sort of ethical argument. He might then wish to *give* the terms a meaning in accordance with D1 and D2, not hoping to remain 'faithful' to the confusions of common usage, but hoping rather to shock people into realizing that if they do not use his sense, or naturalistic ones like it, they will be dealing with pseudo-problems. In the same way a behaviourist might define 'soul' in terms of processes in the higher nervous system. His purpose (whatever one may think of it) would presumably be to shock people into believing, with him, that 'soul' must either mean something like this or else be a label for a confusion.

One *might* proceed in that way, but I for one do not wish to do so. Although ethical terms are used in a manifestly confused way, it is certainly ill-advised to cry '*total* confusion' until all alternatives are carefully tested. It is well, in beginning, to assume that the ethical terms, as usually used, are *not* totally confused. This assumption will lead us to *look for* some salvageable element in their usage. Unless we look for it, we cannot be sure whether or not it exists, and whether or not that very element is the one which presents normative ethics with its most characteristic difficulties. So let us assume, at least for the present, that ethical terms are not totally confused; and let us further assume that *if* Moore's arguments correctly prove his contention—if D1 and D2 distort or ignore the senses that are most interesting to writers on moral matters—then these definitions are question-begging, and productive of greater confusion, rather than of more clearly envisaged issues.

The first argument may be formulated, without significantly altering the force of Moore's own words,[1] as follows:

(1) It may happen that one man, A, approves of X, and another man, B, disapproves of X.

(2) Thus according to D1 and D2, above, A may say 'X is right', and B, 'X is wrong', and both be telling the truth.[2]

(3) Hence if 'right' and 'wrong' are used in accordance with D1 and D2, X may be both right and wrong.

(4) But if 'right' and 'wrong' are used in any typical ethical sense, then X cannot be both right and wrong. (This is evident to 'inspection'.[3])

(5) Therefore the sense ascribed to 'right' and 'wrong' by D1 and D2 is not any typical ethical sense.

Criticism of the first argument must be concerned with the way in which Moore can get to step (3). Is it possible, using innocent premises and valid logic, to prove that if 'right' and 'wrong' are used in accordance with D1 and D2, X may be both right and wrong? We may properly suspect that it is not possible, simply because a quite different conclusion may be derived from D1 and D2. The last part of (3), namely,

(a) X may be both right and wrong,

becomes equivalent by D1 and D2 (as can be seen by simple substitution, with only trivial grammatical changes) to

(b) I may both approve and disapprove of X.

---

[1]*Ethics*, 91: 'If, whenever I judge an action to be right, I am merely judging that I myself have a particular feeling towards it, then it plainly follows that, provided I really have the feeling in question, my judgement is true, and therefore the action in question really is right. And what is true of me, in this respect, will also be true of any other man.... It strictly follows, therefore, from this theory that whenever *any man whatever* really has a particular feeling towards an action, the action really is right; and whenever *any man whatever* really has another particular feeling towards an action, the action really is wrong.' And, 93: 'If we take into account a second fact, it seems plainly to follow that ... the same action must be quite often both right and wrong. This second fact is merely the observed fact, that it seems difficult to deny, that, whatever pair of feelings or single feeling we take, cases do occur in which two different men have opposite feelings towards the same action.'

[2]According to the usual conventions of logic, an 'X' may not undergo substitution when it occurs between quotation marks. For the present, however, I wish 'X' to be used in a different way. If the reader should erase the mark 'X', whether it occurs between quotation marks or not, and replace it, *throughout*, by some one name of a particular action, with the assumption that that name is perfectly unambiguous, he would then have the sort of argument which I intend. This explanation will serve to indicate what I mean in saying that 'X is right' may tell the truth. I simply mean that that expression, when the first letter of it is replaced by a name, may tell the truth.

[3]*Ethics*, 86f.

This latter statement can, within the limits of linguistic propriety, be taken as a contradiction. Hence D1 and D2 imply that (a) may be taken as a contradiction. One may accordingly urge that

(3x) If 'right' and 'wrong' are used in accordance with D1 and D2, X cannot possibly be both right and wrong. Note that this conclusion, so far from pointing to a way in which D1 and D2 distort ordinary usage, point to a way in which they are faithful to it. Note further that if we should accept both (3x) and also Moore's (3), we should have to conclude that D1 and D2 imply the contradiction that X may and also cannot possibly be both right and wrong. Now whether or not D1 and D2 distort ordinary usage, it is scarcely plausible that such innocent definitions should imply so flagrant a contradiction. Hence, if we accept the derivation of (3x), we may properly suspect some error in Moore's derivation of (3).

One *need* not, of course, maintain that (b) above is a contradiction; and since we habitually try to make consistent sense out of any utterance, we might be led to more charitable interpretations. We might take it as a paradoxical way of saying, 'I may approve of certain aspects of X, and also may disapprove of other aspects of it'; or we might take it as testifying to a possible conflict of attitudes—a paradoxical way of saying, 'Certain of my impulses may lead me to approve of X, but others may lead me to disapprove of it'. But if we are content to make these more charitable interpretations of (b), may we not make similarly charitable interpretations of (a), and so proceed to question (4) in the argument? If there is any reason against this, Moore certainly leaves it unmentioned. And in any case there is certainly one way, and a linguistically appropriate way, of interpreting (b) as a contradiction; hence for one use of the definiens, D1 and D2 have not been shown to distort ordinary usage. The definitions may still be objectionable, but Moore's first argument has by no means shown that they are.

It is interesting to see just where Moore's derivation of (3)—in my own, but I think faithful, statement of his first argument—is invalid. This step seems to follow from (2), which in turn is perfectly correct; but it seems to follow only because of a confusion about pronouns.[1] In (2), which reads, 'According to D1 and D2, A may say,

[1] The confusion is one which often attends the use of what Dr. Nelson Goodman has called 'indicator words'. My criticism of Moore's first argument is largely a matter of applying Goodman's work to a special case. See Chapter XI of his *A Study of Qualities*, a doctoral dissertation now available only at the Widener Library, Harvard, but which is to be published by the Harvard University Press.

"X is right", and B may say, "X is wrong", and both be telling the truth', the words 'right' and 'wrong' occur in direct quotations. Hence the word 'I', which by D_1 and D_2 is implicit in the use of the ethical terms, is appropriately taken as referring not to Moore, or any one speaker, but rather to the people quoted as having judged that X was right or wrong. The 'I' implicit in 'right' refers to A, and the 'I' implicit in 'wrong' refers to B. But in (3), which may be abridged as, 'According to D_1 and D_2, X may be both right and wrong', the words 'right' and 'wrong' are not quoted by Moore as having been used by somebody else. Hence by D_1 and D_2 themselves, which are to the effect that ethical terms refer to the speaker who uses them (as distinct from a speaker who quotes how others used them) the implicit 'I' in (3) refers not first to A and then to B, but rather to Moore, or whoever it is that says 'X may be both right and wrong'. Briefly, the implicitly quoted 'I's' in (2) do not refer to the same person as the implicit and unquoted 'I's' refer to in (3). By assuming that they do, Moore makes an invalid step in his argument appear valid.

This point can helpfully be put in another way. It would seem that
(a1) If 'X is right', said by A, is true, then X is right; and that
(a2) If 'X is wrong', said by B, is true, then X is wrong.
And it is certainly true that *if* (a1) and (a2) were both true, and *if* their antecedents could both be true, then their consequents could both be true. Thus if D_1 and D_2 entitled one to accept (a1) and (a2) and also entitled one to accept as possible the conjunction of their antecedents, it would entitle one to accept as possible the conjunction of their consequents, or in other words, to assert that X might be both right and wrong. This is what Moore, by (3), seems to maintain, in part. But unfortunately for Moore's argument, D_1 and D_2 entitle one to accept *neither* (a1) *nor* (a2). For by D_1, (a1) is like:
If 'I approve of X', said by A, is true, then I approve of X.
And by D_2, (a2) is like:
If 'I disapprove of X', said by B, is true, then I disapprove of X.
And neither of these statements is true, so long as the quoted 'I's' in the antecedents each have a different referent from that of the unquoted 'I's' in the consequents. It will thus appear that Moore, who tacitly presupposes (a1) and (a2) in getting from step (2) to step (3) in his argument, fails to show that D_1 and D_2 lead to what, for ordinary usage, would be an absurdity. In the course of showing the alleged absurdity, he unknowingly rejects an implication of these definitions on the falsity of (a1) and (a2), and so, in effect, *rejects* the definitions

in the very course of an argument that tries to show the absurdity of what their *acceptance* would imply.

If D1 and D2 had read, respectively,

'X is right' has the same meaning as '*Somebody* approves of X', and

'X is wrong' has the same meaning as 'Somebody disapproves of X',

where the 'somebody' could be a different person in each case, then Moore would be entitled to step (3), and his argument would be correct in showing that *these* naturalistic definitions distort ordinary usage, so long as (4) is granted. But in showing merely that, he would leave untouched the far more interesting definitions that D1 and D2 actually provide.

Not in Moore's own words,[1] but in words which are faithful, no doubt, to D2, A may say, 'X is right', and B, 'X is wrong', and both be telling the truth. And it may be that Moore could proceed *in another* way from that point on to show that these definitions violate ordinary ethical usage. But the only other plausible way, I think, is that which Moore himself develops in his third argument, as here listed; and that must be discussed in its proper place.

The second argument may be formulated, again not in Moore's own words,[1] but in words which are faithful, no doubt, to their import, as follows:

(1) A may be telling the truth if he says, 'I now approve of X, but I formerly disapproved of X'.

(2) Hence, by D1 and D2, A may be telling the truth if he says, 'X is now right, but X was formerly wrong'.

(3) But in any sense of 'right' and 'wrong' that is typically ethical,

[1] *Ethics*, 97: 'An action ... [which a man] formerly regarded with ... disapproval, he may now regard with ... approval, and *vice versa*. So that, for this reason alone, and quite apart from. differences of feeling between different men, we shall have to admit, according to our theory [i.e., the definitions criticized in the argument in question] that it is often *now* true of an action that it *was* right, although it was formerly true of the same action that it *was* wrong.'

I have tried to preserve the force of these words in steps (1) and (2) of my formulation of the argument. It will be obvious that I have taken liberties; but Moore's words become so entangled with the tense of verbs, as well as with 'now' and 'formerly', and the notion of 'truth at one time but not another', that a more complete investigation into what he actually may have meant would be impossible in limited space. The notion of 'truth at a time', together with the other sources of confusion, are exhaustively analyzed by Goodman, though without any specific reference to Moore, in the work mentioned in note 6, above [note 1, p 19 above. Ed.]; and the reader interested in pursuing these matters will do well to refer to that work. Meanwhile I can only dogmatize in saying that if I had been more faithful to Moore's words, I should have had more fallacies to untangle than my present formulation of the argument involves.

Steps (3) and (4) in my formulation are parallels to the remarks in *Ethics*, 86, and 81 ff.

A may *not* tell the truth in saying 'X is now right but X was formerly wrong'. This could truthfully be said, perhaps, if each 'X' in the statement referred to a *different* action of the *same kind*, for a present and former X could have different consequences; but it would be contradictory, in any ordinary sense of terms, if 'X' referred throughout, as is here intended, to the very same action. (This is evident to 'inspection'.)

(4) Therefore the sense ascribed to 'right' and 'wrong' by D1 and D2 is not any typically ethical sense.

Criticism of the second argument must be concerned with the derivation of step (2). This seems to follow directly from (1) by substitution in accordance with D1 and D2; but in fact it also requires 'corollaries', so to speak, of D1 and D2, namely:

D1c: 'X was (formerly) right' has the same meaning as 'I (formerly) approved of X', and

D2c: 'X was (formerly) wrong' has the same meaning as 'I (formerly) disapproved of X'.

These definitions differ from D1 and D2 only in that the temporal reference, in both definiendum and definiens, is shifted from present to past.[1] It is readily obvious that (2) follows from (1), granted that D1 and D2 are taken to have the above 'corollaries', and since I accept the remainder of the argument (though not without hesitations about (3)), I accept the argument. But I do so *only* with the proviso that D1c and D2c are understood to be implied by D1 and D2.

Now it is certainly a natural thing to assume that D1 and D2 *do* imply D1c and D2c. But there is another possibility which is of no little interest. One might insist that 'right' and 'wrong' always refer to the attitudes that the speaker has *at the time that he uses the words*. Any temporal reference in a sentence that includes these words might always be taken as referring to the time at which the action said to be 'right' or 'wrong' *occurred*, rather than to the time at which it was *approved*. Such a view is provided by the following definitions, which are revised versions of D1 and D2:

$$
\text{D3: 'X} \left\{ \begin{array}{l} \text{is} \\ \text{was} \\ \text{will be} \\ \text{would be} \\ \text{etc.} \end{array} \right\} \text{right' has the same meaning as 'I now approve}
$$

[1] In point of fact, only D2c is needed for the inference from (1) to (2), together with D1; but I list D1c as well simply because the argument could so easily be recast in a way that would require it.

of X, which $\begin{Bmatrix} \text{is} \\ \text{was} \\ \text{will be} \\ \text{would be} \\ \text{etc.} \end{Bmatrix}$ occurring'.

D_4: 'X $\begin{Bmatrix} \text{is} \\ \text{was} \\ \text{will be} \\ \text{would be} \\ \text{etc.} \end{Bmatrix}$ wrong' has the same meaning as 'I now disapprove

of X, which $\begin{Bmatrix} \text{is} \\ \text{was} \\ \text{will be} \\ \text{would be} \\ \text{etc.} \end{Bmatrix}$ occurring'.

Note that by these definitions one cannot say anything equivalent to 'I approve*d* of X' by using 'right', unless, perhaps, in such an idiom as 'I used to feel X to be right'.

It is easy to see that if the second argument were rewritten with references to D_1 and D_2 replaced by references to D_3 and D_4, the argument would not be valid. (2) would then not follow from (1). For the statement,

X is (now) right, but X was formerly wrong

would be equivalent, according to D_3 and D_4, with direct substitution, to,

I now approve of X, which is occurring (now), but I now disapprove of X, which was occurring formerly.

This latter statement could not be true, either on account of the incompatible attitudes asserted or because of the impossibility of making X refer to the same action.[1] Hence the former statement, being equivalent to the latter, could not be true. But according to (2), in the rewritten argument, the former statement *might* be true; for (2) would read:

By D_3 and D_4, A may be telling the truth if he says, 'X is now right but X was formerly wrong'.

---

[1] I am assuming (as one common idiom, at least, permits me to) that the time taken in uttering this sentence is not sufficient to prevent the 'nows' from referring all to the same time, and is not sufficient to justify the change in tense from 'is' to 'was'.

Hence (2), being false, could not follow from the innocent premise, (1); and with the collapse of (2) comes the collapse of the remainder of the argument.

Accordingly, although Moore's second argument holds against D1 and D2, provided that certain rather natural assumptions are made about the temporal references involved, it does not hold against D3 and D4, which specifically rule out such assumptions. Since Moore thinks that his argument holds against *any* definition that makes 'right' and 'wrong' refer solely to the attitudes of the speaker, it is clear that he presses the argument for more than it is worth.

I do not wish to defend D3 and D4 as they stand; for on grounds different from Moore's I consider them misleading, and likely to make people overlook the central issues of ethics. But I do wish to defend these definitions from *Moore's* objections. By so doing I shall be free, as I otherwise should not, to amend the definitions in a very simple way, quite without mention of non-natural qualities, and thereby make them give (as closely as the vagueness of ordinary usage will allow) *one* sense, at least, that I consider to be typically ethical. This will be explained later.

There is one curious consequence of D3 and D4, suggested by Moore's second argument, which may more plausibly cast doubt on the conventionality of these definitions. If A, speaking at t1 should say,

(a) X is right,

and speaking at a later time, t2, should say,

(b) X was wrong,

then his second statement *would not contradict* the first. For by D3 and D4, (a) and (b) would become,

(aa) I now approve of X, which is occurring, and

(bb) I now disapprove of X, which was occurring.

These statements, if A makes them, respectively, at t1 and t2, are compatible: for the 'now' in (aa) would not refer to the same time as the 'now' in (bb). And 'X' might designate (as it must to make these considerations of interest) the very same action in both statements; since the change from 'is occurring' in (aa) to 'was occurring' in (bb) would testify to nothing more than that t1, at which (aa) was said, was earlier than t2, at which (bb) was said. Hence, since (aa), said by A at t1, would be compatible with (bb), said by A at t2, it follows, by D3 and D4, that (a), said by A at t1, is compatible with (b), said by A at t2. And *if* (a) and (b) are not compatible, under any circumstances of utterance, so long as 'right' and 'wrong' are used in any typical ethical sense, then it *would* follow that D3 and D4 do not preserve any typical ethical sense. But is it so obvious that (a) and (b), uttered in the way mentioned, are not compatible? My 'inspection' is not so final on this matter as Moore's might be; but further discussion of this point will be easier after we deal with the third argument, to which we must now turn.

The third argument[1] may be formulated as follows:

(1) If A says, 'I approve of X', and B says, 'I do not approve of X', their statements are logically compatible.

(2) Hence, by D3 and D4,[2] if A says, 'X is right', and B says, 'X is not right', their statements are logically compatible.

(3) Thus, according to D3 and D4, if A says, 'X is right', and B says, 'X is not right', A and B, so far as these statements show, do *not* differ in opinion.

(4) But if A says, 'X is right', and B says, 'X is not right', then, in any typical sense of the terms, they *do* differ in opinion, so far as these statements show.

(5) Therefore D3 and D4 do not give any typical ethical sense of the terms they define.

Criticism of the third argument must be concerned with the inference from (2) to (3), and with the truth of (4). The inference from (2) to (3) is one that Moore would justify, no doubt, by the assumption:

(a) When A and B each make an ethical statement, they differ in opinion, so far as these statements show, only if their statements are logically incompatible.

Now clearly, if 'A and B differ in opinion' is taken as just another way of saying 'A and B have beliefs which, if they expressed them verbally, would lead them to make incompatible statements', then (a) above is true. Let us assume that Moore intends 'differ in opinion' to be understood in this sense, and that he is therefore entitled to

---

[1]*Ethics*, 100ff.: 'If, when one man says, "This action is right", and another answers, "No, it is not right", each of them is always merely making an assertion about *his own* feelings, it plainly follows that there is never really any difference of opinion between them: the one of them is never really contradicting what the other is asserting. They are no more contradicting one another than if, when one had said, "I like sugar", the other had answered, "I *don't* like sugar".... And surely the fact that it [the type of analysis under consideration] involves this consequence is sufficient to condemn it.'

[2] In point of fact, only D3 should be mentioned, since the argument does not use the word 'wrong' which D4 defines. But I mention D4 simply because the argument could so easily be rewritten, using 'wrong' instead of 'right', with no effect on its validity or invalidity. D1 and D2 might also have been referred to, since the argument, if it holds at all, would hold against any definition that made ethical terms refer solely to the speaker's own attitudes.

go from (2) to (3) in the argument, *via* (a). In that case we must, in order to make the argument valid, assume that (4) in the argument uses 'differ in opinion' in this same sense. And the force of my criticism is that (4), so interpreted, is by no means obvious.

It *is* obvious, I grant, that in any typical ethical sense, when A and B assert 'X is right' and 'X is not right', respectively, they are in *some* sense differing or disagreeing. But I do not grant that A and B must, in that case, be 'differing in opinion' in the sense of that phrase that we are assuming Moore to intend. I think Moore was led falsely to affirm (4) simply because, due to an exaggerated emphasis on the purely cognitive aspects of ethical language, he could not understand how people could differ or disagree in any sense without differing in opinion in the narrow sense above defined.

The sense in which A and B, asserting 'X is right' and 'X is not right', respectively, clearly do 'disagree', is a sense which I shall preserve by the phrase, 'disagree in attitude'. A and B will be said to disagree in attitude when they have opposed attitudes to something, and when at least one of them is trying to alter the attitude of the other. I have elsewhere argued that disagreement in this sense is highly typical of ethical arguments, hence I shall not elaborate that point here.[1] It will be enough to point out that disagreement in attitude often leads to *argument*, where each person expresses such beliefs as may, if accepted by his opponent, lead the opponent to have a different attitude at the end of the argument. Attitudes are often functions of beliefs, and so we often express beliefs in the hope of altering attitudes. Perhaps Moore confused disagreement in attitude with 'difference of opinion', and this confusion led him to assert (4).

Of course 'difference of opinion' *might* be understood to mean the same as 'disagreement in attitude'; but if Moore intended that, he would not be entitled to go from (2) to (3), and the third argument would still fail, even though (4) would then be true.

Note that when people disagree in attitude, neither need have any false belief about his own or the other's attitude. If A says, 'X is right', and B says, 'X is not right', and both accept D3, then it is quite possible that A and B should *both* know that A approves of X and that B does not. They may disagree in attitude none the less. They are not describing attitudes to one another—not, in Frank Ramsey's phrase, 'comparing introspective notes'. Neither is exclusively interested in knowing the *truth* about the other's *present* attitudes. Rather, they

---

[1] 'The Emotive Meaning of Ethical Terms', *Mind*, Vol. XLVI, n.s., No. 181. I here use 'attitude' where I there used 'interest'.

are trying to *change* each other's attitudes, hoping that later on their attitudes will be of the same sort. It is not necessary for their ethical judgements to be logically incompatible if they are to indicate disagreement in attitude.

Granted, then, that one has an introspective feeling that verbally-seeming incompatible judgements about right and wrong are actually incompatible, this feeling might testify only to the presence of disagreement in attitude, rather than to logical incompatibility. Or perhaps the fact that people who disagree in attitude often do, as well, make incompatible assertions about the consequences of the object of attitude, etc., in the course of their argument, may lead one to feel, without warrant, that the ethical judgements themselves, in any typical sense, must be incompatible. In my opinion, the ethical terms are in fact used so vaguely that people *have not decided* whether 'X is right', said by A, and 'X is not right', said by B, are to be taken as incompatible or not; nor will Messrs. A and B be likely to have decided it. So *we* may decide it either way we like, so long as we are faithful to the issues which ethical arguments usually raise. We may, under certain circumstances of utterance, though not all, make the judgements incompatible. I have dealt with this in my paper, 'Persuasive Definitions',[1] and have here only time to say that such a procedure can be developed in a way that avoids Moore's objections. On the other hand, we may make the judgements, uttered by A and B respectively, logically compatible, as is done by D_3 and D_4. Either alternative, so far as I can see, will permit the ethical terms to raise the issues which ethical arguments usually raise in common life, though of course they do not permit the terms to be used in the way that some philosophers, in their confusion, may want to use them. I can pretend to no super-human certainty on this last point, of course, nor can I here expatiate as I should like; but I hope I have said enough to show that D_3 and D_4 present serious alternatives to Moore's non-natural quality.

I must add, however, that D_3 and D_4 are misleading in that they do not properly suggest disagreement in attitude. They suggest too strongly a mere 'comparing of introspective notes'. But this can be remedied by qualifying D_3 and D_4, as promised on page 24, in a very simple way. 'Right', 'wrong', and the other ethical terms, all have a stronger emotive meaning than any purely psychological terms. This emotive meaning is not preserved by D_3 and D_4, and must be separately mentioned. It has the effect of enabling ethical judgements to be used to alter the attitudes of the hearer, and so lends itself to argu-

[1] *Mind*, Vol. XLVII, n.s., No. 187.

ments that involve disagreement in attitude. So qualified, D3 and D4 seem to me to be immune from all of Moore's objections.

The consideration that was perplexing on page 24 f.—namely, that 'X is right', said by A at t1, is logically compatible according to D3 and D4 with 'X was wrong', said by A at t2—can now be explained. It is clear that in any typical sense these statements are 'opposed' in some way; but I think it is well within the limits of vague common usage to say that the statements, under the circumstances of utterance mentioned, may be taken as logically compatible, just as D3 and D4, qualified by reference to emotive meaning, would imply. Their *seeming* incompatibility springs from the fact that the judgements exert a different sort of emotive *influence*—that the judgement at t2 undoes the work of the judgement at t1. For instance, if B was led by A's judgement at t1 to agree in attitude with A, he may, if he has not subsequently changed his attitude, find himself disagreeing in attitude with A at t2. So in a rough but intelligible way of speaking, B may properly charge A with 'going back on' his former 'opinion'. But we need not insist that this ready way of speaking maintains that A's statement at t1 was logically incompatible with his statement at t2. May it not be taken to mean that A has come to have an attitude, and to exert an influence, which oppose his former attitude and influence?

It will now be clear that none of the arguments I have criticized is conclusive. Moore's *method* of argument, as I have freely interpreted it, is very useful. It consists of drawing consequences from a proposed definition, and then showing that these consequences are 'odd' according to any *usual* sense of the word defined. This 'oddness' may suggestively raise the question as to whether the proposed definition is issue-begging. But although the method is useful, it may be misapplied, either in drawing the consequences of the proposed definition, or in judging whether these consequences show that the proposed definition is likely to beg issues. I think that Moore has misapplied the method throughout, in one or another of these ways.

Although Moore's arguments do not prove as much as he thinks (or at least, as much as he thought when writing the *Ethics*), they are by no means useless. I hope that his repudiation of much of *Principia Ethica*[1] will not be interpreted by careless critics as implying that his work in ethics has gone for nothing. However much Moore himself may have been misled by language, he is much more sensitive to its pitfalls than many of his naturalistic opponents, and some of his

---

[1] See 'Is Goodness a Quality?', in *Aristotelian Society, Supplementary Volume*, XI, 127.

arguments help one to realize this. In the second and third arguments we have found that D1 and D2 cannot be accepted without qualification. Explicit recognition must be added about the confusing character of tense in ethical judgements, of disagreement in attitude, and of emotive meaning. Naturalistic analyses which are content to ignore these matters—which indeed they all were at the time that Moore wrote—are insensitive in a way that the second and third arguments help to point out.

Lest I myself be accused of linguistic insensitivity, I wish to emphasize that D3 and D4 require further qualifications than those which I have here given. 'Right' and 'wrong', being particularly vague and flexible, may be defined in any number of ways, quite within the limits of that muddy continuum which we call 'ordinary usage'. No *one* definition can possibly deal with their varied usage; and perhaps no *list* of definitions, however long, would be adequate. All that one can do is give 'sample' definitions, and then hope to avoid confusion by coming more adequately to understand (as I. A. Richards has so often urged) the flexibility of ordinary language.

In particular, 'right' and 'wrong' are subject to changes in meaning with different contexts. For instance, when we ask someone the *question*, 'Is X right?', we do not usually want the hearer to tell us whether *we* now approve of X, as D3 and D4 might readily suggest. We should be more likely to want the hearer to say whether *he* approves of X, and to influence us with regard to our subsequent approval. Or we might want to know what attitudes others have to X, and so on. Or, if we know to begin with that the hearer approves of X, we may use the question 'Is X right?' to insinuate that it isn't, and so to indicate that we disagree with the hearer in attitude—a disagreement that may later lead to an argument, in which many beliefs would be expressed of a sort that might lead, as a matter of psychological fact, to the alteration of our own or of our opponent's attitude. And again: if a man is 'trying to decide' whether X is right, he is usually not merely trying to characterize his present attitudes. Such a decision would usually be forced upon him by a conflict of attitudes, and would arise in the course of his efforts to resolve the conflict. It would introduce factual considerations, of precedent, the attitude of society, the nature and consequences of X, etc., that may determine whether or not he will subsequently attain a state of mind in which he approves of X, with all impulses to the contrary being repressed or redirected. These are cases in which 'right' is used in a way that varies, greatly or slightly, from the way in which D3 would suggest. They are a few instances among the many which show that D3 and D4 must be taken only as 'sample' definitions.

But although only 'sample' definitions, D3 and D4, qualified by reference to emotive meaning, are for many purposes very interesting samples. I wish to show that they have consequences which may account for certain of Moore's own conclusions:

It seems quite likely, judging from parallel remarks in *Principia Ethica*, page 7, that Moore would deny that

'If I now approve of X, X is right'

is an analytic statement, in any usual sense of words. By D3 this is analytic; and I am prepared to accept that consequence, and at the same time to insist that D3 is as conventional as any precise definition of a vague common term can be, *if* D3 is qualified with reference to emotive meaning. What I do not admit, however, is that the statement is *trivial*, in the way most analytic statements are. The emotive meaning of 'right', in the above statement, might serve to induce the *hearer* to approve of X, provided the speaker does. Any hearer who does not want to be so influenced may accordingly object to the statement, even though it is analytic. Although trivial in regard to its cognitive aspects, the statement is not trivial in regard to its repercussions on attitude; and one may refuse to make it, as I should, very often, for that reason. There are times when I, and all others, wish to induce others to share our attitudes; but few of us want to do so for every case, or to act as though the hearer is expected to agree with us in attitude even before we assert more than hypothetically what attitude we ourselves have. For that reason the above statement would rarely be made. That is far from what Moore would conclude, but I think it may explain why Moore, consciously sensitive only to the cognitive aspects of language, should insist that the judgement in question, not being trivial, could not be analytic.

In the *Ethics*, 131, Moore makes some penetrating remarks. He mentions, with apparent agreement, certain theorists who

have assumed that the question whether an action *is* right cannot be completely settled by showing that any man or set of men have certain feelings . . . about it. They would admit that the feelings . . . of men may, in various ways, have a bearing on the question; but the mere fact that a given man or set of men has a given feeling . . . can, they would say, never be sufficient, *by itself*, to show that an action is right or wrong.

With this I entirely agree, and in fact it is implied by D3 and D4, provided these definitions are qualified by reference to disagreement in attitude and emotive meaning. To settle a question about 'what is right', is presumably (for this context) to settle a disagreement that may exist between A and B, when the former maintains 'X is right', and the latter maintains 'X is not right'. This disagreement is a disagreement in *attitude*, and will be settled only when A and B come to have similar attitudes. Should any other people take sides with A or B, the settlement of the argument would require these people as well to end by having similar attitudes. Now one cannot hope to bring about such a uniformity of attitudes merely by pointing out what any one man or set of men actually do approve of. Such a procedure may, as Moore says, 'in various ways have a bearing on the question', but a knowledge of what any man approves of *may* totally fail to alter the approval of some other man. If approval is to be altered by means of beliefs, all manner of beliefs may have to be utilized. One may, in fact, have to make use of all the sciences; for the beliefs that will collectively serve to alter attitudes may be of all different sorts; and even so, one cannot be guaranteed success in altering them by this means. It is for that reason that the support of an ethical judgement is so very difficult. To support ethical judgements is not merely to prove their truth; it is to further, *via* changes in beliefs, for instance, the influence which they exert. I accept the above quotation from Moore, then; but it will be obvious how very different my own reasons are.

I wish to make clear that, although an analysis along the lines of D3 and D4, with reference to emotive meaning and disagreement in attitude, stands as an alternative to Moore's non-naturalistic views, it does not positively disprove the view that 'right', whether directly or indirectly, has to do with a non-natural quality. What Moore would now say about 'right' I do not know, but he *could* say, without rejecting emotive meaning or disagreement in attitude, that 'X is right' sometimes means that X has some quality, or is related to something else that has some quality, which is wholly inaccessible to discovery by scientific means. 'Right' could then be granted an emotive meaning, but only because it designates such a quality. If the quality is assumed to be one that arouses approval, its name would acquire a laudatory aura. And people could be acknowledged to disagree in attitude about what is right, but only because they approve or do not approve of something, depending on whether or not they believe that this quality is in some way connected with it. If Moore wishes to maintain this, and if he actually is confident that he encounters this quality in his experience or 'intuition', and if he is sure that the quality is non-natural, then I cannot pretend to have said anything here which is likely to convince him to the contrary— even though I should privately suspect him of building up elaborately sophisticated fictions in the name of common sense. I do contend, however, that if Moore is to support such a view, he must argue for it in a more positive way. He cannot hold it up as the only alternative to manifest weaknesses of naturalism. The kind of naturalism which he was combatting, which ignores disagreement in attitude and emotive meaning, does indeed require an alternative; but unless new arguments can be found to the contrary, such an alternative can be developed along the lines I have here suggested.[1]

The present alternative, I must add, is far from crying that ethical judgements represent a 'total confusion'. To ascribe to a judgement a meaning that is partly emotive is by no means to insist that it is confused. Should emotive meaning be taken for something that it is not, that would indeed be a confusion; but if emotive meaning is taken for what it is, it remains as an unconfused part of the meaning that ethical judgements manifestly do have. Nor does this type of analysis imply the curious view that ethical issues are 'artificial'. Issues that spring from disagreement in attitude, so far from being artificial, are the very issues which we all have overwhelmingly compelling motives for resolving. None of us is so remote from society that he can survey the divergent attitudes of others without feeling insurmountable urges to take sides, hoping to make some attitudes preponderate over others. We are none of us 'isolationists' on *all* matters, simply because what others do and approve of doing is so often of near concern to us. I have here, temporarily, suspended any taking of sides on moral matters; but that is only to keep my *analysis* of moral judgements distinct from any efforts of mine to exert a moral influence. This temporary detachment in no way implies—as it is scarcely necessary to insist—that I consider ethical issues to be artificial, or that I maintain, with gross paradox, that it is wrong to discuss what is right or wrong.

[1] For analyses which closely resemble the one I defend here, see: A. J. Ayer's *Language, Truth and Logic*, Ch. VI; B. Russell's *Religion and Science*, Ch. IX; W. H. F. Barnes's 'A Suggestion about Values', in *Analysis* (Mar., 1934); C. D. Broad's 'Is "Goodness" a Name of a Simple, Non-natural Quality?', in *Proceedings of the Aristotelian Society* (1933–4) (where acknowledgment is given to Duncan Jones); and R. Carnap's *Philosophy and Logical Syntax*, Sect. 4.

II

A REPLY TO MY CRITICS

G. E. MOORE

ETHICS

1. *Is 'right' the name of a characteristic?*

On pp. 57–8 of his essay, Mr. Broad says that a complete discussion of my 'doctrine', that the word 'good', when used in one particular way which I had in mind, 'is a name for a characteristic which is simple and "non-natural"', would have to begin by raising the question 'Is "good" a name of a characteristic at all?' Of course, the question he means is the question whether 'good', *when used in that particular way*, is a name of a characteristic; and I quite agree with him that this is the first question which should be discussed, if one wished to discuss completely the 'doctrine' in question.

He himself, however, has chosen not to discuss this particular question on this occasion, and I do not think that any of the other contributors have discussed it either. I do not therefore propose to discuss it myself. Fortunately, however, Mr. Stevenson has put forward a view about 'typically ethical' uses of the words 'right' and 'wrong', which seems to me to raise exactly the same issues. If Mr. Stevenson's view is true, then, I think, an analogous view about the particular use of the word 'good', which is in question, must be true also; and it would follow that 'good', in this usage, is *not* the name of any characteristic at all. I propose therefore to begin by discussing this view of Mr. Stevenson's.

Consider the sentence 'It was right of Brutus to stab Caesar' or the sentence 'Brutus' action in stabbing Caesar was right' or the sentence 'When Brutus stabbed Caesar, he was acting rightly'—three sentences which seem all to have much the same meaning. Mr. Stevenson thinks (p. 80)[1] that the definition ' "It was right of Brutus to stab Caesar" has

From *The Philosophy of G. E. Moore,* ed, P. A. Schilpp, Vol. IV of the Library of Living Philosophers (Northwestern University Press, Evanston, Ill., 1942), pp. 535–54. (Future editions to be published by Open Court, La Salle, Ill. and by Cambridge University Press, London.) Reprinted by permission of the Library of Living Philosophers, Inc.

[1] [p. 24 of this volume. Ed.]

the same meaning as "I now approve of Brutus' stabbing of Caesar, which was occurring"' gives, *if amended in a particular way*, at least *one* 'typically ethical' sense of these sentences. But he adds that he only thinks it does this 'as closely as the vagueness of ordinary usage will allow'. I take it that by the last clause he means that the sense which his amended definition would give to these sentences is more precise than any with which they would actually be used by any one who was using them in a way that was in accordance with ordinary usage; but he thinks that, though more precise, it *approaches* at least *one* sense in which such a person might use them. He thinks moreover that the sense which it approaches is a 'typically ethical' one; but in saying that his amended definition gives (approximately) at least *one* 'typically ethical' sense, he is allowing that there may possibly be other 'typically ethical' senses, equally in accordance with ordinary usage, which it does not give even approximately; and allowing also that there may possibly be other senses, equally in accordance with ordinary usage, which are not 'typically ethical' and which also his amended definition does not give even approximately. This is a generous allowance of possible senses, all of them in accordance with ordinary usage, with which these simple sentences might be used. But perhaps it is not too generous; and, guarded and limited as Mr. Stevenson's statement is, I think it is sufficient to raise important questions.

It would seem that, before we can discuss whether Mr. Stevenson is right in this guarded statement, we ought to know what his amended definition is. And he professes to give it on p. 84.[1] He says that his amendment is a very simple one, and possibly it may be; but it is certainly not a simple matter to discover from what he says on this page, what the amendment he has in mind is. Let us, for the sake of brevity, call the sentence 'It was right of Brutus to stab Caesar' 'the *definiendum*', and the sentence 'I now approve of Brutus' stabbing of Caesar, which was occurring' 'the *definiens*'. The original definition stated that the *definiendum*, when used in the particular sense (approximating to an ordinary one) which Mr. Stevenson wants to 'give' us, has the same meaning as the *definiens*. This definition, Mr. Stevenson now says, does not, *as it stands*, give us the sense he means, but must be amended. And it is obvious, from what he says, that the required amendment will have something to do with 'emotive meaning': it will either mention the conception 'emotive meaning' itself, or will mention some particular emotive meaning which a

[1][p. 27 Ed.]

sentence might have. In order to help us to see what the required
amendment (or, as he now calls it, 'qualification') is, Mr. Stevenson
tell us: ' "Right", "wrong", and the other ethical terms, all have a
stronger emotive meaning than any purely psychological terms.' By
this, I take it, he means to imply that the *definiendum* has a stronger
emotive meaning than the *definiens*. And then he adds: 'This emotive
meaning is not preserved by' the original definition 'and must be
separately mentioned'. And here, I take it, by '*must* be separately
mentioned' he means 'must' in the amended definition—in any
definition which is to 'give' the sense of the *definiendum* he wants to
give. These two sentences are, I think, all the help he gives us. Well
now, using this help, what *is* the amended definition? Does it merely
say: The *definiendum* (when used in the sense in question) has the same
meaning as the *definiens*, but it has an emotive meaning which the
definiens lacks? Or does it say: It has the same meaning, but it has a
stronger emotive meaning than the *definiens*? If either of these is all,
it certainly does not *give* us any sense whatever of the *definiendum* over
and above what the *definiens* gives; it only tells us something *about* a
possible sense. Or would it be a statement, which mentioned some
particular emotive meaning, and said: The *definiendum* (when used in
the sense in question) has the same meaning as the *definiens*, but it has
also *this* emotive meaning which the *definiens* lacks? Or would it
mention *both* some particular emotive meaning, *and* some particular
degree of strength in which a sentence might have that emotive
meaning, and say: The *definiendum* (when used in the sense in question)
has the same meaning as the *definiens*, but it has *this* emotive meaning
in a degree of strength above *this* degree, whereas the *definiens* only
has it in a degree of strength below *this* degree? In these two cases,
the amended definition really would give us a sense of the *definiendum*;
but it is certain that Mr. Stevenson has not given us any amendment
of this sort. Perhaps there are other alternatives besides these four:
how on earth are we to tell which Mr. Stevenson means? The bare fact
is that he has not given us *any* sense whatever of the *definiendum* over
and above what the *definiens* gives, nor any amended definition which
gives such a sense. But nevertheless I think it is possible to gather
from what he says that he holds the following views. Let us, in
analogy with a way in which Mr. Stevenson himself uses the word
'cognitive' and also in analogy with the way in which he uses the
phrase 'emotive meaning', distinguish between the 'cognitive
meaning' of a sentence and its 'emotive meaning'. I think we can then
say Mr. Stevenson thinks that the *definiendum*, when used in the sense

he has in mind, has exactly the same 'cognitive meaning' as the *definiens*, but nevertheless has not the same *sense*, because it has a different 'emotive meaning'. But what does this mean? How are we using the term 'cognitive meaning'? I think this can be explained as follows. Some sentences can (in accordance with ordinary usage) be used in such a way that a person who is so using them can be said to be *making an assertion* by their means. E.g., our *definiendum*, the sentence 'It was right of Brutus to stab Caesar', can be used in such a way that the person who so uses it can be correctly said to be asserting that it *was* right of Brutus to stab Caesar. But, sometimes at least, when a sentence is used in such a way that the person who uses it is making an assertion by its means, he is asserting something which might conceivably be true or false—something such that it is logically possible that it should be true or should be false. Let us say that a sentence has 'cognitive meaning', if and only if it is both true that it can be used to make an assertion, and also that anyone who was so using it would be asserting something which might be true or might be false; and let us say that a sentence, *p*, has *the same cognitive meaning* as another, *q*, if and only if both *p* and *q* have cognitive meaning, and also, *so far as* anybody who used *p* to make an assertion was asserting something which might be true or might be false, he would have been asserting exactly the same if he had used *q* instead. If so, then the view I am attributing to Mr. Stevenson is that if a person were using our *definiendum* to make an assertion, and were using it in the sense Mr. Stevenson has in mind, then so far as he was asserting anything which might be true or might be false, he might have asserted exactly the same by using the *definiens* instead, but that, if he had done this, he would *not* have been using the *definiens* in the same *sense* in which he actually used the *definiendum*, and would not therefore have been asserting that it was right of Brutus to stab Caesar, in the sense Mr. Stevenson means. In short, Mr. Stevenson is holding that there is at least one 'typically ethical' sense in which a man may assert that it was right of Brutus to stab Caesar, which is such that, though the only assertion which might be true or false that he is making will be that he himself, at the moment of speaking, 'approves of Brutus' stabbing of Caesar, which was occurring', yet from the mere fact that he is making this assertion it will not follow that he is asserting that Brutus' action was right, in the sense in question: that he is doing so will only follow from the *conjunction* of the fact that he is asserting that he 'approves of Brutus' stabbing of Caesar which was occurring', with the fact that he is using words which have a certain emotive meaning (*what* emotive meaning, Mr. Stevenson has not told us). There is, Mr. Stevenson seems to imply, at least one type of ethical assertion such that an assertion of that type is distinguished from a possible assertion, which would not be ethical at all, not by the fact that it asserts anything which might be true or false, which the other would not assert, but simply by its 'emotive meaning'.

Mr. Stevenson holds, then, if I understand him rightly, that there is at least one 'typically ethical' sense in which a man might assert that it was right of Brutus to stab Caesar, which is such that (1) the man *would* be asserting that he, at the time of speaking, approved of this action of Brutus' and (2) would *not* be asserting anything, which might conceivably be true or false, *except* this or, possibly also, things entailed by it, as, for instance, that Brutus did stab Caesar. And I think he is right in supposing that, limited as this statement is, it is inconsistent with what I have stated or implied in my ethical writings. I have, I think, implied that there is *no* 'typically ethical' sense in which a man might assert this, of which *both* these two things are true; and I have also implied, I think, that there is no 'typically ethical' sense of which *either* is true. I will say something separately about each of these two separate contentions of Mr. Stevenson's.

(1) I am still inclined to think that there is no 'typically ethical' sense of 'It was right of Brutus to stab Caesar', such that a man, who asserted that it was right in that sense, would, as a rule, be *asserting* that he approved of this action of Brutus'. I think there certainly is a 'typically ethical' sense such that a man who asserted that Brutus' action was right in that sense would be *implying* that at the time of speaking he approved of it, or did not disapprove, or at least had some kind of mental 'attitude' towards it. (I do not think Mr. Stevenson means to insist on the word 'approve' as expressing quite accurately what he means: I think the essence of his view is only that there is *some* kind of 'attitude', such that a man would be asserting, if he used the words in the sense Mr. Stevenson means, that he had, at the time of speaking, that attitude towards it.) But I think that, as a rule at all events, a man would only be *implying* this, in a sense in which to say that he *implies* it, is *not* to say that he asserts it nor yet that it *follows* from anything which he does assert. I think that the sense of 'imply' in question is similar to that in which, when a man asserts anything which might be true or false, he *implies* that he himself, at the time of speaking, believes or knows the thing in question—a sense in which he *implies* this, even if he is lying. If, for instance, I assert, on a particular day, that I went to the pictures the preceding

Tuesday, I *imply*, by asserting this, that, at the time of speaking, I believe or know that I did, though I do not *say* that I believe or know it. But in this case, it is quite clear that this, which I *imply*, is no part of what I *assert*; since, if it were, then in order to discover whether I did go to the pictures that Tuesday, a man would need to discover whether, when I said I did, I believed or knew that I did, which is clearly not the case. And it is also clear that from what I assert, namely that I went to the pictures that Tuesday, it does not *follow* that I believe or know that I did, when I say so: for it might have been the case that I did go, and yet that I did not, when I spoke, either believe or know that I did. Similarly, I think that, if a person were to assert that it was right of Brutus to stab Caesar, though he would be *implying* that, at the time of speaking, he approved, or had some similar attitude towards, this action of Brutus', yet he would *not* be *asserting* this that he would be implying, nor would this follow from anything, possibly true or false, which he was asserting. He would be implying by *saying* that Brutus' action was right, that he approved of it; but he would not be *saying* that he did, nor would anything that he said (if anything) *imply* (in the sense of 'entail') that he did approve of it: just as, if I say that I went to the pictures last Tuesday, I *imply* by *saying* so that I believe or know that I did, but I do not *say* that I believe or know this, nor does *what* I say, namely that I went to the pictures, *imply* (in the sense of 'entail') that I do believe or know it. I think Mr. Stevenson's apparent confidence that, in at least one 'typically ethical' sense, a man who asserted that it was right of Brutus to stab Caesar, would be *asserting* that he approved of this action, may be partly due to his having never thought of this alternative that he might be only *implying* it. But I think it may also be partly due to his shrinking from the paradox which would be involved in saying that, even where it can quite properly be said that a man is *asserting* that Brutus' action was right, yet he may be asserting *nothing whatever that could possibly be true or false*—that his words have absolutely no *cognitive* meaning—except, perhaps, that Brutus did stab Caesar. This paradox, however, is, I think, no greater than paradoxes which Mr. Stevenson is willing to accept, and I think that very possibly it may be true. So far as I can understand it, I think Mr. Stevenson's actual view is that sometimes, when a man *asserts* that it was right of Brutus to stab Caesar, the sense of his words is (roughly) much the same as if he had said 'I approve of Brutus' action: do approve of it too!' the former clause giving the *cognitive* meaning, the latter the *emotive*. But why should he not say instead, that the sense of the man's words is *merely* 'Do approve of Brutus' stabbing of Caesar!'—an imperative, which has absolutely no *cognitive* meaning, in the sense I have tried to explain? If this were so, the man might perfectly well be *implying* that he approved of Brutus' action, though he would not be *saying* so, and would be asserting nothing whatever, that might be true or false, except, perhaps, that Brutus did stab Caesar. It certainly seems queer—paradoxical—that it should be correct to say that the man was *asserting* that Brutus' action was right, when the only meaning his words had was this imperative. But may it not, nevertheless, actually be the case? It seems to me more likely that it is the case, than that Mr. Stevenson's actual view is true.

There seems to me to be nothing mysterious about this sense of 'imply', in which if you assert that you went to the pictures last Tuesday, you *imply*, though you don't *assert*, that you believe or know that you did; and in which, if you assert that Brutus' action was right, you *imply*, but don't *assert*, that you approve of Brutus' action. In the first case, that you do imply this proposition about your present attitude, although it is not implied by (i.e., does not follow from) *what* you assert, simply arises from the fact, which we all learn by experience, that in the immense majority of cases a man who makes such an assertion as this does believe or know what he asserts: lying, though common enough, is vastly exceptional. And this is why to say such a thing as 'I went to the pictures last Tuesday, but I don't believe that I did' is a perfectly absurd thing to say, although *what* is asserted is something which is perfectly possible logically: it is perfectly possible that you did go to the pictures and yet you do not believe that you did; the proposition that you did does not 'imply' that you believe you did—that you believe you did does not *follow from* the fact that you did. And of course, also, from the fact that you say that you did, it does not follow that you believe that you did: you might be lying. But nevertheless your saying that you did, does *imply* (in another sense) that you believe you did; and this is why 'I went, but I don't believe I did' is an absurd thing to say. Similarly the fact that, if you assert that it was right of Brutus to stab Caesar, you *imply* that you approve of or have some such attitude to this action of Brutus', simply arises from the fact, which we have all learnt by experience, that a man who makes this kind of assertion does in the vast majority of cases approve of the action which he asserts to be right. Hence, if we hear a man assert that the action was right, we should all take it that, unless he is lying, he does, at the time of speaking, approve, although he has *not* asserted that he does.

(2) Let us next consider the second part of Mr. Stevenson's view: namely the part which asserts that in some 'typically ethical' cases, a man who asserts that it was right of Brutus to stab Caesar, is not asserting anything that might conceivably be true or false, *except* that he approves of Brutus' action, and possibly also that Brutus did stab Caesar. By this I mean a view which is merely negative: which does *not* assert that there are any cases in which such a man *is* asserting that he approves of Brutus' action; but which only asserts that there are cases in which he is *not* asserting anything *else*, leaving perfectly open the possibility that in all such cases he is not asserting *anything at all*, which could conceivably be true or false. Mr. Stevenson, of course, does not express any belief that there are any cases in which such a man, using the *definiendum* in a 'typically ethical' sense, would not be asserting *anything at all*, which might conceivably be true or false. But he does imply that, if you consider all propositions, other than the propositions (1) that he now approves of Brutus' action and (2) that Brutus did stab Caesar and (3) the conjunction of these two, then there are cases in which such a man is not asserting any single one of these *other* propositions. This is the view of his I want now to consider.

It certainly is inconsistent with views which I have expressed or implied. I have certainly implied that in all cases in which a man were to assert in a 'typically ethical' sense that it was right of Brutus to stab Caesar, he would be asserting something, capable of truth or falsity (some proposition, that is) which both (a) is not identical with any of the three propositions just mentioned, (b) does not follow from (3), and (c) is also a proposition from which (1) does not follow: some proposition, therefore, which might have been true, even if he had not approved of Brutus' action, and which may be false, even though he does approve of it—which is, in short, completely independent logically of the proposition that he does approve of the action.

What are we to say about these two incompatible views—the second part of Mr. Stevenson's view, and the view, implied in my writings, which I have just formulated?

I think I ought, first of all, to make as clear as I can what my present personal attitude to them is. I certainly think that this second part of Mr. Stevenson's view *may* be true: that is to say, I certainly think that I don't *know* that it is not true. But this is not all. I certainly have some inclination to think that it *is* true, and that therefore my own former view is false. And, thinking as I do, that the first part of Mr. Stevenson's view is false, this means that I have some inclination to think that there is at least *one* 'typically ethical' sense of the sentence 'It was right of Brutus to stab Caesar', such that a man who used this sentence in that sense and used it in such a way that he could be properly said to be *asserting* that this action of Brutus' was right, would nevertheless not be asserting anything at all that could conceivably be true or false, except, perhaps, that Brutus did stab Caesar: nothing, that is, *about* Brutus' action except simply that it occurred. And, going far beyond Mr. Stevenson's cautious assertion, I have a very strong inclination to think that, *if* there is at least *one* 'typically ethical' sense of which these things are true, then of *all* 'typically ethical' senses these things are true. So that I have some inclination to think that in *any* 'typically ethical' sense in which a man might assert that Brutus' action was right, he would be asserting nothing whatever which could conceivably be true or false, except, perhaps, that Brutus' action occurred—no more than, if he said, 'Please, shut the door'. I certainly have *some* inclination to think all this, and that therefore not merely the contradictory, but the contrary, of my former view is true. But then, on the other hand, I also still have *some* inclination to think that my former view *is* true. And, if you ask me to which of these incompatible views I have the *stronger* inclination, I can only answer that I simply do not know whether I am any more strongly inclined to take the one than to take the other.—I think this is at least an honest statement of my present attitude.

Secondly, I want to call attention to the fact that, so far as I can discover, Mr. Stevenson neither gives nor attempts to give any reason whatever for thinking that his view is true. He asserts that it *may* be true, i.e., that he does not know that it's not, and that he *thinks* it is true; but, so far as I can see, he gives absolutely no positive arguments in its favour: he is only concerned with showing that certain arguments which might be used against it are inconclusive. Perhaps, he *could* give some positive reasons for thinking that it is true. But, so far as I am concerned, though, as I say, I have some inclination to think it is true, and even do not know whether I have not as much inclination to think so as to think that my former view is so, I can give no positive reasons in its favour.

But now, how about reasons for thinking that Mr. Stevenson's view is false and my former one true? I can give at least one reason for this, namely that it *seems as if* whenever one man, using 'right' in a 'typically ethical' sense, asserts that a particular action was right, then, if another, using 'right' in the same sense, asserts that it was not, they are making assertions which are logically incompatible. If this, which seems to be the case, really were the case, it would follow that Mr. Stevenson's view is false. But, of course, from the fact that it *seems* to be the case, it does not follow that it really is the case; and Mr. Stevenson suggests that it seems to be the case, not because it really is the case, but because, when such a thing happens, the two men, if both are sincere, really are *differing in attitude* towards the action in question, and we mistake this difference of attitude for the holding of logically incompatible opinions. He even says, in one place (p. 82),[1] that he thinks I was led falsely to affirm that two such men really are holding logically incompatible opinions, because I 'could not understand how people could differ or disagree in any sense' without holding logically incompatible opinions.

Now I think that as regards this suggestion as to how I was led to affirm that two such men are holding logically incompatible opinions, Mr. Stevenson has certainly not hit the right nail on the head. I think that, even when I wrote *Principia Ethica*, I was quite capable of understanding that, if one member of a party, A, says 'Let's play poker', and another, B, says 'No; let's listen to a record', A and B can be quite properly said to be disagreeing. What is true, I think, is that, when I wrote the *Ethics*, it simply had not occurred to me that in the case of our two men, who assert sincerely, in a 'typically ethical' sense of 'right', and both in the same sense, the one that Brutus' action was right, the other that it was not, the disagreement between them might possibly be merely of that sort. Now that Mr. Stevenson has suggested that it may, I do feel uncertain whether it is not merely of that sort: that is to say, I feel uncertain whether they are holding incompatible opinions: and therefore I completely agree with Mr. Stevenson that, when I used the argument 'Two such men can't be merely asserting the one that he approves of Brutus' action, the other that he does not, because, if so, their assertions would not be logically incompatible', this argument was inconclusive. It is inconclusive, because it is not certain that their assertions are logically incompatible. I even go further, I feel some inclination to think that those two men are *not* making incompatible assertions: that their disagreement· *is* merely a disagreement in attitude, like that between the man who says 'Let's play poker' and the other who says 'No; let's listen to a record': and I do not know that I am not *as much* inclined to think this as to think that they are making incompatible assertions. But I certainly still have *some* inclination to think that my old view was true and that they *are* making incompatible assertions. And I think

[1] [p. 26 of this volume. Ed.]

that the mere fact that they *seem to be* is *a* reason in its favour, though, of course, not a conclusive one. As for Mr. Stevenson's cautious view that, in at least *one* 'typically ethical' case, they are merely disagreeing in attitude and not making logically incompatible assertions, he, of course, gives no reason whatever for thinking it true, and I can see none, though I am perhaps as much inclined to think it is true, as to think that my old view is. How on earth is it to be settled whether they *are* making incompatible assertions or not? There are hosts of cases where we do know for certain that people *are* making incompatible assertions; and hosts of cases where we know for certain that they are not, as, for instance, if one man merely asserts 'I approve of Brutus' action' and the other merely asserts 'I don't approve of it'. Why should there be this doubt in the case of ethical assertions? And how is it to be removed?

I think, therefore, that Mr. Stevenson has certainly not *shewn* that my old view was wrong; and he has not even *shewn* that this particular argument which I used for it is not conclusive. I agree with him that it is not conclusive. But he has not *shewn* that it is not; since he has simply asserted that in at least one 'typically ethical' case two such men *may* be merely differing in attitude and not holding incompatible opinions: he has not shewn even that they *may*, i.e., that it is not certain that they aren't, far less that it is ever the case that they *are*. But there is one statement which I made in my *Ethics*, which he has definitely shewn to be a mistake; and I think this mistake is perhaps of sufficient interest to be worth mentioning.

I asserted that from the two premises (1) that, whenever any man asserts an action to be right or wrong, he is *merely* making an assertion about his own feelings towards it, and (2) that sometimes one man really has towards a given action the kind of feeling, which he would be asserting that he had to it if he said it was right, while another man really has towards the same action the kind of feeling, which he would be asserting that he had to it if he said it was wrong—that from these two premises there *follows* that the same action is sometimes both right and wrong. But this was a sheer mistake: that conclusion does *not* follow from these two premises. In order to see that it does not, and why it does not, let us take a particular case. Suppose it were true (a) that the best English usage is such that a man will be using the words 'It was wrong of Brutus to stab Caesar' *correctly*, i.e., in accordance with the best English usage, if and only if he means by them neither more nor less than that he himself, at the time of speaking, disapproves of this action of Brutus'; and that hence he will be using them *both* correctly *and* in such a way that what he means by them is *true*, if and only if, at the time when he says them, he does disapprove of this action. (Of course, a man may be using a sentence perfectly correctly, even when what he means by it is *false*, either because he is lying or because he is making a mistake; and, similarly, a man may be using a sentence in such a way that what he means by it is *true*, even when he is not using it correctly, as, for instance, when he uses the wrong word for what he means, by a slip or because he has made a mistake as to what the correct usage is. Thus using a sentence *correctly*—in the sense explained—and using it in such a way that what you mean by it is *true*, are two things which are completely logically independent of one another: either may occur without the other.) Let us, for the sake of brevity, use the phrase 'could say *with perfect truth* the words "It was wrong of Brutus to stab Caesar"', to mean 'could, if he said them, be using them *both* correctly *and* in such a way that what he meant by them was true'. It will then follow from the supposition made above that a man could, at a given time, say with perfect truth the words 'It was wrong of Brutus to stab Caesar', if and only if, at the time in question, he was disapproving of this action of Brutus'; that from the fact that he is disapproving of this action it will *follow* that he could say those words with perfect truth, and from the fact that he could say them with perfect truth it will *follow* that he is disapproving of that action. Let us similarly suppose it were true (b) that a man could at a given time say with perfect truth the words 'It was right of Brutus to stab Caesar', if and only if at that time he were approving of this action of Brutus'. And let us finally suppose it were also true (c) that some man, A, has actually at some time disapproved of this action of Brutus', and that *either* the same man, A, has also, at another time, approved of it *or* some other man, B, has at some time approved of it. The question is: Does it follow from (a) (b) and (c) taken jointly, that Brutus' action in stabbing Caesar was both right and wrong? If this does not follow, in this particular case, then from my two premises (1) and (2) it does not follow that sometimes an action is both right and wrong, and I was making a sheer mistake when I said it did.

Now from (a) (b) and (c) together it *does* follow that at some time somebody could have said with perfect truth the words 'It was wrong of Brutus to stab Caesar' and also that at some time somebody could have said with perfect truth the words 'It was right of Brutus to stab Caesar'. And at first sight it is very natural to think that if somebody could have said with perfect truth the words 'It was wrong of Brutus to stab Caesar', it *does* follow that it *was* wrong of Brutus to stab Caesar, and similarly in the other case. It is very natural to identify the statement 'Somebody could have said with perfect truth *the* words "Brutus' action was wrong"' with the statement 'Somebody could have said with perfect truth that Brutus' action was wrong'; and then to ask: If Brutus' action wasn't wrong, how could anybody possibly have ever said with perfect truth that it was? Indeed, I think the latter form of statement very often is used, and can be correctly used, to mean the same as the former; and it is a peculiarity of premises (1), and therefore also of (a), that it follows from them that it *could* be correctly used in a different sense, and that, if so used, then from 'Somebody could have said with perfect truth that Brutus' action was wrong' it really would follow that Brutus' action was wrong, although from 'Somebody could have said with perfect truth *the words* "Brutus' action was wrong"' it would *not* follow that it was wrong. But, even apart from this identification, there are thousands of cases in which from a proposition of the form 'Somebody could have said with perfect truth *the words* "*p*"' *p* does follow: e.g., from 'Somebody could have said with perfect truth the words "Brutus stabbed Caesar"' it really does follow that Brutus did stab Caesar; if he didn't, then nobody could ever possibly have said these words with perfect truth. It was, therefore, very natural that I should think that from (a) and (c) taken together it really would follow that Brutus' action was wrong, and from (b) and (c) taken together that it was right. But nevertheless it was a sheer mistake. What I had failed to notice was that from (a) it follows that from 'Somebody could have said with perfect truth *the words* "Brutus' action was wrong"' it does *not* follow that Brutus' action was wrong. For we saw that, if (a) were true, then 'Somebody could have said with perfect truth *the words* "Brutus' action was wrong"' would be simply equivalent to 'Somebody has at some time disapproved of Brutus' action'; while, also, anybody who was using the words 'Brutus' action was wrong' correctly would mean by them simply that he himself, at the time of speaking, disapproved of Brutus' action. Hence, if (a) were true, anybody who said 'From the fact that somebody could have said with perfect truth "Brutus' action was wrong" it follows that Brutus' action was wrong' would, if he were using the last four words *correctly*, be committing himself to the proposition that from the fact that somebody has at some time disapproved of Brutus' action it follows that he himself, at the time of speaking, disapproves of it—which is, of course, absurdly false. If, on the other hand, he were not using the last four words correctly, what he was asserting to follow from the fact that somebody had at some time disapproved of Brutus' action would not be that Brutus' action was wrong, but something else which he was incorrectly using those words to mean. Hence, if (a) were true, it would not follow from the fact that some-one could at some time have said with perfect truth 'Brutus' action was wrong', that Brutus' action was wrong. Anybody who said that it did, would mean by saying so (if speaking correctly), something different from what anyone else who said it would mean; and each of all those different things would be absurdly false. And hence it was a sheer mistake to infer that because from (a) and (c) jointly, it would follow that some-one could have said with perfect truth *the words* 'Brutus' action was wrong', therefore it would also follow that Brutus' action was wrong: the latter would not follow, though the former would. If on the other hand, instead of the statement 'Some-one could have said with perfect truth *the words* "Brutus' action was wrong"', we consider the statement which I contrasted with it above, namely, 'Some-one could have said with perfect truth that Brutus' action was wrong', this latter, if (a) were true, *could* mean, if said by me, 'Some-one could have said with perfect truth that I now disapprove of Brutus' action' from which, of course, it would follow that I do now disapprove of Brutus' action.

Perhaps, all this could have been said much more simply. Perhaps Mr. Stevenson has said it more simply. But in any case I completely agree with him that it was a sheer mistake on my part to say that from premises (1) and (2) it would follow that the same action was sometimes both right and wrong; and it is he who has convinced me that it was a mistake.

Perhaps, I ought, finally, to explain why I said above that, if Mr. Stevenson's view about 'typically ethical' uses of the word 'right' were true, then 'right' when used in a typically ethical way would not be 'the name of a characteristic'; and that if 'right' were not, then 'good', in the sense I was principally concerned with, would also not be.

Of course, it is not strictly true that this follows from Mr. Stevenson's view. As I have emphasized, he cautiously limits himself to saying that in at least *one* typically ethical use, 'right' is used in a particular way, leaving open the possibility that, even if, when used in that way, it would not be 'the name of a characteristic', yet there may be other ethical uses in which it is the name of a characteristic. But it seems to me that if there is even *one* ethical use such as Mr. Stevenson holds that there is, then probably *all* ethical uses are like it in the respect which makes me say that if used as Mr. Stevenson thinks it sometimes is, it would not be the 'name of a characteristic'.

Why, then, did I say that 'right', if used in the way Mr. Stevenson describes, would not be 'the name of a characteristic'? I am afraid my reason was no better than this. If 'right' were used in the way in question, it would follow both (1) that no two people, who, using it in that way, said of the same action that it was right or would be right, would ever be saying the same thing about it, since one would be saying that he, at the time of speaking, approved of it, while the other would be saying that *he* did, and also (2) that no single person who said of the same action on two different occasions that it was right or would be right, would ever be saying the same thing about it on the one occasion as he said about it on the other, since on the one occasion he would be saying that he approved of it at *that* time, and on the other would be saying that he approved of it at that other, different, time. In short, 'right', if used in Mr. Stevenson's way, would mean something different every time it was used in predication. And it seemed to me, and does still seem to me, that to say of a word that, in one particular use, it is 'the name of a characteristic' would naturally be understood to mean that, when used in that way, it does mean the same both when used at different times and when used by different persons. If it does not, then, there is no one characteristic of which it is the name. Of course, it might be said, that 'right', when used in the way Mr. Stevenson describes, would be the name of one and only one 'characteristic' each time it was used, though of a different one each time; though this would have to be qualified by saying that on each occasion, though it was the name of a characteristic, it was not *merely* the name of a characteristic, since it also had 'emotive meaning'. I think this would be in accordance with the way in which philosophers use the term 'characteristic' (and, I imagine, the way in which Mr. Broad was using it), since they do some-times so use it, that if I say now 'I approve of Brutus' stabbing of Caesar', I am attributing to this action of Brutus' a certain 'charac-teristic', namely that of being appoved by me now. This is, of course, a very different use of the word 'characteristic' from any which is established in ordinary speech: nobody would think of saying, in ordinary conversation, that this action of Brutus' has, if I do approve of it now, a characteristic which it would not have had, if I had not: we ordinarily so use 'characteristic' that 'being approved of now by me' or 'being spoken of now by me' could not be 'character-istics' of that action at all: but nevertheless there is, I think, a well-established philosophical usage in which they would be, provided I do now approve of that action or do now speak of it; and I imagine that Mr. Broad was using 'characteristic' in this philosophic way. It must then be admitted that 'right', if used in the way Mr. Stevenson describes, would, in this sense of 'characteristic' be the name of a characteristic each time it was used, though of a different one each time, and though it would never be *merely* the name of a characteristic, since it would also always have 'emotive meaning'. But this fact, it seems to me, would not justify us in saying that, in this use, it was the name of a characteristic; since this latter phrase would naturally be understood to mean that, in this use, it was the name of *one and the same characteristic when used at different times and by different persons.*

But to say that 'right', in its ethical uses, is not 'the name of a characteristic' might also mean something else, which I think probably Mr. Broad had in mind, when he said it was a question whether 'good' (in that particular usage) is a name for a characteristic at all. Suppose it were the case that, as regards at least *one* 'typically ethical' use of 'right', what I called above the first part of Mr. Stevenson's view were false, while the second were true, so that 'It was right of Brutus to stab Caesar', when used in this way, had absolutely no *cognitive* meaning at all (except, perhaps, that Brutus did stab Caesar) but were merely equivalent to some such imperative or petition as 'Do approve of Brutus' stabbing of Caesar!' Then, in this case, 'right', so used, would not be the name of a characteristic, in the sense that a person who asserted, in this sense, that it was right of Brutus to stab Caesar, would not be asserting anything at all that could possibly be true or false, except, perhaps, simply that Brutus did stab Caesar: by asserting that Brutus' action was right, he would not be asserting anything at all *about* that action, beyond its mere occurrence. That 'right' is, in this sense, not the name of a characteristic, is, of course, not a view which can be attributed to Mr. Stevenson, since he only maintains that the second part of his view is true in cases where the first part is true too i.e., where 'It was right of Brutus to stab Caesar' has *some* cognitive meaning each time it is uttered, though a different one every time and for every person that utters it. But I said above that I thought it more likely that the second part of his view is true, and the first false, than that both are true together; and if this were so then 'right' would, in this more radical sense, not be 'the name of a characteristic'.

I must say again that I am inclined to think that 'right', in all ethical uses, and, of course, 'wrong', 'ought', 'duty' also, are, in this more radical sense, not the names of characteristics at all, that they have merely 'emotive meaning' and no 'cognitive meaning' at all: and, if this is true of them, it must also be true of 'good', in the sense I have been most concerned with. I am *inclined* to think that this is so, but I am also inclined to think that it is not so; and I do not know which way I am inclined most strongly. If these words, in their ethical uses, have only emotive meaning, or if Mr. Stevenson's view about them is true, then it would seem that all else I am going to say about them must be either nonsense or false (I don't know which). But it does not seem to me that what I am going to say is either nonsense or false; and this, I think, is an additional reason (though, of course, not a conclusive one) for supposing both that they have a 'cognitive' meaning, and that Mr. Stevenson's view as to the nature of this cognitive meaning is false.

THE NATURALISTIC FALLACY

W. K. FRANKENA

THE FUTURE HISTORIAN of 'thought and expression' in the twentieth century will no doubt record with some amusement the ingenious trick, which some of the philosophical controversialists of the first quarter of our century had, of labelling their opponents' views 'fallacies'. He may even list some of these alleged fallacies for a certain sonority which their inventors embodied in their titles: the fallacy of initial predication, the fallacy of simple location, the fallacy of misplaced concreteness, the naturalistic fallacy.

Of these fallacies, real or supposed, perhaps the most famous is the naturalistic fallacy. For the practitioners of a certain kind of ethical theory, which is dominant in England and capably represented in America, and which is variously called objectivism, non-naturalism, or intuitionism, have frequently charged their opponents with committing the naturalistic fallacy. Some of these opponents have strongly repudiated the charge of fallacy, others have at least commented on it in passing, and altogether the notion of a naturalistic fallacy has had a considerable currency in ethical literature. Yet, in spite of its repute, the naturalistic fallacy has never been discussed at any length, and, for this reason, I have elected to make a study of it in this paper. I hope incidentally to clarify certain confusions which have been made in connexion with the naturalistic fallacy, but my main interest is to free the controversy between the intuitionists and their opponents of the notion of a logical or quasi-logical fallacy, and to indicate where the issue really lies.

The prominence of the concept of a naturalistic fallacy in recent moral philosophy is another testimony to the great influence of the Cambridge philosopher, Mr. G. E. Moore, and his book, *Principia Ethica*. Thus Mr. Taylor speaks of the 'vulgar mistake' which Mr. Moore has taught us to call 'the naturalistic fallacy',[1] and Mr. G. S. Jury, as if to illustrate how well we have learned this lesson, says, with

From *Mind*, Vol. 48 (1939), pp. 464–77. Reprinted by permission of the author and the Editor of *Mind*.

[1] A. E. Taylor, *The Faith of a Moralist*, vol. i, p. 104 n.

reference to naturalistic definitions of value, 'All such definitions stand charged with Dr. Moore's "naturalistic fallacy"'.[1] Now, Mr. Moore coined the notion of the naturalistic fallacy in his polemic against naturalistic and metaphysical systems of ethics. 'The naturalistic fallacy is a fallacy,' he writes, and it 'must not be committed.' All naturalistic and metaphysical theories of ethics, however, 'are *based* on the naturalistic fallacy, in the sense that the commission of this fallacy has been the main cause of their wide acceptance'.[2] The best way to dispose of them, then, is to expose this fallacy. Yet it is not entirely clear just what is the status of the naturalistic fallacy in the polemics of the intuitionists against other theories. Sometimes it is used as a weapon, as when Miss Clarke says that if we call a thing good simply because it is liked we are guilty of the naturalistic fallacy.[3] Indeed, it presents this aspect to the reader in many parts of *Principia Ethica* itself. Now, in taking it as a weapon, the intuitionists use the naturalistic fallacy as if it were a logical fallacy on all fours with the fallacy of composition, the revelation of which disposes of naturalistic and metaphysical ethics and leaves intuitionism standing triumphant. That is, it is taken as a fallacy in advance, for use in controversy. But there are signs in *Principia Ethica* which indicate that the naturalistic fallacy has a rather different place in the intuitionist scheme, and should not be used as a weapon at all. In this aspect, the naturalistic fallacy must be proved to be a fallacy. It cannot be used to settle the controversy, but can only be asserted to be a fallacy when the smoke of battle has cleared. Consider the following passages: (*a*) 'the naturalistic fallacy consists in the contention that good *means* nothing but some simple or complex notion, that can be defined in terms of natural qualities'; (*b*) 'the point that good is indefinable and that to deny this involves a fallacy, is a point capable of strict proof'.[4] These passages seem to imply that the fallaciousness of the naturalistic fallacy is just what is at issue in the controversy between the intuitionists and their opponents, and cannot be wielded as a weapon in that controversy. One of the points I wish to make in this paper is that the charge of committing the naturalistic fallacy can be made, if at all, only as a conclusion from the discussion and not as an instrument of deciding it.

The notion of a naturalistic fallacy has been connected with the

---

[1] *Value and Ethical Objectivity*, p. 58.

[2] *Principia Ethica*, pp. 38, 64.

[3] M. E. Clarke, 'Cognition and Affection in the Experience of Value', *Journal of Philosophy* (1938).

[4] *Principia Ethica*, pp. 73, 77. See also p. xix.

notion of a bifurcation between the 'ought' and the 'is', between value and fact, between the normative and the descriptive. Thus Mr. D. C. Williams says that some moralists have thought it appropriate to chastise as the naturalistic fallacy the attempt to derive the Ought from the Is.[1] We may begin, then, by considering this bifurcation, emphasis on which, by Sidgwick, Sorley, and others, came largely as a reaction to the procedures of Mill and Spencer. Hume affirms the bifurcation in his *Treatise*: 'I cannot forbear adding to these reasonings an observation, which may, perhaps, be found of some importance. In every system of morality which I have hitherto met with, I have always remarked, that the author proceeds for some time in the ordinary way of reasoning, and establishes the being of a God, or makes observations concerning human affairs; when of a sudden I am surprised to find, that instead of the usual copulations of propositions, *is*, and *is not*, I meet with no proposition that is not connected with an *ought*, or an *ought not*. This change is imperceptible; but is, however, of the last consequence. For as this *ought*, or *ought not*, expresses some new relation or affirmation, it is necessary that it should be observed and explained; and at the same time that a reason should be given, for what seems altogether inconceivable, how this new relation can be a deduction from others, which are entirely different from it. But as authors do not commonly use this precaution, I shall presume to recommend it to the readers; and am persuaded, that this small attention would subvert all the vulgar systems of morality, and let us see that the distinction of vice and virtue is not founded merely on the relations of objects, nor is perceived by reason.'[2]

Needless to say, the intuitionists *have* found this observation of some importance.[3] They agree with Hume that it subverts all the vulgar systems of morality, though, of course, they deny that it lets us see that the distinction of virtue and vice is not founded on the relations of objects, nor is perceived by reason. In fact, they hold that a small attention to it subverts Hume's own system also, since this gives naturalistic definitions of virtue and vice and of good and evil.[4]

Hume's point is that ethical conclusions cannot be drawn validly

---

[1] 'Ethics as Pure Postulate'. *Philosophical Review* (1933). See also T. Whittaker. *The Theory of Abstract Ethics*, pp. 19 f.

[2] Book III, part ii, section i.

[3] See J. Laird, *A Study in Moral Theory*, pp. 16 f.; Whittaker, op. cit., p. 19.

[4] See C. D. Broad, *Five Types of Ethical Theory*, ch. iv.

from premises which are non-ethical. But when the intuitionists affirm the bifurcation of the 'ought' and the 'is', they mean more than that ethical propositions cannot be deduced from non-ethical ones. For this difficulty in the vulgar systems of morality could be remedied, as we shall see, by the introduction of definitions of ethical notions in non-ethical terms. They mean, further, that such definitions of ethical notions in non-ethical terms are impossible. 'The essential point,' says Mr. Laird, 'is the irreducibility of values to non-values.'[1] But they mean still more. Yellow and pleasantness are, according to Mr. Moore, indefinable in non-ethical terms, but they are natural qualities and belong on the 'is' side of the fence. Ethical properties, however, are not, for him, mere indefinable natural qualities, descriptive or expository. They are properties of a different *kind*—non-descriptive or non-natural.[2] The intuitionist bifurcation consists of three statements:—

(1) Ethical propositions are not deducible from non-ethical ones.[3]

(2) Ethical characteristics are not definable in terms of non-ethical ones.

(3) Ethical characteristics are different in kind from non-ethical ones.

Really it consists of but one statement, namely, (3), since (3) entails (2) and (2) entails (1). It does not involve saying that any ethical characteristics are absolutely indefinable. That is another question, although this is not always noticed.

What, now, has the naturalistic fallacy to do with the bifurcation of the 'ought' and the 'is'? To begin with, the connexion is this: many naturalistic and metaphysical moralists proceed as if ethical conclusions can be deduced from premises all of which are non-ethical, the classical examples being Mill and Spencer. That is, they violate (1). This procedure has lately been referred to as the 'factualist fallacy' by Mr. Wheelwright and as the 'valuational fallacy' by Mr. Wood.[4] Mr. Moore sometimes seems to identify it with the naturalistic fallacy, but in the main he holds only that it involves, implies, or rests upon this fallacy.[5] We may now consider the charge that the procedure in question is or involves a fallacy.

---

[1] *A Study in Moral Theory*, p. 94 n.

[2] See *Philosophical Studies*, pp. 259, 273 f.

[3] See J. Laird, op. cit., p. 318. Also pp. 12 ff.

[4] P. E. Wheelwright, *A Critical Introduction to Ethics*, pp. 40–51, 91 f.; L. Wood, 'Cognition and Moral Value', *Journal of Philosophy*, (1937), p. 237.

[5] See *Principia Ethica*, pp. 114, 57, 43, 49. Whittaker identifies it with the naturalistic fallacy and regards it as a 'logical' fallacy, op. cit., pp. 19 f.

It may be noted at once that, even if the deduction of ethical conclusions from non-ethical premises is in no way a fallacy, Mill certainly did commit a fallacy in drawing an analogy between visibility and desirability in his argument for hedonism; and perhaps his committing *this* fallacy, which, as Mr. Broad has said, we all learn about at our mothers' knees, is chiefly responsible for the notion of a naturalistic *fallacy*. But is it a fallacy to deduce ethical conclusions from non-ethical premises? Consider the Epicurean argument for hedonism which Mill so unwisely sought to embellish: pleasure is good, since it is sought by all men. Here an ethical conclusion is being derived from a non-ethical premise. And, indeed, the argument, taken strictly as it stands, *is* fallacious. But it is not fallacious because an *ethical* term occurs in the conclusion which does not occur in the premise. It is fallacious because any argument of the form 'A is B, therefore A is C' is invalid, if taken strictly as it stands. For example, it is invalid to argue that Crœsus is rich because he is wealthy. Such arguments are, however, not intended to be taken strictly as they stand. They are enthymemes and contain a suppressed premise. And, when this suppressed premise is made explicit, they are valid and involve no logical fallacy.[1] Thus the Epicurean inference from psychological to ethical hedonism is valid when the suppressed premise is added to the effect that what is sought by all men is good. Then the only question left is whether the premises are true.

It is clear, then, that the naturalistic fallacy is not a logical fallacy, since it may be involved even when the argument is valid. How does the naturalistic fallacy enter such 'mixed ethical arguments'[2] as that of the Epicureans? Whether it does or not depends on the nature of the suppressed premise. This may be either an induction, an intuition, a deduction from a 'pure ethical argument', a definition, or a proposition which is true by definition. If it is one of the first three, then the naturalistic fallacy does not enter at all. In fact, the argument does not then involve violating (1), since one of its premises will be ethical. But if the premise to be supplied is a definition or a proposition which is true by definition, as it probably was for the Epicureans, then the argument, while still valid, involves the naturalistic fallacy, and will run as follows:—

(*a*) Pleasure is sought by all men.

(*b*) What is sought by all men is good (by definition).

(*c*) Therefore, pleasure is good.

[1] See ibid., pp. 50, 139; Wheelwright, loc. cit.
[2] See C. D. Broad, *The Mind and its Place in Nature*, pp. 488 f.; Laird, loc. cit.

Now I am not greatly interested in deciding whether the argument as here set up violates (1). If it does not, then no 'mixed ethical argument' actually commits any factualist or valuational fallacy, except when it is unfairly taken as complete in its enthymematic form. If it does, then a valid argument may involve the deduction of an ethical conclusion from non-ethical premises and the factualist or valuational fallacy is not really a fallacy. The question depends on whether or not (b) and (c) are to be regarded as ethical propositions. Mr. Moore refuses so to regard them, contending that, by hypothesis, (b) is analytic or tautologous, and that (c) is psychological, since it really says only that pleasure is sought by all men.[1] But to say that (b) is analytic and not ethical and that (c) is not ethical but psychological is to prejudge the question whether 'good' can be defined; for the Epicureans would contend precisely that if their definition is correct then (b) is ethical but analytic and (c) ethical though psychological. Thus, unless the question of the definability of goodness is to be begged, (b) and (c) must be regarded as ethical, in which case our argument does not violate (1). However, suppose, if it be not nonsense, that (b) is non-ethical and (c) ethical, then the argument will violate (1), but it will still obey all of the canons of logic, and it is only confusing to talk of a 'valuational logic' whose basic rule is that an evaluative conclusion cannot be deduced from non-evaluative premises.[2]

For the only way in which either the intuitionists or postulationists like Mr. Wood can cast doubt upon the conclusion of the argument of the Epicureans (or upon the conclusion of any parallel argument) is to attack the premises, in particular (b). Now, according to Mr. Moore, it is due to the presence of (b) that the argument involves the naturalistic fallacy. (b) involves the identification of goodness with 'being sought by all men', and to make this or any other such identification is to commit the naturalistic fallacy. The naturalistic fallacy is not the procedure of violating (1). It is the procedure, implied in many mixed ethical arguments and explicitly carried out apart from such arguments by many moralists, of defining such characteristics as goodness or of substituting some other characteristic for them. To quote some passages from *Principia Ethica*:—

(a) '... far too many philosophers have thought that when they named those other properties [belonging to all things which are good] they were actually defining good; that these properties, in

[1] See op. cit., pp. 11 f.; 19, 38, 73, 139.
[2] See L. Wood, loc. cit.

fact, were simply not "other", but absolutely and entirely the same with goodness. This view I propose to call the "naturalistic fallacy"....'[1]

(b) 'I have thus appropriated the name Naturalism to a particular method of approaching Ethics. . . . This method consists in substituting for "good" some one property of a natural object or of a collection of natural objects. . . .'[2]

(c) '. . . the naturalistic fallacy [is] the fallacy which consists in identifying the simple notion which we mean by "good" with some other notion.'[3]

Thus, to identify 'better' and 'more evolved', 'good' and 'desired', etc., is to commit the naturalistic fallacy.[4] But just why is such a procedure fallacious or erroneous? And is it a fallacy only when applied to good? We must now study Section 12 of *Principia Ethica*. Here Mr. Moore makes some interesting statements:—

'. . . if anybody tried to define pleasure for us as being any other natural object; if anybody were to say, for instance that pleasure *means* the sensation of red. . . . Well, that would be the same fallacy which I have called the naturalistic fallacy. . . . I should not indeed call that a naturalistic fallacy, although it is the same fallacy as I have called naturalistic with reference to Ethics. . . . When a man confuses two natural objects with one another, defining the one by the other . . . then there is no reason to call the fallacy naturalistic. But if he confuses "good", which is not . . . a natural object, with any natural object whatever, then there is a reason for calling that a naturalistic fallacy. . . .'[5]

Here Mr. Moore should have added that, when one confuses 'good', which is not a metaphysical object or quality, with any metaphysical object or quality, as metaphysical moralists do, according to him, then the fallacy should be called the metaphysical fallacy. Instead he calls it a naturalistic fallacy in this case too, though he recognizes that the case is different since metaphysical properties are non-natural[6]—a procedure which has misled many readers of *Principia Ethica*. For example, it has led Mr. Broad to speak of 'theological naturalism'.[7]

[1] p. 10.
[2] p. 40.
[3] p. 58, cf. pp. xiii, 73.
[4] Cf. pp. 49, 53, 108, 139.
[5] p. 13.
[6] See pp. 38–40, 110–112.
[7] *Five Types of Ethical Theory*, p. 259.

To resume: 'Even if [goodness] were a natural object, that would not alter the nature of the fallacy nor diminish its importance one whit.'[1]

From these passages it is clear that the fallaciousness of the procedure which Mr. Moore calls the naturalistic fallacy is not due to the fact that it is applied to good or to an ethical or non-natural characteristic. When Mr. R. B. Perry defines 'good' as 'being an object of interest' the trouble is not merely that he is defining *good*. Nor is the trouble that he is defining an *ethical* characteristic in terms of *non-ethical* ones. Nor is the trouble that he is regarding a *non-natural* characteristic as a *natural* one. The trouble is more generic than that. For clarity's sake I shall speak of the definist fallacy as the generic fallacy which underlies the naturalistic fallacy. The naturalistic fallacy will then, by the above passages, be a species or form of the definist fallacy, as would the metaphysical fallacy if Mr. Moore had given that a separate name.[2] That is, the naturalistic fallacy, as illustrated by Mr. Perry's procedure, is a fallacy, not because it is naturalistic or confuses a non-natural quality with a natural one, but solely because it involves the definist fallacy. We may, then, confine our attention entirely to an understanding and evaluation of the definist fallacy.

To judge by the passages I have just quoted, the definist fallacy is the process of confusing or identifying two properties, of defining one property by another, or of substituting one property for another. Furthermore, the fallacy is always simply that two properties are being treated as one, and it is irrelevant, if it be the case, that one of them is natural or non-ethical and the other non-natural or ethical. One may commit the definist fallacy without infringing on the bifurcation of the ethical and the non-ethical, as when one identifies pleasantness and redness or rightness and goodness. But even when one infringes on that bifurcation in committing the definist fallacy, as when one identifies goodness and pleasantness or goodness and satisfaction, then the *mistake* is still not that the bifurcation is being infringed on, but only that two properties are being treated as one. Hence, on the present interpretation, the definist *fallacy* does not, in any of its forms, consist in violating (3), and has no essential connexion with the bifurcation of the 'ought' and the 'is'.

This formulation of the definist fallacy explains or reflects the motto of *Principia Ethica*, borrowed from Bishop Butler: 'Everything is what

---

[1] p. 14.
[2] As Whittaker has, loc. cit.

it is, and not another thing'. It follows from this motto that goodness is what it is and not another thing. It follows that views which try to identify it with something else are making a mistake of an elementary sort. For it *is* a mistake to confuse or identify two properties. If the properties really are two, then they simply are not identical. But do those who define ethical notions in non-ethical terms make this mistake? They will reply to Mr. Moore that they are not identifying two properties; what they are saying is that two words or sets of words stand for or mean one and the same property. Mr. Moore was being, in part, misled by the material mode of speech, as Mr. Carnap calls it, in such sentences as 'Goodness is pleasantness', 'Knowledge is true belief', etc. When one says instead. 'The word "good" and the word "pleasant" mean the same thing', etc., it is clear that one is not identifying two things. But Mr. Moore kept himself from seeing this by his disclaimer that he was interested in any statement about the use of words.[1]

The definist fallacy, then, as we have stated it, does not rule out any naturalistic or metaphysical definitions of ethical terms. Goodness is not identifiable with any 'other' characteristic (if it is a characteristic at all). But the question is: *which* characteristics are other than goodness, which names stand for characteristics other than goodness? And it is begging the question of the definability of goodness to say out of hand that Mr. Perry, for instance, is identifying goodness with something else. The point is that goodness is what it is, even if it is definable. That is why Mr. Perry can take as the motto of his naturalistic *Moral Economy* another sentence from Bishop Butler: 'Things and actions are what they are, and the consequences of them will be what they will be; why then should we desire to be deceived?' The motto of *Principia Ethica* is a tautology, and should be expanded as follows: Everything is what it is, and not another thing, unless it is another thing, and even then it is what it is.

On the other hand, if Mr. Moore's motto (or the definist fallacy) rules out any definitions, for example of 'good', then it rules out all definitions of any term whatever. To be effective at all, it must be understood to mean, 'Every term means what it means, and not what is meant by any other term'. Mr. Moore seems implicitly to understand his motto in this way in Section 13, for he proceeds as if 'good' has no meaning, if it has no unique meaning. If the motto be taken in this way, it will follow that 'good' is an indefinable term, since no

[1] See op. cit., pp. 6, 8, 12.

synonyms can be found. But it will also follow that no term is definable. And then the method of analysis is as useless as an English butcher in a world without sheep.

Perhaps we have misinterpreted the definist fallacy. And, indeed, some of the passages which I quoted earlier in this paper seem to imply that the definist fallacy is just the error of defining an indefinable characteristic. On this interpretation, again, the definist fallacy has, in all of its forms, no essential connexion with the bifurcation of the ethical and the non-ethical. Again, one may commit the definist fallacy without violating that bifurcation, as when one defines pleasantness in terms of redness or goodness in terms of rightness (granted Mr. Moore's belief that pleasantness and goodness are indefinable). But even when one infringes on that bifurcation and defines goodness in terms of desire, the *mistake* is not that one is infringing on the bifurcation by violating (3), but only that one is defining an indefinable characteristic. This is possible because the proposition that goodness is indefinable is logically independent of the proposition that goodness is non-natural: as is shown by the fact that a characteristic may be indefinable and yet natural, as yellowness is; or non-natural and yet definable, as rightness is (granted Mr. Moore's views about yellowness and rightness).

Consider the definist fallacy as we have just stated it. It is, of course, an error to define an indefinable quality. But the question, again, is: which qualities are indefinable? It is begging the question in favour of intuitionism to say in advance that the quality goodness is indefinable and that, therefore, all naturalists commit the definist fallacy. One must know that goodness is indefinable before one can argue that the definist fallacy *is* a fallacy. Then, however, the definist fallacy can enter only at the end of the controversy between intuitionism and definism, and cannot be used as a weapon in the controversy.

The definist fallacy may be stated in such a way as to involve the bifurcation between the 'ought' and the 'is'.[1] It would then be committed by anyone who offered a definition of any ethical characteristic in terms of non-ethical ones. The trouble with such a definition, on this interpretation, would be that an *ethical* characteristic is being reduced to a *non-ethical* one, a *non-natural* one to a *natural* one. That is, the definition would be ruled out by the fact that the characteristic being defined is ethical or non-natural and therefore cannot be defined in non-ethical or natural terms. But on this interpretation,

[1] See J. Wisdom, *Mind* (1931), p. 213, note 1.

too, there is danger of a *petitio* in the intuitionist argumentation. To assume that the ethical characteristic is exclusively ethical is to beg precisely the question which is at issue when the definition is offered. Thus, again, one must know that the characteristic is non-natural and indefinable in natural terms before one can say that the definists are making a mistake.

Mr. Moore, McTaggart, and others formulate the naturalistic fallacy sometimes in a way somewhat different from any of those yet discussed. They say that the definists are confusing a universal synthetic proposition about *the good* with a definition of *goodness*.[1] Mr. Abraham calls this the 'fallacy of misconstrued proposition'.[2] Here again the difficulty is that, while it is true that it is an error to construe a universal synthetic proposition as a definition, it is a *petitio* for the intuitionists to say that what the definist is taking for a definition is really a universal synthetic proposition.[3]

At last, however, the issue between the intuitionists and the definists (naturalistic or metaphysical) is becoming clearer. The definists are all holding that certain propositions involving ethical terms are analytic, tautologous, or true by definition, e.g., Mr. Perry so regards the statement, 'All objects of desire are good'. The intuitionists hold that such statements are synthetic. What underlies this difference of opinion is that the intuitionists claim to have at least a dim awareness of a simple unique quality or relation of goodness or rightness which appears in the region which our ethical terms roughly indicate, whereas the definists claim to have no awareness of any such quality or relation in that region, which is different from all other qualities and relations which belong to the same context but are designated by words other than 'good' and 'right' and their obvious synonyms.[4] The definists are in all honesty claiming to find but one characteristic where the intuitionists claim to find two, as Mr. Perry claims to find only the property of being desired where Mr. Moore claims to find both it and the property of being good. The issue, then, is one of inspection or intuition, and concerns the awareness or discernment of qualities and relations.[5] That is why it cannot be decided by the use of the notion of a fallacy.

---

[1] See *Principia Ethica*, pp. 10, 16, 38; *The Nature of Existence*, vol. ii, p. 398.

[2] Leo Abraham, 'The Logic of Intuitionism', *International Journal of Ethics*, (1933).

[3] As Mr. Abraham points out, loc. cit.

[4] See R. B. Perry, *General Theory of Value*, p. 30; cf.; *Journal of Philosophy*, (1931), p. 520.

[5] See H. Osborne, *Foundations of the Philosophy of Value,* pp. 15, 19, 70.

If the definists may be taken at their word, then they are not actually confusing two characteristics with each other, nor defining an indefinable characteristic, not confusing definitions and universal synthetic propositions—in short they are not committing the naturalistic or definist fallacy in any of the interpretations given above. Then the only fallacy which they commit—the real naturalistic or definist fallacy—is the failure to descry the qualities and relations which are central to morality. But this is neither a logical fallacy nor a logical confusion. It is not even, properly speaking, an error. It is rather a kind of blindness, analogous to colour-blindness. Even this moral blindness can be ascribed to the definists only if they are correct in their claim to have no awareness of any unique ethical characteristics and if the intuitionists are correct in affirming the existence of such characteristics, but certainly to call it a 'fallacy', even in a loose sense, is both unamiable and profitless.

On the other hand, of course, if there are no such characteristics in the objects to which we attach ethical predicates, then the intuitionists, if we may take them at their word, are suffering from a corresponding moral hallucination. Definists might then call this the intuitionistic or moralistic fallacy, except that it is no more a 'fallacy' than is the blindness just described. Anyway, they do not believe the claim of the intuitionists to be aware of unique ethical characteristics, and consequently do not attribute to them this hallucination. Instead, they simply deny that the intuitionists really do find such unique qualities or relations, and then they try to find some plausible way of accounting for the fact that very respectable and trustworthy people think they find them.[1] Thus they charge the intuitionists with verbalism, hypostatization, and the like. But this half of the story does not concern us now.

What concerns us more is the fact that the intuitionists do not credit the claim of the definists either. They would be much disturbed, if they really thought that their opponents were morally blind, for they do not hold that we must be regenerated by grace before we can have moral insight, and they share the common feeling that morality is something democratic even though not all men are good. Thus they hold that 'we are all aware' of certain unique characteristics when we use the terms 'good', 'right', etc., only due to a lack of analytic clearness of mind, abetted perhaps by a philosophical prejudice, we may not be aware at all that they are different from other character-

---

[1] Cf. R. B. Perry, *Journal of Philosophy*, (1931), pp. 520 ff.

istics of which we are also aware.[1] Now, I have been arguing that the intuitionists cannot charge the definists with committing any fallacy unless and until they have shown that we are all, the definists included, aware of the disputed unique characteristics. If, however, they were to show this, then, at least at the end of the controversy, they could accuse the definists of the error of confusing two characteristics, or of the error of defining an indefinable one, and these errors might, since the term is somewhat loose in its habits, be called 'fallacies', though they are not logical fallacies in the sense in which an invalid argument is. The fallacy of misconstrued proposition depends on the error of confusing two characteristics, and hence could also on our present supposition, be ascribed to the definists, but it is not really a *logical* confusion,[2] since it does not actually involve being confused about the difference between a proposition and a definition.

Only it is difficult to see how the intuitionists can prove that the definists are at least vaguely aware of the requisite unique characteristics.[3] The question must surely be left to the inspection or intuition of the definists themselves, aided by whatever suggestions the intuitionists may have to make. If so, we must credit the verdict of their inspection, especially of those among them who have read the writings of the intuitionists reflectively, and, then, as we have seen, the most they can be charged with is moral blindness.

Besides trying to discover just what is meant by the naturalistic fallacy, I tried to show that the notion that a logical or quasi-logical fallacy is committed by the definists only confuses the issue between the intuitionists and the definists (and the issue between the latter and the emotists or postulationists), and misrepresents the way in which the issue is to be settled. No logical fallacy need appear anywhere in the procedure of the definists. Even fallacies in any less accurate sense cannot be implemented to decide the case against the definists; at best they can be ascribed to the definists only after the issue has been decided against them on independent grounds. But the only defect which can be attributed to the definists, *if* the intuitionists are right in affirming the existence of unique indefinable ethical characteristics, is a peculiar moral blindness, which is not a fallacy even in the looser sense. The issue in question must be decided by

---

[1] *Principia Ethica*, pp. 17, 38, 59, 61.

[2] But see H. Osborne, op. cit., pp. 18 f.

[3] For a brief discussion of their arguments, see ibid., p. 67; L. Abraham, op. cit. I think they are all inconclusive, but cannot show this here.

whatever method we may find satisfactory for determining whether or not a word stands for a characteristic at all, and, if it does, whether or not it stands for a unique characteristic. What method is to be employed is, perhaps, in one form or another, the basic problem of contemporary philosophy, but no generally satisfactory solution of the problem has yet been reached. I shall venture to say only this: it does seem to me that the issue is not to be decided against the intuitionists by the application *ab extra* to ethical judgements of any empirical or ontological meaning dictum.[1]

[1] See *Principia Ethica*, pp. 124 f., 140.

IV

GOOD AND EVIL[1]

P. T. GEACH

MY FIRST TASK will be to draw a logical distinction between two sorts of adjectives, suggested by the distinction between *attributive* adjectives (e.g. 'a red book') and *predicative* adjectives (e.g. 'this book is red'); I shall borrow this terminology from the grammars. I shall say that in a phrase 'an A B' ('A' being an adjective and 'B' being a noun) 'A' is a (logically) predicative adjective if the predication 'is an A B' splits up logically into a pair of predications 'is a B' and 'is A'; otherwise I shall say that 'A' is a (logically) attributive adjective. Henceforth I shall use the terms 'predicative adjective' and 'attributive adjective' always in my special logical sense, unless the contrary is shown by my inserting the adverb 'grammatically'.

There are familiar examples of what I call attributive adjectives. 'Big' and 'small' are attributive; 'x is a big flea' does not split up into 'x is a flea' and 'x is big', nor 'x is a small elephant' into 'x is an elephant' and 'x is small'; for if these analyses were legitimate, a simple argument would show that a big flea is a big animal and a small elephant a small animal. Again, the sort of adjective that the mediaevals called *alienans* is attributive; 'x is a forged banknote' does not split up into 'x is a banknote' and 'x is forged', nor 'x is the putative father of y' into 'x is the father of y' and 'x is putative'. On the other hand, in the phrase 'a red book' 'red' is a predicative adjective in my sense, although not grammatically so, for 'is a red book' logically splits up into 'is a book' and 'is red'.

I can now state my first thesis about good and evil: 'good' and 'bad' are always attributive, not predicative, adjectives. This is fairly clear about 'bad' because 'bad' is something like an *alienans* adjective; we cannot safely predicate of a bad A what we predicate of an A, any

From *Analysis*, Vol. 17 (1956), pp. 33–42. Reprinted by permission of the author, *Analysis*, and Basil Blackwell.

[1] [This article is discussed in A. Duncan-Jones, 'Good Things and Good Thieves'. *Analysis* (1966). Also relevant are P. R. Foot, 'Goodness and Choice', *Aristotelian Society Supplementary Volume*, XXXV (1961); Z. Vendler, 'The Grammar of Goodness', *Philosophical Review* (1963); and T. E. Patton and P. Ziff, 'On Vendler's Grammar of "Good"', *Philosophical Review* (1964). Ed.]

more than we can predicate of a forged banknote or a putative father what we predicate of a banknote or a father. We actually call forged money 'bad'; and we cannot infer e.g. that because food supports life bad food supports life. For 'good' the point is not so clear at first sight, since 'good' is not *alienans*—whatever holds true of an A as such holds true of a good A. But consider the contrast in such a pair of phrases as 'red car' and 'good car'. I could ascertain that a distant object is a red car because I can see it is red and a keener-sighted but colour-blind friend can see it is a car; there is no such possibility of ascertaining that a thing is a good car by pooling independent information that it is good and that it is a car. This sort of example shows that 'good' like 'bad' is essentially an attributive adjective. Even when 'good' or 'bad' stands by itself as a predicate, and is thus grammatically predicative, some substantive has to be understood; there is no such thing as being just good or bad, there is only being a good or bad so-and-so. (If I say that something is a good or bad *thing*, either 'thing' is a mere proxy for a more descriptive noun to be supplied from the context; or else I am trying to use 'good' or 'bad' predicatively, and its being grammatically attributive is a mere disguise. The latter attempt is, on my thesis, illegitimate.)

We can indeed say *simpliciter* 'A is good' or 'A is bad', where 'A' is a proper name; but this is an exception that proves the rule. For Locke was certainly wrong in holding that there is no nominal essence of individuals; the continued use of a proper name 'A' always presupposes a continued reference to an individual as being the same X, where 'X' is some common noun; and the 'X' expresses the nominal essence of the individual called 'A'. Thus use of the proper name 'Peter Geach' presupposes a continuing reference to the same *man*; use of 'the Thames' a continuing reference to the same *river*; and so on. In modern logic books you often read that proper names have no meaning, in the sense of 'meaning' in which common nouns are said to have meaning; or (more obscurely) that they have no 'connotation'. But consider the difference between the understanding that a man has of a conversation overheard in a country house when he knows that 'Seggie' stands for a man, and what he has if he is uncertain whether 'Seggie' stands for a man, a Highland stream, a village, or a dog. In the one case he knows *what* 'Seggie' means, though not *whom*; in the other case he does not know *what* 'Seggie' means and cannot follow the drift of the conversation. Well, then if the common noun 'X' expresses the nominal essence of the individual called 'A'; if *being the same X* is a condition whose fulfilment is presupposed by our

still calling an individual 'A'; then the meaning of 'A is good/bad'
said *simpliciter*, will be 'A is a good/bad X'. E.g. if 'Seggie' stands for
a man, 'Seggie is good' said *simpliciter* will mean 'Seggie is a good
man', though context might make it mean 'Seggie is a good deer-
stalker', or the like.

The moral philosophers known as Objectivists[1] would admit all
that I have said as regards the ordinary uses of the terms 'good'
and 'bad'; but they allege that there is an essentially different, predicative, use of the terms in such utterances as 'pleasure is good' and
'preferring inclination to duty is bad', and that this use alone is of
philosophical importance. The ordinary uses of 'good' and 'bad' are
for Objectivists just a complex tangle of ambiguities. I read an article
once by an Objectivist exposing these ambiguities and the baneful
effects they have on philosophers not forewarned of them. One
philosopher who was so misled was Aristotle; Aristotle, indeed, did
not talk English, but by a remarkable coincidence ἀγαθός had ambiguities quite parallel to those of 'good'. Such coincidences are, of
course, possible; puns are sometimes translatable. But it is also
possible that the uses of ἀγαθός and 'good' run parallel because they
express one and the same concept; that this is a philosophically
important concept, in which Aristotle did well to be interested;
and that the apparent dissolution of this concept into a mass of ambiguities results from trying to assimilate it to the concepts expressed
by ordinary predicative adjectives. It is mere prejudice to think that
either all things called 'good' must satisfy some one condition, or the
term 'good' is hopelessly ambiguous. A philosopher who writes off
most of the uses of 'good' as trivial facts about the English language
can, of course, with some plausibility, represent the remaining uses
of 'good' as all expressing some definite condition fulfilled by good
things—e.g. that they either contain, or are conducive to, pleasure;
or again that they satisfy desire. Such theories of goodness are, however, open to well-known objections; they are cases of the Naturalistic
Fallacy, as Objectivists say. The Objectivists' own theory is that 'good'
in the selected uses they leave to the word does not supply an ordinary,
'natural', description of things, but ascribes to them a simple and
indefinable *non*-natural attribute. But nobody has ever given a coherent
and understandable account of what it is for an attribute to be non-
natural. I am very much afraid that the Objectivists are just playing
fast and loose with the term 'attribute'. In order to assimilate 'good'

---

[1] [Geach seems to have had Moore and Ross in mind; perhaps also Prichard. Ed.]

to ordinary predicative adjectives like 'red' and 'sweet' they call goodness an attribute; to escape undesired consequences drawn from the assimilation, they can always protest, 'Oh no, not like that. Goodness isn't a *natural* attribute like redness and sweetness, it's a non-natural attribute'. It is just as though somebody thought to escape the force of Frege's arguments that the number 7 is not a figure, by saying that it is a figure, only a non-natural figure, and that this is a possibility Frege failed to consider.

Moreover, can a philosopher offer philosophical utterances like 'pleasure is good' as an *explanation* of how he means 'good' to be taken in his discussions? 'Forget the uses of "good" in ordinary language' says the Objectivist; 'in our discussion it shall mean what I mean by it in such typical remarks as "pleasure is good". You, of course, know just how I want you to take these. No, of course I cannot explain further: don't you know that "good" in my sense is a simple and undefinable term?' But how can we be asked to take for granted at the outset that a peculiarly philosophical use of words necessarily means anything at all? Still less can we be expected at the outset to know what this use means.

I conclude that Objectivism is only the pretence of a way out of the Naturalistic Fallacy: it does not really give an account of how 'good' differs in its logic from other terms, but only darkens counsel by words without knowledge.

What I have said so far would meet with general approval by contemporary ethical writers at Oxford (whom I shall henceforth call the Oxford Moralists); and I now have to consider their positive account of 'good'. They hold that the features of the term's use which I have described derive from its function's being primarily not descriptive at all but commendatory. 'That is a good book' means something like 'I recommend that book' or 'choose that book'. They hold, however, that although the primary force of 'good' is commendation there are many cases where its force is purely descriptive—'Hutton was batting on a good wicket', in a newspaper report, would not mean 'What a wonderful wicket Hutton was batting on. May you have such a wicket when you bat'.[1] The Oxford Moralists account for such cases by saying that here 'good' is, so to say, in quotation marks; Hutton was batting on a 'good' wicket, i.e. a wicket such as cricket fans would call 'good', i.e. would commend and choose.

I totally reject this view that 'good' has not a primarily descriptive

[1][The text is here slightly altered to remove a misunderstanding that arose over the first version. Ed.]

force. Somebody who did not care two pins about cricket, but fully understood how the game worked (not an impossible supposition), could supply a purely descriptive sense for the phrase 'good batting wicket' regardless of the tastes of cricket fans. Again if I call a man a good burglar or a good cut-throat I am certainly not commending him myself; one can imagine circumstances in which these descriptions would serve to guide another man's choice (e.g. if a commando leader were choosing burglars and cut-throats for a special job), but such circumstances are rare and cannot give the primary sense of the descriptions. It ought to be clear that calling a thing a good A does not influence choice unless the one who is choosing happens to want an A; and this influence on action is not the logically primary force of the word 'good'. 'You have ants in your pants', which obviously has a primarily descriptive force, is far closer to affecting action than many uses of the term 'good'. And many uses of the word 'good' have no reference to the tastes of a panel of experts or anything of the sort; if I say that a man has a good eye or a good stomach my remark has a very clear descriptive force and has no reference to any panel of eye or stomach fanciers.

So far as I can gather from their writings, the Oxford Moralists would develop two lines of objection against the view that 'good' has a primarily descriptive force. First, if we avoid the twin errors of the Naturalistic Fallacy and of Objectivism we shall see that there is no one description, 'natural' or 'non-natural', to which all good things answer. The traits for which a thing is called 'good' are different according to the kind of thing in question; a knife is called 'good' if it is UVW, a stomach if it is XYZ, and so on. So, if 'good' did have a properly descriptive force this would vary from case to case: 'good' applied to knives would express the attributes UVW, 'good' as applied to stomachs would express the attributes XYZ, and so on. If 'good' is not to be merely ambiguous its primary force must be taken to be the unvarying commendatory force, not the indefinitely varying descriptive force.

This argument is a mere fallacy; it is another example of assimilating 'good' to ordinary predicative adjectives, or rather it assumes that this assimilation would have to be all right if the force of 'good' were descriptive. It would not in fact follow, even if 'good' were an ordinary predicative adjective, that if 'good knife' means the same as 'knife that is UVW', 'good' means the same as 'UVW'. 'Triangle with all its sides equal' means the same as 'triangle with three sides equal', but you cannot cancel out 'triangle' and say that 'with all its sides equal' means the same as 'with three sides equal'. In the case of 'good' the fallacy is even grosser; it is like thinking that 'square of' means the same as 'double of' because 'the square of 2' means the same as 'the double of 2'. This mathematical analogy may help to get our heads clear. There is no one number by which you can always multiply a number to get its square: but it does not follow either that 'square of' is an ambiguous expression meaning sometimes 'double of', sometimes 'treble of', etc., or that you have to do something other than multiplying to find the square of a number; and, given a number, its square is determinate. Similarly, there is no one description to which all things called 'good so-and-so's' answer; but it does not follow either that 'good' is a very ambiguous expression or that calling a thing good is something different from describing it; and given the descriptive force of 'A', the descriptive force of 'a good A' does not depend upon people's tastes.

'But I could know what "good hygrometer" meant without knowing what hygrometers were for; I could not, however, in that case be giving a definite descriptive force to "good hygrometer" as opposed to "hygrometer"; so "good" must have commendatory not descriptive force.' The reply to this objection (imitated from actual arguments of the Oxford Moralists) is that if I do not know what hygrometers are for, I do not really know what 'hygrometer' means, and *therefore* do not really know what 'good hygrometer' means; I merely know that I could find out its meaning by finding out what hygrometers were for—just as I know how I could find out the value of the square of the number of the people in Sark if I knew the number of people, and *so far* may be said to understand the phrase, 'the square of the number of the people in Sark'.

The Oxford Moralists' second line of objection consists in first asking whether the connexion between calling a thing 'a good A' and advising a man who wants an A to choose this one is analytic or empirical, and then developing a dilemma. It sounds clearly wrong to make the connexion a mere empirical fact; but if we make it analytic, then 'good' cannot have descriptive force, for from a mere description advice cannot be logically inferred.

I should indeed say that the connexion is not merely empirical; but neither is it analytic. It belongs to the *ratio* of 'want', 'choose', 'good', and 'bad', that, normally, and other things being equal, a man who wants an A will choose a good A and will not choose a bad A—or rather will choose an A that he thinks good and will not choose an A that he thinks bad. This holds good whether the A's we are choosing between are knives, horses, or thieves; *quidquid appetitur, appetitur sub specie boni*. Since the qualifying phrase, 'normally and other things being equal', is necessary for the truth of this statement, it is not an analytic statement. But the presence of these phrases does *not* reduce the statement to a mere rough empirical generalization: to think this would be to commit a crude empiricist fallacy, exposed once for all by Wittgenstein. Even if not all A's are B's, the statement that A's are normally B's may belong to the *ratio* of an A. Most chess moves are valid, most intentions are carried out, most statements are veracious; none of these statements is just a rough generalization, for if we tried to describe how it would be for most chess moves to be invalid, most intentions not to be carried out, most statements to be lies, we should soon find ourselves talking nonsense. We shall equally find ourselves talking nonsense if we try to describe a people whose custom it was, when they wanted A's, to choose A's they thought bad and reject A's they thought good. (And this goes for *all* interpretations of 'A'.)

There is, I admit, much more difficulty in passing from 'man' to 'good/bad/man', or from 'human act' to 'good/bad/human act', if these phrases are to be taken as purely descriptive and in senses determined simply by those of 'man' and 'human act'. I think this difficulty could be overcome; but even so the Oxford Moralists could now deploy a powerful weapon of argument. Let us suppose that we have found a clear descriptive meaning for 'good human act' and for 'bad human act', and have shown that adultery answers to the description 'bad human act'. Why should this consideration deter an intending adulterer? By what logical step can we pass from the supposedly descriptive sentence 'adultery is a bad human act' to the imperative 'you must not commit adultery'? It is useless to say 'It is your duty to do good and avoid doing evil'; either this is much the same as the unhelpful remark 'It is good to do good and avoid doing evil', or else 'It is your duty' is a smuggling in of an imperative force not conveyed by the terms 'good' and 'evil' which are *ex hypothesi* purely descriptive.

We must allow in the first place that the question, 'Why should I?' or 'Why shouldn't I?' is a reasonable question, which calls for an answer, not for abusive remarks about the wickedness of asking; and I think that the only relevant answer is an appeal to something the questioner *wants*. Since Kant's time people have supposed that there is another sort of relevant reply—an appeal not to inclination but to the Sense of Duty. Now indeed a man may be got by training into a state of mind in which 'You *must* not' is a sufficient answer to 'Why shouldn't I?'; in which, giving this answer to himself, or hearing it given by others, strikes him with a quite peculiar awe; in which, perhaps, he even thinks he 'must not' ask why he 'must not'. (Cf. Lewis Carroll's juvenile poem 'My Fairy', with its devastating 'Moral: You mustn't'.) Moral philosophers of the Objectivist school, like Sir David Ross, would call this 'apprehension of one's obligations'; it does not worry them that, but for God's grace, this sort of training can make a man 'apprehend' practically anything as his 'obligations'. (Indeed, they admire a man who does what he thinks he *must* do regardless of what he actually does; is he not acting from the Sense of Duty which is the highest motive?) But even if *ad hominem* 'You mustn't' is a final answer to 'Why shouldn't I?', it is no rational answer at all.

It can, I think, be shown that an action's being a good or bad human action is of itself something that touches the agent's desires. Although calling a thing 'a good A' or 'a bad A' does not of itself work upon the hearer's desires, it may be expected to do so if the hearer happens to be choosing an A. Now what a man cannot fail to be choosing is his manner of acting; so to call a manner of acting good or bad cannot but serve to guide action. As Aristotle says, acting well, $\epsilon \dot{v} \pi \rho \alpha \xi \acute{\iota} \alpha$, is a man's aim *simpliciter*, $\dot{\alpha} \pi \lambda \tilde{\omega} \varsigma$, and *qua* man; other objects of choice are so only relatively, $\pi \rho \acute{o} \varsigma \; \tau \iota$, or are the objects of a particular man, $\tau \iota v \acute{o} \varsigma$[1]; but *any* man has to choose how to act, so calling an action good or bad does not depend for its effect as a suasion upon any individual peculiarities of desire.

I shall not here attempt to explicate the descriptive force of 'good (bad) human action': but some remarks upon the logic of the phrase seem to be called for. In the first place, a tennis stroke or chess move is a human act. Are we to say, then, that the description 'good tennis stroke' or 'good chess move' is of itself something that must appeal to the agent's desire? Plainly not; but this is no difficulty. Although a tennis stroke or a chess move is a human act, it does not follow that a good tennis stroke or a good chess move is a good human act, because of the peculiar logic of the term 'good'; so calling a tennis stroke or a chess move good is not *eo ipso* an appeal to what an agent must be wanting.

Secondly, though we can sensibly speak of a good or bad human act, we cannot sensibly speak of a good or bad event, a good or bad thing to happen. 'Event', like 'thing', is too empty a word to convey either a criterion of identity or a standard of goodness; to ask 'Is

[1] E. N. 1139*b* 2–4.

this a good or bad thing (to happen)?' is as useless as to ask 'Is this the same thing that I saw yesterday?' or 'Is the same event still going on?', unless the emptiness of 'thing' or 'event' is filled up by a special context of utterance. Caesar's murder was a bad thing to happen to a living organism, a good fate for a man who wanted divine worship for himself, and again a good or bad act on the part of his murderers; to ask whether it was a good or bad event would be senseless.

Thirdly, I am deliberately ignoring the supposed distinction between the Right and the Good. In Aquinas there is no such distinction. He finds it sufficient to talk of good and bad human acts. When Ross would say that there is a morally good action but not a right act, Aquinas would say that a good human intention had issued in what was, in fact, a bad action; and when Ross would say that there was a right act but not a morally good action, Aquinas would say that there was a bad human act performed in circumstances in which a similar act with a different intention would have been a good one (e.g. giving money to a beggar for the praise of men rather than for the relief of his misery).

Since the English word 'right' has an idiomatic predilection for the definite article—we speak of a good chess move but of the right move— people who think that doing right is something other than doing good will regard virtuous behaviour as consisting, not just in doing good and eschewing evil, but in doing, on every occasion, the right act for the occasion. This speciously strict doctrine leads in fact to quite laxist consequences. A man who just keeps on doing good and eschewing evil, if he knows that adultery is an evil act, will decide that (as Aristotle says) there can be no deliberating when or how or with whom to commit adultery.[1] But a man who believes in discerning, on each occasion, the right act for the occasion, may well decide that on this occasion, all things considered, adultery is the right action. Sir David Ross explicitly tells us that on occasion the right act may be the judicial punishment of an innocent man 'that the whole nation perish not': for in this case 'the *prima facie* duty of consulting the general interest has proved more obligatory than the perfectly distinct *prima facie* duty of respecting the rights of those who have respected the rights of others'.[2] (We must charitably hope that for him the words of Caiaphas that he quotes just had the vaguely hallowed associations of a Bible text, and that he

[1] E. N. 1107a 16.
[2] *The Right and the Good*, p. 61.

did not remember whose judicial murder was being counselled.)[1]

I am well aware that much of this discussion is unsatisfying; some points on which I think I do see clear I have not been able to develop at proper length; on many points (e.g. the relation between desire and good, and the precise *ratio* of evil in evil acts), I certainly do not see clear. Moreover, though I have argued that the characteristic of being a good or bad human action is of itself bound to influence the agent's desires, I have not discussed whether an action of its nature bad is always and on all accounts to be avoided, as Aristotle thought. But perhaps, though I have not made everything clear, I have made some things clearer.

[1] Holding this notion of *the* right act, people have even held that some creative act would be *the* right act for a God—e.g. that a God would be obliged to create the best of all possible worlds, so that either this world of ours is the best possible or there is no good God. I shall not go further into this; it will be enough to say that what is to be expected of a good Creator is *a* good world, not *the* right world.

V

GEACH: GOOD AND EVIL

R. M. HARE

MR. GEACH has suggested to me that I publish a reply to his article on Good and Evil.[1] From this I conclude that he regards me as a constituent part of the composite Aunt Sally which he calls 'The Oxford Moralists'. I am not, however, concerned to defend this heterogeneous monster. In the stage-battle which Geach has with his creature I find myself engaged on both sides; for although some of the views of 'The Oxford Moralists' are more or less recognizable versions of mine, so also are a good many of Geach's own arguments and in some cases examples. Neither am I going to attack his main thesis that 'good' is an attributive adjective, since I agree with it.[2]

How composite a creature Geach's Aunt Sally is, may be seen by considering a typical paragraph of his paper—the third complete paragraph on p. 36.[3] There 'The Oxford Moralists' are said to hold the following positions:

(1) The function of 'good' is primarily not descriptive at all but commendatory.

(2) 'That is a good book' means something like 'I recommend that book'.

(3) 'That is a good book' means something like 'Choose that book'.

From *Analysis*, Vol. 18 (1957), pp. 103–12. Reprinted by permission of the author and *Analysis*. Apart from small alterations to the second and third paragraphs, which were consequential on changes in Professor Geach's article, Professor Hare's reply is reprinted without revision.

[1] Analysis, Vol. 17, No. 2, pp. 33–42. I wish to thank Mr. Geach for his kindness in lending me the full typescript of a longer paper of which his published article forms the opening section; and also for elucidating, in correspondence, the meaning which he attaches to the word *ratio*, and the use to which he wishes to put this concept in his theory.

[2] This thesis has been common form among Oxford moralists for many years; so far as I remember, it first entered my own mind when discussing Frege with Professor Austin. In *Foundations of Arithmetic* (ed. and tr. Austin, pp. 28ff.) Frege, following a suggestion of Baumann, points out that cardinal numbers are, in Geach's sense, attributive. But some acknowledgement is also due to Joseph and ultimately to Aristotle, *Eth. Nic.*, I, 6. The thesis, without the terminology, is to be found in my *Language of Morals* (*LM*), p. 133.

[3] [Paragraph 4, p. 67 of this volume, Ed.]

It may be that Geach has not noticed the difference between commending and recommending.[1] or between either of them and the various purposes for which the imperative is used; or between any of these various things and the two different things which are expressed by the sentences 'What a wonderful wicket Hutton was batting on' and 'May you have such a wicket when you bat', which he manages to cram into this mixed bag. That the last example comes from *LM*, p. 118, makes it look as if, according to that book, the commendatory meaning of 'good' is to be identified with the expression of exclamation or wishes. But this view does not occur in the text of the book. If Geach wishes to attribute these confusions to others besides himself, ought they not to be named?[2]

It is not clear to me, either, why it should be thought that 'Oxford Moralists', when confronted with the 'good wicket' example, would use the argument which Geach puts in their mouths. The example is given by Geach as a case where 'the force of "good" is purely descriptive'. 'Oxford Moralists' says Geach, 'account for such cases by saying that here "good" is so to say in quotation marks; Hutton was batting on a "good" wicket, i.e. a wicket such as cricket fans would call "good", i.e. would commend and choose'. Now there are indeed cases in which 'good' is used in this 'inverted-commas' way[3]; but this is not one of them. Those are cases where the word 'good' has no evaluative meaning, because the speaker is not himself commending, but only alluding to the commendation of some other (normally well-known) set of people. But in the present case the writer is certainly commending the wicket (though he is not doing some of the other things which Geach confuses with commending). In this context, no doubt, the primary purpose of saying, in a newspaper report, that it was a good wicket is 'to inform readers what description of wicket it was'[4]; but it can surely be supposed that the writer and most of his readers are

---

[1]According to the O.E.D. 'commend' is sometimes used with the sense 'recommend'; but this use is not common, and it is not in this sense that the word occurs in *LM*. We normally use 'recommend' when a *particular* choice is in question, but 'commend' when a thing is being mentioned as in general 'worthy of acceptance or approval'.

[2]I myself claim no property in any of these positions attributed to 'The Oxford Moralists'. My view is that 'good' has, normally, both descriptive and evaluative (commendatory) meaning, and that the evaluative meaning is primary. This position is to be distinguished from (1) above, in which the words 'at all' *seem* to imply that the word has 'primarily' (whatever that means) no meaning at all but commendation; and this latter position I specifically reject in *LM*, pp. 121 f.

[3]See *LM*, p. 124.
[4]See *LM*, p. 118.

themselves cricket-fans and therefore accept the standard of commendation which is attached to the phrase. If this standard of commendation were not, by common use, attached to the phrase, it could not be used, as it is here, for giving information. Moreover, Geach's reasoning depends on the assumption that you can prove the meaning of an expression to be not primarily evaluative by adducing *one* context in which it is used with a primarily descriptive purpose. There could scarcely be a weaker argument. It is strange, too, that Geach should think that someone who fully understood the game could 'supply a purely descriptive sense for the phrase "good batting wicket" regardless of the tastes of cricket-fans'. Would he say that the standards according to which this phrase is applied to wickets have nothing to do with the preferences of batsmen?

Another instance of confusion in the minds of 'The Oxford Moralists' is to be found in the immediately succeeding passage. They evidently do not distinguish between saying that to call a thing a good A is to *guide* choice and saying that it is to *influence* or *affect* choice. To commend may be to seek to guide choice; but it certainly is not necessarily to seek to influence or affect choice.[1] It is not (as Geach might put it) part of the *ratio* of the word 'good', or of the word 'commend', or even of imperatives, that 'good'-sentences or commendations or imperatives have a causal influence on our behaviour. Against such a theory Geach's 'ants in your pants' example provides an objection, though one which is not by itself conclusive. It is, indeed, a vulgarized version of an example which I myself used, in the first of the articles referred to, to show this in the case of imperatives: 'If you want a man to take off his trousers, you will more readily succeed by saying "a scorpion has just crawled up your trouser-leg" than by saying "Take off your trousers"'. Some philosophers, such as that distinguished Cambridge and Ann Arbor moralist Professor Stevenson, have held that both moral judgements and imperatives are, *de ratione*, action-affecting; others, like Dr. Falk, have held that imperatives are, but moral judgements not. It is certainly objection-

---

[1] I have tried to make this distinction clear in my articles 'Imperative Sentences', *Mind* (1949), esp. p. 39; and 'Freedom of the Will', *Ar. Soc. Supp. Vol.* xxv, esp. pp. 206–216; and in *LM* pp. 13–16. Similar distinctions are made by Dr. Falk, 'Goading and Guiding', *Mind* (1953), p. 145, and by Professor Cross, 'The Emotive Theory of Ethics', *Ar. Soc. Supp. Vol.* xxii, esp. pp. 139 f.; but Cross does not deal with the matter very fully, and Falk seems to me to put imperatives on the wrong side of the divide. Perhaps the matter will become clearer if and when Professor Austin puts something in print about his general distinction between illocutionary and perlocutionary force (that is to say, between what we are doing *in* saying P—and what we are trying to do *by* saying P—).

able to say that moral judgements are; and in this I agree with Geach. But, again, if he thinks that this objectionable view is current in Oxford, should not its holders be identified by name?

In short, to be a prescriptivist (which is perhaps the best name for what I am) is not necessarily to be an emotivist of any kind; and in particular, it is not to be an emotivist of the kind which confuses moral judgements with propaganda. Perhaps, if Geach reflects on this distinction, 'commending' will in future cause him no greater discomfort than 'good' itself does. For, once this misunderstanding is cleared away, the chief reason is removed for doubting what the *O.E.D.* says about 'good'. The very first thing which this dictionary says about the meaning of 'good' is that it is 'the most general adjective of commendation'. The fact that this definition is quoted without dissent by Sir David Ross (than whom nobody could be a stauncher descriptivist) strengthens the link between 'good' and commending[1]; and it really becomes very hard to deny this association when we consider what the same dictionary says about the word 'commend'. This it defines as 'To mention as worthy of acceptance or approval'; 'approve' is defined as 'to pronounce to be good, commend'. Putting these two definitions together we get: 'Commend: to mention as worthy of . . . being pronounced to be good', or, for short, 'to mention as being good'. If this is what 'commend' means, how can it be as improper as Geach evidently thinks it is to say that 'good' has as its primary function to commend?

It might at this point be objected that, although the dictionary is quite right to connect 'good' with 'commend' in the way that it does, I am wrong to take the further step of connecting commending with the guidance of choices. This objection might be made by someone who wished at all costs to keep 'good' a purely descriptive word, in spite of its connexion (which can hardly be denied) with commending. But this argument is not open to Geach; for on pp. 38 f. of his paper[2] he says 'It belongs to the *ratio* of "want", "choose", "good" and "bad", that, normally, and other things being equal, a man who wants an A will . . . choose an A that he thinks good and will not choose an A that he thinks bad'. Geach is no doubt right to say that the doctrine *quidquid appetitur, appetitur sub specie boni* is not as it stands analytic, 'since the qualifying phrase "normally and other things being equal" is necessary for the truth of this statement'. But

---

[1] See *The Right and the Good*, p. 66.

[2] [p. 69 of this volume. Ed.]

if this qualifying phrase is added to the statement, it becomes, not merely true, but analytically so; and this is all that is required in order to show that the meaning of the word 'good' is *not* purely descriptive.

My principal purpose in this article, to which I now turn, is to appraise Geach's own suggestion as to how the word 'good' has descriptive force. That it *has* descriptive force I have said many times; but Geach wants to go further. Whereas I maintain that the meaning which is common to all instances of the word's use cannot be descriptive, and that this common meaning is to be sought in the evaluative (commendatory) function of the word, Geach maintains that this common meaning is a kind of descriptive meaning. Thus, he thinks, 'good' has the same descriptive meaning in the expressions 'good knife' and 'good stomach' although, as he and I agree, 'the traits for which a thing is called "good" are different according to the kind of thing in question'.[1] He thinks that this can be so because, although there are no common traits, the meaning of the word 'good', taken in conjunction with that of the word 'knife' or that of the word 'stomach', enables us to specify the traits which things of these kinds have to have in order to be called 'good'. He compares this with the way in which, though we do not have to multiply 2 by the same factor, in order to get its square, as we do 3 in order to get *its* square, nevertheless the expression 'the square of' has a common meaning; given a number, its square is determinate.[2]

I was aware of this possible line of argument when I wrote *LM* pp. 99–103; and that passage contains the considerations which in my view provide an answer to it. There is a certain class of words (called in *LM* 'functional words') for which this manoeuvre is very inviting. 'A word is a functional word if, in order to explain its meaning fully, we have to say what the object it refers to is *for*, or what it is supposed to do.'[3] Examples of functional words are 'auger', 'knife' and 'hygrometer'. The dictionary-definitions of all these words include a reference to the functions of objects so called. Therefore, if we know the meaning of 'good', and also that of 'hygrometer', we are in the way of knowing what traits a hygrometer has to have in order to be called

---

[1] p. 37. [p. 68 of this volume. Ed.]

[2] This example gives rise to much useful reflection; some materials for this reflection are to be found on p. 36 of *LM*, where a similar example occurs. For the connexion between my use of the example and Geach's, see below, p. 108 n. 1. [p. 80. Ed.]

[3] *LM*, p. 100; cf. Geach, p. 38. [p. 69. Ed.]

a good one (indeed, we know very well one of the traits which would entitle us to call it a bad one, viz., habitually registering as the moisture-content of a gas a different moisture-content from that actually possessed by the gas).

Where 'good' precedes a functional word, most of what Geach says is correct. He passes uncritically, however, from this truth about functional words to the much more sweeping claim (which is unjustified) that the same can be said of all uses of 'good'. This is what he would have to show, if he wished to establish his contention that the common meaning of 'good' is descriptive. 'Good' often precedes words which are not functional. In such cases, in order to know what traits the thing in question would have to have in order to be called good, it is not sufficient to know the meaning of the word. We have also to know what standard is to be adopted for judging the goodness of this sort of thing; and the standard is not even partly (as in the case of functional words) revealed to us by the meaning of the word which follows 'good'. Thus, we may know, not only the meaning of 'good', but also the meaning of 'sunset' (and thus know the meaning of the whole expression, 'good sunset'), without thereby having determined for us the traits which a sunset must have in order to be called good. There is, indeed, general agreement among those who are interested in looking at sunsets, what a sunset has to be like to be called a good one (it has to be bright but not dazzling, and cover a wide area of sky with varied and intense colours, etc.); but this standard is not even hinted at in the meaning of 'sunset', let alone in that of 'good'.

It must be emphasized that this difference between the behaviour of 'good' when it precedes a functional word, and its behaviour when it precedes a non-functional word, is not due to any difference in the meaning of 'good' itself. We may say, roughly, that it means in both cases 'having the characteristic qualities (whatever they are) which are commendable in the kind of object in question'. The difference between the two cases is that the functional word does, and the non-functional word does not, give us clues as to what these qualities are. This is because, in classifying a thing as a hygrometer, for example, we have already determined that evaluation of it is to be according to a certain standard, whereas in classifying something else as a sunset we have not. Thus the word 'hygrometer' is, unlike the word 'sunset', not purely descriptive. To know the meaning of 'hygrometer', we do not only have to know what observable properties a thing must have to be called a hygrometer; we have also to know something about what would justify us in commending or condemning something as a hygrometer. None of this is true of 'sunset'; to know the meaning of 'sunset' we have merely to know that we can give this name to what we see in the western sky when the sun visibly sinks beneath the horizon.[1]

Now it is obviously Geach's intention that what he says about 'good' in general should be applicable to moral uses of the word. The question therefore arises whether the words which succeed 'good' in moral contexts are ever functional words. My own view is that the mere occurrence of a functional word after 'good' is normally an indication that the context is *not* a moral one. There are some possible exceptions to this rule; for instance, the phrase 'good example' occurs in moral contexts, and 'example' in such contexts is possibly a functional word, meaning 'thing to imitate'. I am not sure what account is to be given of this expression; but fortunately I do not, for the purposes of this argument, need to maintain that in moral contexts 'good' is never used with functional words, but only that it is sometimes used with non-functional words. For I shall then have shown that, at any rate in those contexts, neither 'good' itself, nor the whole expression in which it occurs, is purely descriptive. And thus I shall have shown that, if there is a common meaning of 'good' which it has in all cases, Geach's account of this common meaning is inadequate.

'He is a good man' is a moral judgement in some contexts, though in some it is not. If 'man' is being used (as it sometimes is) to mean 'soldier' or 'servant' (both functional words), the expression 'good man' is non-moral, just because the word 'man' is being used functionally. It is part of the definitions of a soldier or a servant that they have certain duties; a servant who acts contrary to his master's wishes or interests is *eo ipso* a bad servant, and a soldier whose conduct is conducive to the losing of wars by his side is *eo ipso* a bad soldier. But if 'man' is being used in the ordinary, general way to mean 'member of the human species', it is not functional; and this is the way in which it is used in moral contexts. I think that the same is true of the expression 'good human action' which Geach uses; but since this expression is not in common use, it is hard to be sure. At any rate, in the common expression 'good action', 'action' is not functional. One may know the meaning of 'action' without knowing anything which determines, even

---

[1] The explanation of the paradox that the expression 'good hygrometer' has a fixed *descriptive* meaning just because the two words composing it are both partly *evaluative* will be evident to anyone who compares *LM* pp. 100–101 with *ibid* pp. 36–7; the two evaluations 'cancel one another out'.

to the smallest degree, what actions are to be called good or bad. And if 'human', like 'man', is a non-functional word, the same will be true of 'human action'.

It is not, however, necessary for my argument to make any assumptions about what is or is not included in the meaning of the word 'man'. It will suffice to consider various things that *might* be included, and to notice the logical consequences of their inclusion. As often in philosophy, nothing here hangs upon the *actual* current use of words; but, *if* we decide to use them in a certain way, we must abide by the consequences. We might decide to mean by 'man' simply 'living creature having the following physical shape . . .' followed by a specification of his shape. If this were what we meant by 'man', the word would clearly not be functional, and so the whole expression 'good man' would not be descriptive. But I would be prepared to agree with Geach if he protested that we mean more by 'man' than this. For, as he has pointed out to me, there might be creatures having the same shape as man, but to whom, because they lacked certain intellectual capacities, for example the power of rational speech, we would not allow the name. True, we call by the name 'man' an offspring of human parents who lacks this power. But if we discovered a *race* of creatures who lacked this power, we might hesitate to call them men.

So far, Geach and I can perhaps agree. But it is one thing to say that by calling a creature a man we imply that he belongs to a species having certain *capacities*, and quite another thing to say that by so calling him we imply that he belongs to a species whose *specific good*[1] is of a certain kind. We might, for example, refuse to allow the name 'men' to a species of creatures who, though otherwise like the men we know, were psychologically incapable of lying, or murdering, or doing any other of the things commonly called sinful. We might say 'They aren't human; we would do better to call them "angels", or (if there are theological objections to that) by some new distinctive name'. If this were how we used the word 'man', the possession of these *powers* (of lying, murdering, etc.) would be part of the *ratio* of the word 'man', so used. But from this it would not follow that the exercise of these powers, or even their possession, is conducive to the specific good of man, or that to impair these powers or restrain their exercise (for example by a thorough-going moral education) is contrary to the specific good of man.[2]

---

[1] I take this expression from a letter of Geach's.

[2] Geach is the latest of a famous succession of thinkers who have systematically confused 'what a thing *can* (or, alternatively, *can typically*, or *does typically*) do', with

If Geach wants to make it possible to draw from the meaning of 'man' conclusions about what is contrary to or conducive to a man's being a good man, he will have to include in the meaning of the word not only certain stipulations about the *capacities* of those entitled to the name 'man', but also something about what it is to be a *good* man. He will, in short, have to make 'man' into a functional word. Now let us suppose that Geach takes this liberty. Then the whole expression 'good man', and perhaps also such expressions as 'good human action', will receive fixed descriptive meanings. But he will have paid a severe penalty for this achievement. It will mean that what he says on p. 40[1] is no longer true: 'What a man cannot fail to be choosing is his manner of acting, so to call a manner of acting good or bad cannot but serve to guide action'. On the suggested definition of 'man', and hence of 'human', this will no longer be the case, if 'action' (as Geach implies in the first line of the paragraph from which this quotation comes) is short for 'human action'. For in choosing what to do I may be choosing, not within the class of comparison '*human* actions', but within some other, larger class. Similarly, if 'horse' is used as a functional word, meaning 'charger', a horse that throws his rider becomes *eo ipso* a bad one; but the *horse* might say to himself 'I'm not trying to be a horse in *that* sense; I'm only a solid-hoofed perissodactyl quadruped (*equus caballus*), having a flowing mane and tail', and proceed to throw his rider without offence to anything except the rider's standards. For, though the meaning of the word 'charger' determines some of the qualities of a good charger, that of the word 'horse', in the more general definition given by the *O.E.D.*, does not; in this sense of 'horse', the question of what horses ought to do with themselves remains open. Just *because* the horse cannot choose but be a horse in this general sense, the fact that it is a horse in this general sense does not determine whether or not it ought to choose to be a good charger. It may not regard the choice before it as a choice, what sort of charger to be, but only, more generally, what sort of horse to be. The horsebreaker's art would be easy if one could turn horses into chargers by definition.

the quite different notion 'what a thing *ought* to do (or, alternatively, what it is specifically *good* for it to do)'. Plato was of course the principal culprit. The word 'function' has perhaps been used to cover all these notions. The assimilation between them is only justified if we accept the assumed premise *Natura (sive Deus) nihil facit inane*. Anyone who feels attracted by Geach's use of this kind of reasoning should first read Aristotle, *Politics* 1252 a 35, where a similar premise is used in order to justify slavery and the subjection of women (cf. also 1253 a 9).

[1] [p. 71 of this volume. Ed.]

VI

MORAL BELIEFS[1]

PHILIPPA FOOT

To MANY PEOPLE it seems that the most notable advance in moral philosophy during the past fifty years or so has been the refutation of naturalism; and they are a little shocked that at this late date such an issue should be reopened. It is easy to understand their attitude: given certain apparently unquestionable assumptions, it would be about as sensible to try to reintroduce naturalism as to try to square the circle. Those who see it like this have satisfied themselves that they know in advance that any naturalistic theory must have a catch in it somewhere, and are put out at having to waste more time exposing an old fallacy. This paper is an attempt to persuade them to look critically at the premises on which their arguments are based.

It would not be an exaggeration to say that the whole of moral philosophy, as it is now widely taught, rests on a contrast between statements of fact and evaluations, which runs something like this: 'The truth or falsity of statements of fact is shewn by means of evidence; and what counts as evidence is laid down in the meaning of the expressions occurring in the statement of fact. (For instance, the meaning of "round" and "flat" made Magellan's voyages evidence for the roundness rather than the flatness of the Earth; someone who went on questioning whether the evidence was evidence could eventually be shewn to have made some linguistic mistake.) It follows that no two people can make the same statement and count completely different things as evidence; in the end one at least of them could be convicted of linguistic ignorance. It also follows that if a man is given good evidence for a factual conclusion he cannot just refuse to accept the conclusion on the ground that in his scheme of things this evidence is not evidence at all. With evaluations, however, it is different. An evaluation is not connected logically with the factual

From *Proceedings of the Aristotelian Society*, Vol. 59 (1958–9), pp. 83–104. Reprinted by courtesy of the author and the Editor of the Aristotelian Society.
[1] [This article has been criticized e.g. by M. Tanner, 'Examples in Moral Philosophy', *Proceedings of the Aristotelian Society* (1964–5); D. Z. Phillips, 'Does it Pay to be Good?', ibid; D. Z. Phillips, 'On Morality's Having a Point', *Philosophy* (1965). Ed.]

statements on which it is based. One man may say that a thing is good because of some fact about it, and another may refuse to take that fact as any evidence at all, for nothing is laid down in the meaning of "good" which connects it with one piece of "evidence" rather than another. It follows that a moral eccentric could argue to moral conclusions from quite idiosyncratic premises; he could say, for instance, that a man was a good man because he clasped and unclasped his hands, and never turned N.N.E. after turning S.S.W. He could also reject someone else's evaluation simply by denying that his evidence was evidence at all.

'The fact about "good" which allows the eccentric still to use this term without falling into a morass of meaninglessness, is its "action-guiding" or "practical" function. This it retains; for like everyone else he considers himself bound to choose the things he calls "good" rather than those he calls "bad". Like the rest of the world he uses "good" in connexion only with a "pro-attitude"; it is only that he has pro-attitudes to quite different things, and therefore calls them good.'

There are here two assumptions about 'evaluations', which I will call assumption (1) and assumption (2).

Assumption (1) is that some individual may, without logical error, base his beliefs about matters of value entirely on premises which no one else would recognize as giving any evidence at all. Assumption (2) is that, given the kind of statement which other people regard as evidence for an evaluative conclusion, he may refuse to draw the conclusion because *this* does not count as evidence for *him*.

Let us consider assumption (1). We might say that this depends on the possibility of keeping the meaning of 'good' steady through all changes in the facts about anything which are to count in favour of its goodness. (I do not mean, of course, that a man can make changes as fast as he chooses; only that, whatever he has chosen, it will not be possible to rule him out of order.) But there is a better formulation, which cuts out trivial disputes about the meaning which 'good' happens to have in some section of the community. Let us say that the assumption is that the evaluative function of 'good' can remain constant through changes in the evaluative principle; on this ground it could be said that even if no one can call a man *good* because he clasps and unclasps his hands, he can commend him or express his *pro-attitude* towards him, and if necessary can invent a new moral vocabulary to express his unusual moral code.

Those who hold such a theory will naturally add several qualific-ations. In the first place, most people now agree with Hare, against

Stevenson, that such words as 'good' only apply to individual cases through the application of general principles, so that even the extreme moral eccentric must accept principles of commendation. In the second place 'commending', 'having a pro-attitude', and so on, are supposed to be connected with doing and choosing, so that it would be impossible to say, e.g., that a man was a good man only if he lived for a thousand years. The range of evaluation is supposed to be restricted to the range of possible action and choice. I am not here concerned to question these supposed restrictions on the use of evaluative terms, but only to argue that they are not enough.

The crucial question is this. Is it possible to extract from the meaning of words such as 'good' some element called 'evaluative meaning' which we can think of as externally related to its objects? Such an element would be represented, for instance, in the rule that when any action was 'commended' the speaker must hold himself bound to accept an imperative 'let me do these things'. This is externally related to its object because, within the limitation which we noticed earlier, to possible actions, it would make sense to think of anything as the subject of such 'commendation'. On this hypothesis a moral eccentric could be described as commending the clasping of hands as the action of a good man, and we should not have to look for some background to give the supposition sense. That is to say, on this hypothesis the clasping of hands could be commended without any explanation; it could be what those who hold such theories call 'an ultimate moral principle'.

I wish to say that this hypothesis is untenable, and that there is no describing the evaluative meaning of 'good', evaluation, commending, or anything of the sort, without fixing the object to which they are supposed to be attached. Without first laying hands on the proper object of such things as evaluation, we shall catch in our net either something quite different such as accepting an order or making a resolution, or else nothing at all.

Before I consider this question, I shall first discuss some other mental attitudes and beliefs which have this internal relation to their object. By this I hope to clarify the concept of internal relation to an object, and incidentally, if my examples arouse resistance, but are eventually accepted, to show how easy it is to overlook an internal relation where it exists.

Consider, for instance, pride.

People are often surprised at the suggestion that there are limits to the things a man can be proud of, about which indeed he can feel pride.

I do not know quite what account they want to give of pride;
perhaps something to do with smiling and walking with a jaunty air,
and holding an object up where other people can see it; or perhaps
they think that pride is a kind of internal sensation, so that one
might naturally beat one's breast and say 'pride is something I feel
here'. The difficulties of the second view are well known; the logically
private object cannot be what a name in the public language is the
name of.[1] The first view is the more plausible, and it may seem reasonable to say that given certain behaviour a man can be described as
showing that he is proud of something, whatever that something may
be. In one sense this is true, and in another sense not. Given any
description of an object, action, personal characteristic, etc., it is
not possible to rule it out as an object of pride. Before we can do so
we need to know what would be said about it by the man who is to be
proud of it, or feels proud of it; but if he does not hold the right
beliefs about it then whatever his attitude is it is not pride. Consider,
for instance, the suggestion that someone might be proud of the sky
or the sea: he looks at them and what he feels is *pride*, or he puffs out
his chest and gestures with *pride* in their direction. This makes sense
only if a special assumption is made about his beliefs, for instance
that he is under some crazy delusion and believes that he has saved the
sky from falling, or the sea from drying up. The characteristic object
of pride is something seen (*a*) as in some way a man's own, and (*b*) as
some sort of achievement or advantage; without this object pride
cannot be described. To see that the second condition is necessary,
one should try supposing that a man happens to feel proud because
he has laid one of his hands on the other, three times in an hour.
Here again the supposition that it is pride that he feels will make
perfectly good sense if a special background is filled in. Perhaps he
is ill, and it is an achievement even to do this; perhaps this gesture
has some religious or political significance, and he is a brave man who
will so defy the gods or the rulers. But with no special background
there can be no pride, not because no one could psychologically
speaking feel pride in such a case, but because whatever he did feel
could not logically be pride. Of course, people can see strange things
as achievements, though not just anything, and they can identify
themselves with remote ancestors, and relations, and neighbours, and
even on occasions with Mankind. I do not wish to deny there are
many far-fetched and comic examples of pride.

[1] See Wittgenstein, *Philosophical Investigations*, especially §§243–315.

We could have chosen many other examples of mental attitudes which are internally related to their object in a similar way. For instance, fear is not just trembling, and running, and turning pale; without the thought of some menacing evil no amount of this will add up to fear. Nor could anyone be said to feel dismay about something he did not see as bad; if his thoughts about it were that it was altogether a good thing, he could not say that (oddly enough) what he felt about it was dismay. 'How odd, I feel dismayed when I ought to be pleased' is the prelude to a hunt for the adverse aspect of the thing, thought of as lurking behind the pleasant façade. But someone may object that pride and fear and dismay are feelings or emotions and therefore not a proper analogy for 'commendation', and there will be an advantage in considering a different kind of example. We could discuss, for instance, the belief that a certain thing is dangerous, and ask whether this could logically be held about anything whatsoever. Like 'this is good', 'this is dangerous' is an assertion, which we should naturally accept or reject by speaking of its truth or falsity; we seem to support such statements with evidence, and moreover there may seem to be a 'warning function' connected with the word 'dangerous' as there is supposed to be a 'commending function' connected with the word 'good'. For suppose that philosophers, puzzled about the property of dangerousness, decided that the word did not stand for a property at all, but was essentially a practical or action-guiding term, used for *warning*. Unless used in an 'inverted comma sense' the word 'dangerous' was used to warn, and this meant that anyone using it in such a sense committed himself to avoiding the things he called dangerous, to preventing other people from going near them, and perhaps to running in the opposite direction. If the conclusion were not obviously ridiculous, it would be easy to infer that a man whose application of the term was different from ours throughout might say that the oddest things were dangerous without fear of disproof; the idea would be that he could still be described as 'thinking them dangerous', or at least as 'warning', because by his attitude and actions he would have fulfilled the conditions for these things. This is nonsense because without its proper object *warning*, like *believing dangerous*, will not be there. It is logically impossible to warn about anything not thought of as threatening evil, and for danger we need a particular kind of serious evil such as injury or death.

There are, however, some differences between thinking a thing dangerous and feeling proud, frightened or dismayed. When a man says that something is dangerous he must support his statement with a special kind of evidence; but when he says that he feels proud or frightened or dismayed the description of the object of his pride or fright or dismay does not have quite this relation to his original statement. If he is shown that the thing he was proud of was not his after all, or was not after all anything very grand, he may have to say that his pride was not justified, but he will not have to take back the statement that he was proud. On the other hand, someone who says that a thing is dangerous, and later sees that he made a mistake in thinking that an injury might result from it, has to go back on his original statement and admit that he was wrong. In neither case, however, is the speaker able to go on as before. A man who discovered that it was not his pumpkin but someone else's which had won the prize could only say that he still felt proud, if he could produce some other ground for pride. It is in this way that even feelings are logically vulnerable to facts.

It will probably be objected against these examples that for part of the way at least they beg the question. It will be said that indeed a man can be proud only of something he thinks a good action, or an achievement, or a sign of noble birth; as he can feel dismay only about something which he sees as bad, frightened at some threatened evil; similarly he can warn only if he is also prepared to speak, for instance, of injury. But this will limit the range of possible objects of those attitudes and beliefs only if the range of these terms is limited in its turn. To meet this objection I shall discuss the meaning of 'injury' because this is the simplest case. Anyone who feels inclined to say that anything could be counted as an achievement, or as the evil of which people were afraid, or about which they felt dismayed, should just try this out. I wish to consider the proposition that anything could be thought of as dangerous, because if it causes injury it is dangerous, and anything could be counted as an injury. I shall consider bodily injury because this is the injury connected with danger; it is not correct to put up a notice by the roadside reading 'Danger!' on account of bushes which might scratch a car. Nor can a substance be labelled 'dangerous' on the ground that it can injure delicate fabrics; although we can speak of the danger that it may do so, that is not the use of the word which I am considering here.

When a body is injured it is changed for the worse in a special way, and we want to know which changes count as injuries. First of all, it matters how an injury comes about; e.g., it cannot be caused by natural decay. Then it seems clear that not just any kind of thing will do, for instance, any unusual mark on the body, however much trouble a man might take to have it removed. By far the most important class of injuries are injuries to a part of the body, counting as injuries because there is interference with the function of that part; injury to a leg, an eye, an ear, a hand, a muscle, the heart, the brain, the spinal cord. An injury to an eye is one that affects, or is likely to affect, its sight; an injury to a hand one which makes it less well able to reach out and grasp, and perform other operations of this kind. A leg can be injured because its movements and supporting power can be affected; a lung because it can become too weak to draw in the proper amount of air. We are most ready to speak of an injury where the function of a part of the body is to perform a characteristic operation, as in these examples. We might hesitate to say that a skull can be injured, and might prefer to speak of damage to it, since although there is indeed a function (a protective function) there is no operation. But thinking of the protective function of the skull we may want to speak of injury here. In so far as the concept of *injury* depends on that of *function* it is narrowly limited, since not even every use to which a part of the body is put will count as its function. Why is it that, even if it is the means by which they earn their living, we would never consider the removal of the dwarf's hump or the bearded lady's beard as a bodily injury? It will be tempting to say that these things are disfigurements, but this is not the point; if we suppose that a man who had some invisible extra muscle made his living as a court jester by waggling his ears, the ear would not have been injured if this were made to disappear. If it were natural to men to communicate by movements of the ear, then ears would have the function of signalling (we have no word for this kind of 'speaking') and an impairment of this function would be an injury; but things are not like this. This court jester would use his ears to make people laugh, but this is not the function of ears.

No doubt many people will feel impatient when such facts are mentioned, because they think that it is quite unimportant that this or that *happens* to be the case, and it seems to them arbitrary that the loss of the beard, the hump, or the ear muscle would not be called an injury. Isn't the loss of that by which one makes one's living a pretty catastrophic loss? Yet it seems quite natural that these are not counted as injuries if one thinks about the conditions of human life, and contrasts the loss of a special ability to make people gape or laugh with the ability to see, hear, walk, or pick things up. The first is only needed for one very special way of living; the other in any foreseeable

future for any man. This restriction seems all the more natural when
we observe what other threats besides that of injury can constitute
danger: of death, for instance, or mental derangement. A shock which
could cause mental instability or impairment of memory would be
called dangerous, because a man needs such things as intelligence,
memory, and concentration as he needs sight or hearing or the use of
hands. Here we do not speak of injury unless it is possible to connect
the impairment with some physical change, but we speak of danger
because there is the same loss of a capacity which any man needs.

There can be injury outside the range we have been considering;
for a man may sometimes be said to have received injuries where no
part of his body has had its function interfered with. In general, I
think that any blow which disarranged the body in such a way that
there was lasting pain would inflict an injury, even if no other ill
resulted, but I do not know of any other important extension of the
concept.

It seems therefore that since the range of things which can be
called injuries is quite narrowly restricted, the word 'dangerous' is
restricted in so far as it is connected with injury. We have the right to
say that a man cannot decide to call just anything dangerous, however
much he puts up fences and shakes his head.

So far I have been arguing that such things as pride, fear, dismay,
and the thought that something is dangerous have an internal relation
to their object, and hope that what I mean is becoming clear. Now we
must consider whether those attitudes or beliefs which are the moral
philosopher's study are similar, or whether such things as 'evaluation'
and 'thinking something good' and 'commendation' could logically
be found in combination with any object whatsoever. All I can do here
is to give an example which may make this suggestion seem implausible, and to knock away a few of its supports. The example will come
from the range of trivial and pointless actions such as we were
considering in speaking of the man who clasped his hands three times
an hour, and we can point to the oddity of the suggestion that this can
be called a good action. We are bound by the terms of our question to
refrain from adding any special background, and it should be stated
once more that the question is about what can count in favour of the
goodness or badness of a man or an action, and not what could be, or
be thought, good or bad with a special background. I believe that the
view I am attacking often seems plausible only because the special
background is surreptitiously introduced.

Someone who said that clasping the hands three times in an hour was a good action would first have to answer the question 'How do you mean?' For the sentence 'this is a good action' is not one which has a clear meaning. Presumably, since our subject is moral philosophy, it does not here mean 'that was a good thing to do' as this might be said of a man who had done something sensible in the course of any enterprise whatever; we are to confine our attention to 'the moral use of "good"'. I am not clear that it makes sense to speak of 'a moral use of "good"', but we can pick out a number of cases which raise moral issues. It is because these are so diverse and because 'this is a good action' does not pick out any one of them, that we must ask 'How do you mean?' For instance, some things that are done fulfil a duty, such as the duty of parents to children or children to parents. I suppose that when philosophers speak of good actions they would include these. Some come under the heading of a virtue such as charity, and they will be included too. Others again are actions which require the virtues of courage or temperance, and here the moral aspect is due to the fact that they are done in spite of fear or the temptation of pleasure; they must indeed be done for the sake of some real or fancied good, but not necessarily what philosophers would want to call a moral good. Courage is not *particularly* concerned with saving other people's lives, or temperance with leaving them their share of the food and drink, and the goodness of *what is done* may here be all kinds of usefulness. It is because there are these very diverse cases included (I suppose) under the expression 'a good action' that we should refuse to consider applying it without asking what is meant, and we should now ask what is intended when someone is supposed to say that 'clasping the hands three times in an hour is a good action'. Is it supposed that this action fulfils a duty? Then in virtue of what does a man have this duty, and to whom does he owe it? We have promised not to slip in a special background, but he cannot possibly have a *duty* to clasp his hands unless such a background exists. Nor could it be an act of charity, for it is not thought to do anyone any good, nor again a gesture of humility unless a special assumption turns it into this. The action could be courageous, but only if it were done both in the face of fear and for the sake of a good; and we are not allowed to put in special circumstances which could make this the case.

I am sure that the following objection will now be raised. 'Of course clasping one's hands three times in an hour cannot be brought under one of the virtues which we recognize, but that is only to say that it is not a good action by our current moral code. It is logically possible that in a quite different moral code quite different virtues should be recognized, for which we have not even got a name.' I cannot answer this objection properly, for that would need a satisfactory account of the concept of a virtue. But anyone who thinks it would be easy to describe a new virtue connected with clasping the hands three times in an hour should just try. I think he will find that he has to cheat, and suppose that in the community concerned the clasping of hands has been given some special significance, or is thought to have some special effect. The difficulty is obviously connected with the fact that without a special background there is no possibility of answering the question 'What's the point?' It is no good saying that there would be a point in doing the action because the action was a morally good action: the question is how it can be given any such description if we cannot first speak about the point. And it is just as crazy to suppose that we can call *anything* the point of doing something without having to say what the point of *that* is. In clasping one's hands one may make a slight sucking noise, but what is the point of that? It is surely clear that moral virtues must be connected with human good and harm, and that it is quite impossible to call anything you like good or harm. Consider, for instance, the suggestion that a man might say he had been harmed because a bucket of water had been taken out of the sea. As usual it would be possible to think up circumstances in which this remark would make sense; for instance, when coupled with a belief in magical influences; but then the harm would consist in what was done by the evil spirits, not in the taking of the water from the sea. It would be just as odd if someone were supposed to say that harm had been done to him because the hairs of his head had been reduced to an even number.[1]

I conclude that assumption (1) is very dubious indeed, and that no one should be allowed to speak as if we can understand 'evaluation' 'commendation' or 'pro-attitude', whatever the actions concerned.

II

I propose now to consider what was called Assumption (2), which said that a man might always refuse to accept the conclusion of an argument about values, because what counted as evidence for other people did not count for him. Assumption (2) could be true even if

---

[1] In face of this sort of example many philosophers take refuge in the thicket of aesthetics. It would be interesting to know if they are willing to let their whole case rest on the possibility that there might be aesthetic objections to what was done.

Assumption (1) were false, for it might be that once a particular question of values—say a moral question—had been accepted, any disputant was bound to accept particular pieces of evidence as relevant, the same pieces as everyone else, but that he could always refuse to draw any moral conclusions whatsoever or to discuss any questions which introduced moral terms. Nor do we mean 'he might refuse to draw the conclusion' in the trivial sense in which anyone can perhaps refuse to draw *any* conclusion; the point is that any statement of value always seems to go beyond any statement of fact, so that he might have a reason for accepting the factual premises but refusing to accept the evaluative conclusion. That this is so seems to those who argue in this way to follow from the practical implication of evaluation. When a man uses a word such as 'good' in an 'evaluative' and not an 'inverted comma' sense, he is supposed to commit his will. From this it has seemed to follow inevitably that there is a logical gap between fact and value; for is it not one thing to say that a thing is so, and another to have a particular attitude towards its being so; one thing to see that certain effects will follow from a given action, and another to care? Whatever account was offered of the essential feature of evaluation—whether in terms of feelings, attitudes, the acceptance of imperatives or what not—the fact remained that with an evaluation there was a committal in a new dimension, and that this was not guaranteed by any acceptance of facts.

I shall argue that this view is mistaken; that the practical implication of the use of moral terms has been put in the wrong place, and that if it is described correctly the logical gap between factual premises and moral conclusion disappears.

In this argument it will be useful to have as a pattern the practical or 'action-guiding' force of the word 'injury', which is in some, though not all, ways similar to that of moral terms. It is clear I think that an injury is necessarily something bad and therefore something which as such anyone always has a reason to avoid, and philosophers will therefore be tempted to say that anyone who uses 'injury' in its full 'action-guiding' sense commits himself to avoiding the things he calls injuries. They will then be in the usual difficulties about the man who says he knows he ought to do something but does not intend to do it; perhaps also about weakness of the will. Suppose that instead we look again at the kinds of things which count as injuries, to see if the connexion with the will does not start here. As has been shown, a man is injured whenever some part of his body, in being damaged, has become less well able to fulfil its ordinary function. It follows that he suffers a disability, or is liable to do so; with an injured hand he will be less well able to pick things up, hold on to them, tie them together or chop them up, and so on. With defective eyes there will be a thousand other things he is unable to do, and in both cases we should naturally say that he will often be unable to get what he wants to get or avoid what he wants to avoid.

Philosophers will no doubt seize on the word 'want', and say that if we suppose that a man happens to want the things which an injury to his body prevents him from getting, we have slipped in a supposition about a 'pro-attitude' already; and that anyone who does not happen to have these wants can still refuse to use 'injury' in its prescriptive, or 'action-guiding' sense. And so it may seem that the only way to make a *necessary* connexion between 'injury' and the things that are to be avoided, is to say that it is used in an 'action-guiding sense' only when applied to something the speaker intends to avoid. But we should look carefully at the crucial move in that argument, and query the suggestion that someone might happen not to want anything for which he would need the use of hands or eyes. Hands and eyes, like ears and legs, play a part in so many operations that a man could only be said not to need them if he had no wants at all. That such people exist, in asylums, is not to the present purpose at all; the proper use of his limbs is something a man has reason to want if he wants anything.

I do not know just what someone who denies this proposition could have in mind. Perhaps he is thinking of changing the facts of human existence, so that merely wishing, or the sound of the voice, will bring the world to heel? More likely he is proposing to rig the circumstances of some individual's existence within the framework of the ordinary world, by supposing for instance that he is a prince whose servant will sow and reap and fetch and carry for him, and so use their hands and eyes in his service that he will not need the use of his. Let us suppose that such a story could be told about a man's life; it is wildly implausible, but let us pretend that it is not. It is clear that in spite of this we could say that any man had a reason to shun injury; for even if at the end of his life it could be said that by a strange set of circumstances he had never needed the use of his eyes, or his hands, this could not possibly be foreseen. Only by once more changing the facts of human existence, and supposing every vicissitude foreseeable, could such a supposition be made.

This is not to say that an injury might not bring more incidental gain than necessary harm; one has only to think of times when the order has gone out that able-bodied men are to be put to the sword. Such a gain might even, in some peculiar circumstances, be reliably foreseen, so that a man would have even better reason for seeking than for avoiding injury. In this respect the word 'injury' differs from terms such as 'injustice'; the practical force of 'injury' means only that anyone has *a* reason to avoid injuries, not that he has an over-riding reason to do so.

It will be noticed that this account of the 'action-guiding' force of 'injury' links it with reasons for acting rather than with actually doing something. I do not think, however, that this makes it a less good pattern for the 'action-guiding' force of moral terms. Philoso-phers who have supposed that actual action was required if 'good' were to be used in a sincere evaluation have got into difficulties over weakness of will, and they should surely agree that enough has been done if we can show that any man has reason to aim at virtue and avoid vice. But is this impossibly difficult if we consider the kinds of things that count as virtue and vice? Consider, for instance, the cardinal virtues, prudence, temperance, courage and justice. Obviously any man needs prudence, but does he not also need to resist the temptation of pleasure when there is harm involved? And how could it be argued that he would never need to face what was fearful for the sake of some good? It is not obvious what someone would mean if he said that temperance or courage were not good qualities, and this not because of the 'praising' sense of these *words*, but because of the things that courage and temperance are.

I should like to use these examples to show the artificiality of the notions of 'commendation' and of 'pro-attitudes' as these are commonly employed. Philosophers who talk about these things will say that after the facts have been accepted—say that X is the kind of man who will climb a dangerous mountain, beard an irascible em-ployer for a rise in pay, and in general face the fearful for the sake of something he thinks worth while—there remains the question of 'commendation' or 'evaluation'. If the word 'courage' is used they will ask whether or not the man who speaks of another as having courage is supposed to have commended him. If we say 'yes' they will insist that the judgement about courage *goes beyond the facts*, and might therefore be rejected by someone who refused to do so; if we say 'no' they will argue that 'courage' is being used in a purely des-criptive or 'inverted comma sense', and that we have not got an example of the evaluative use of language which is the moral philosopher's special study. What sense can be made, however, of the question 'does he commend?' What is this extra element which is supposed to be present or absent after the facts have been settled? It is not a matter of liking the man who has courage, or of thinking him altogether good, but of 'commending him for his courage'. How are we supposed to do that? The answer that will be given is that we only commend someone else in speaking of him as courageous if we accept the imperative 'let me be courageous' for ourselves. But this is quite unnecessary. I can speak of someone else as having the virtue of courage, and of course recognize it as a virtue in the proper sense, while knowing that I am a complete coward, and making no resolution to reform. I know that I should be better off if I were courageous, and so have a reason to cultivate courage but I may also know that I will do nothing of the kind.

If someone were to say that courage was not a virtue he would have to say that it was not a quality by which a man came to act well. Perhaps he would be thinking that someone might be worse off for his courage, which is true, but only because an incidental harm might arise. For instance, the courageous man might have underestimated a risk, and run into some disaster which a cowardly man would have avoided because he was not prepared to take any risk at all. And his courage, like any other virtue, could be the cause of harm to him because possessing it he fell into some disastrous state of pride.[1] Similarly, those who question the virtue of temperance are probably thinking not of the virtue itself but of men whose temperance has consisted in resisting pleasure for the sake of some illusory good, or those who have made this virtue their pride.

But what, it will be asked, of justice? For while prudence, courage and temperance are qualities which benefit the man who has them, justice seems rather to benefit others, and to work to the disadvantage of the just man himself. Justice as it is treated here, as one of the cardinal virtues, covers all those things owed to other people: it is under injustice that murder, theft and lying come, as well as the withholding of what is owed for instance by parents to children and by children to parents, as well as the dealings which would be called unjust in everyday speech. So the man who avoids injustice will find himself in need of things he has returned to their owner, unable to obtain an advantage by cheating and lying; involved in all those difficulties painted by Thrasymachus in the first book of the Republic, in order to show that injustice is more profitable than justice to a man

---

[1] Cp. Aquinas, *Summa Theologica*, I–II, q. 55, Art. 4.

of strength and wit. We will be asked how, on our theory, justice can be a virtue and injustice a vice, since it will surely be difficult to show that any man whatsoever must need to be just as he needs the use of his hands and eyes, or needs prudence, courage and temperance?

Before answering this question I shall argue that if it cannot be answered, then justice can no longer be recommended as a virtue. The point of this is not to show that it must be answerable, since justice is a virtue, but rather to suggest that we should at least consider the possibility that justice is not a virtue. This suggestion was taken seriously by Socrates in the Republic, where it was assumed by everyone that if Thrasymachus could establish his premise—that injustice was more profitable than justice—his conclusion would follow: that a man who had the strength to get away with injustice had reason to follow this as the best way of life. It is a striking fact about modern moral philosophy that no one sees any difficulty in accepting Thrasymachus' premise and rejecting his conclusion, and it is because Nietzsche's position is at this point much closer to that of Plato that he is remote from academic moralists of the present day.

In the Republic it is assumed that if justice is not a good to the just man, moralists who recommend it as a virtue are perpetrating a fraud. Agreeing with this, I shall be asked where exactly the fraud comes in; where the untruth that justice is profitable to the individual is supposed to be told? As a preliminary answer we might ask how many people are prepared to say frankly that injustice is more profitable than justice? Leaving aside, as elsewhere in this paper, religious beliefs which might complicate the matter, we will suppose that some tough atheistical character has asked 'Why should I be just?' (Those who believe that this question has something wrong with it can employ their favourite device for sieving out 'evaluating meaning', and suppose that the question is 'Why should I be "just"?') Are we prepared to reply 'As far as you are concerned you will be better off if you are unjust, but it matters to the rest of us that you should be just, so we are trying to get you to be just'? He would be likely to enquire into our methods, and then take care not to be found out, and I do not think that many of those who think that it is not necessary to show that justice is profitable to the just man would easily accept that there was nothing more they could say.

The crucial question is: 'Can we give anyone, strong or weak, a reason why he should be just?'—and it is no help at all to say that since 'just' and 'unjust' are 'action-guiding words' no one can even ask 'Why should I be just?' Confronted with that argument the man who wants to do unjust things has only to be careful to avoid the *word*, and he has not been given a reason why he should not do the things which other people call 'unjust'. Probably it will be argued that he has been given a reason so far as anyone can ever be given a reason for doing or not doing anything, for the chain of reasons must always come to an end somewhere, and it may seem that one may always reject the reason which another man accepts. But this is a mistake; some answers to the question 'why should I?' bring the series to a close and some do not. Hume showed how *one* answer closed the series in the following passage:

'Ask a man *why he uses exercise*; he will answer, *because he desires to keep his health*. If you then enquire, *why he desires health*, he will readily reply, *because sickness is painful*. If you push your enquiries farther, and desire a reason *why he hates pain*, it is impossible he can ever give any. This is an ultimate end, and is never referred to any other object.' (*Enquiries*, Appendix I, V.) Hume might just as well have ended this series with boredom: sickness often brings boredom, and no one is required to give a reason why he does not want to be bored, any more than he has to give a reason why he does want to pursue what interests him. In general, anyone is given a reason for acting when he is shown the way to something he wants; but for some wants the question 'Why do you want that?' will make sense, and for others it will not.[1] It seems clear that in this division justice falls on the opposite side from pleasure and interest and such things. 'Why shouldn't I do that?' is not answered by the words 'because it is unjust' as it is answered by showing that the action will bring boredom, loneliness, pain, discomfort or certain kinds of incapacity, and this is why it is not true to say that 'it's unjust' gives a reason in so far as any reasons can ever be given. 'It's unjust' gives a reason only if the nature of justice can be shown to be such that it is necessarily connected with what a man wants.

This shows why a great deal hangs on the question of whether justice is or is not a good to the just man, and why those who accept Thrasymachus' premise and reject his conclusion are in a dubious position. They recommend justice to each man, as something he has a reason to follow, but when challenged to show why he should do so they will not always be able to reply. This last assertion does not depend on any 'selfish theory of human nature' in the philosophical sense. It is often possible to give a man a reason for acting by showing

[1] For an excellent discussion of reasons for action, see G. E. M. Anscombe, *Intention* §34-40.

him that someone else will suffer if he does not; someone else's good may really be more to him than his own. But the affection which mothers feel for children, and lovers for each other, and friends for friends, will not take us far when we are asked for reasons why a man should be just; partly because it will not extend far enough, and partly because the actions dictated by benevolence and justice are not always the same. Suppose that I owe someone money; ' . . . what if he be my enemy, and has given me just cause to hate him? What if he be a vicious man, and deserves the hatred of all mankind? What if he be a miser, and can make no use of what I would deprive him of? What if he be a profligate debauchee, and would rather receive harm than benefit from large possessions?'[1] Even if the general practice of justice could be brought under the motive of universal benevolence—the desire for the greatest happiness of the greatest number—many people certainly do not have any such desire. So that if justice is only to be recommended on these grounds a thousand tough characters will be able to say that they have been given no reason for practising justice, and many more would say the same if they were not too timid or too stupid to ask questions about the code of behaviour which they have been taught. Thus, given Thrasymachus' premise Thrasymachus' point of view is reasonable; we have no particular reason to admire those who practise justice through timidity or stupidity.

It seems to me, therefore, that if Thrasymachus' thesis is accepted things cannot go on as before; we shall have to admit that the belief on which the status of justice as a virtue was founded is mistaken, and if we still want to get people to be just we must recommend justice to them in a new way. We shall have to admit that injustice is more profitable than justice, at least for the strong, and then do our best to see that hardly anyone can get away with being unjust. We have, of course, the alternative of keeping quiet, hoping that for the most part people will follow convention into a kind of justice, and not ask awkward questions, but this policy might be overtaken by a vague scepticism even on the part of those who do not know just what is lacking; we should also be at the mercy of anyone who was able and willing to expose our fraud.

Is it true, however, to say that justice is not something a man needs in his dealings with his fellows, supposing only that he be

---

[1] Hume, *Treatise* Book III, Part II, Sect. 1.

strong? Those who think that he can get on perfectly well without being just should be asked to say exactly how such a man is supposed to live. We know that he is to practise injustice whenever the unjust act would bring him advantage; but what is he to say? Does he admit that he does not recognize the rights of other people, or does he pretend? In the first case even those who combine with him will know that on a change of fortune, or a shift of affection, he may turn to plunder them, and he must be as wary of their treachery as they are of his. Presumably the happy unjust man is supposed, as in Book II of the Republic, to be a very cunning liar and actor, combining complete injustice with the appearance of justice: he is prepared to treat others ruthlessly, but pretends that nothing is further from his mind. Philosophers often speak as if a man could thus hide himself even from those around him, but the supposition is doubtful, and in any case the price in vigilance would be colossal. If he lets even a few people see his true attitude he must guard himself against them; if he lets no one into the secret he must always be careful in case the least spontaneity betray him. Such facts are important because the need a man has for justice in dealings with other men depends on the fact that they are men and not inanimate objects or animals. If a man only needed other men as he needs household objects, and if men could be manipulated like household objects, or beaten into a reliable submission like donkeys, the case would be different. As things are, the supposition that injustice is more profitable than justice is very dubious, although like cowardice and intemperance it might turn out incidentally to be profitable.

The reason why it seems to some people so impossibly difficult to show that justice is more profitable than injustice is that they consider in isolation particular just acts. It is perfectly true that if a man is just it follows that he will be prepared, in the event of very evil circumstances, even to face death rather than to act unjustly—for instance, in getting an innocent man convicted of a crime of which he has been accused. For him it turns out that his justice brings disaster on him, and yet like anyone else he had good reason to be a just and not an unjust man. He could not have it both ways and while possessing the virtue of justice hold himself ready to be unjust should any great advantage accrue. The man who has the virtue of justice is not ready to do certain things, and if he is too easily tempted we shall say that he was ready after all.

VII

HOW TO DERIVE 'OUGHT' FROM 'IS'[1]

JOHN R. SEARLE

I

IT IS OFTEN SAID that one cannot derive an 'ought' from an 'is'. This thesis, which comes from a famous passage in Hume's *Treatise*, while not as clear as it might be, is at least clear in broad outline: there is a class of statements of fact which is logically distinct from a class of statements of value. No set of statements of fact by themselves entails any statement of value. Put in more contemporary terminology, no set of *descriptive* statements can entail an *evaluative* statement without the addition of at least one evaluative premise. To believe otherwise is to commit what has been called the naturalistic fallacy.

I shall attempt to demonstrate a counterexample to this thesis.[2] It is not of course to be supposed that a single counterexample can refute a philosophical thesis, but in the present instance if we can present a plausible counterexample and can in addition give some account or explanation of how and why it is a counterexample, and if we can further offer a theory to back up our counterexample—a theory which will generate an indefinite number of counterexamples— we may at the very least cast considerable light on the original thesis; and possibly, if we can do all these things, we may even incline our- selves to the view that the scope of that thesis was more restricted than we had originally supposed. A counterexample must proceed

From *Philosophical Review*, Vol. 73 (1964), pp. 43–58. Reprinted by permission of the author and the *Philosophical Review*.

[1] Earlier versions of this paper were read before the Stanford Philosophy Colloqium and the Pacific Division of the American Philosophical Association. I am indebted to many people for helpful comments and criticisms, especially Hans Herzberger, Arnold Kaufmann, Benson Mates, A. I. Melden, and Dagmar Searle.

[This article has been much discussed. See e.g. J. and J. Thomson, 'How not to Derive "Ought" from "Is"', *Philosophical Review*, (1964); also A. Flew and others in *Analysis* from 1964 to 1966. Also relevant are J. Searle, 'Meaning and Speech Acts', *Philosophical Review* (1962), and Searle's contribution ('What is a Speech Act?') to M. Black (ed.) *Philosophy in America* (George Allen and Unwin, London, 1965). Ed.]

[2] In its modern version. I shall not be concerned with Hume's treatment of the problem.

by taking a statement or statements which any proponent of the thesis would grant were purely factual or 'descriptive' (they need not actually contain the word 'is') and show how they are logically related to a statement which a proponent of the thesis would regard as clearly 'evaluative'. (In the present instance it will contain an 'ought'.)[1]

Consider the following series of statements:

(1) Jones uttered the words 'I hereby promise to pay you, Smith, five dollars'.

(2) Jones promised to pay Smith five dollars.

(3) Jones placed himself under (undertook) an obligation to pay Smith five dollars.

(4) Jones is under an obligation to pay Smith five dollars.

(5) Jones ought to pay Smith five dollars.

I shall argue concerning this list that the relation between any statement and its successor, while not in every case one of 'entailment', is nonetheless not just a contingent relation; and the additional statements necessary to make the relationship one of entailment do not need to involve any evaluative statements, moral principles, or anything of the sort.

Let us begin. How is (1) related to (2)? In certain circumstances, uttering the words in quotation marks in (1) is the act of making a promise. And it is a part of or a consequence of the meaning of the words in (1) that in those circumstances uttering them is promising. 'I hereby promise' is a paradigm device in English for performing the act described in (2), promising.

Let us state this fact about English usage in the form of an extra premise:

(1a) Under certain conditions *C* anyone who utters the words (sentence) 'I hereby promise to pay you, Smith, five dollars' promises to pay Smith five dollars.

What sorts of things are involved under the rubric 'conditions *C*'? What is involved will be all those conditions, those states of affairs, which are necessary and sufficient conditions for the utterance of the words (sentence) to constitute the successful performance of the act

---

[1] If this enterprise succeeds, we shall have bridged the gap between 'evaluative' and 'descriptive' and consequently have demonstrated a weakness in this very terminology. At present, however, my strategy is to play along with the terminology, pretending that the notions of evaluative and descriptive are fairly clear. At the end of the paper I shall state in what respects I think they embody a muddle.

of promising. The conditions will include such things as that the speaker is in the presence of the hearer Smith, they are both conscious, both speakers of English, speaking seriously. The speaker knows what he is doing, is not under the influence of drugs, not hypnotized or acting in a play, not telling a joke or reporting an event, and so forth. This list will no doubt be somewhat indefinite because the boundaries of the concept of a promise, like the boundaries of most concepts in a natural language, are a bit loose.[1] But one thing is clear; however loose the boundaries may be, and however difficult it may be to decide marginal cases, the conditions under which a man who utters 'I hereby promise' can correctly be said to have made a promise are straightforwardly empirical conditions.

So let us add as an extra premise the empirical assumption that these conditions obtain.

(1b) Conditions C obtain.

From (1), (1a), and (1b) we derive (2). The argument is of the form: If C then (if U then P): C for conditions, U for utterance, P for promise. Adding the premises U and C to this hypothetical we derive (2). And as far as I can see, no moral premises are lurking in the logical woodpile. More needs to be said about the relation of (1) to (2), but I reserve that for later.

What is the relation between (2) and (3)? I take it that promising is, by definition, an act of placing oneself under an obligation. No analysis of the concept of promising will be complete which does not include the feature of the promiser placing himself under or undertaking or accepting or recognizing an obligation to the promisee, to perform some future course of action, normally for the benefit of the promisee. One may be tempted to think that promising can be analyzed in terms of creating expectations in one's hearers, or some such, but a little reflection will show that the crucial distinction between statements of intention on the one hand and promises on the other lies in the nature and degree of commitment or obligation undertaken in promising.

I am therefore inclined to say that (2) entails (3) straight off, but I can have no objection if anyone wishes to add—for the purpose of formal neatness—the tautological premise:

---

[1] In addition the concept of a promise is a member of a class of concepts which suffer from looseness of a peculiar kind, viz. defeasibility. Cf. H. L. A. Hart, 'The Ascription of Responsibility and Rights', *Logic and Language*, First Series, ed. by A. Flew (Oxford, 1951).

(2a) All promises are acts of placing oneself under (undertaking) an obligation to do the thing promised.

How is (3) related to (4)? If one has placed oneself under an obligation, then, other things being equal, one is under an obligation. That I take it also is a tautology. Of course it is possible for all sorts of things to happen which will release one from obligations one has undertaken and hence the need for the *ceteris paribus* rider. To get an entailment between (3) and (4) we therefore need a qualifying statement to the effect that:

(3a) Other things are equal.

Formalists, as in the move from (2) to (3), may wish to add the tautological premise:

(3b) All those who place themselves under an obligation are, other things being equal, under an obligation.

The move from (3) to (4) is thus of the same form as the move from (1) to (2): If *E* then (if *PUO* then *UO*): *E* for other things are equal, *PUO* for place under obligation and *UO* for under obligation. Adding the two premises *E* and *PUO* we derive *UO*.

Is (3a), the *ceteris paribus* clause, a concealed evaluative premise? It certainly looks as if it might be, especially in the formulation I have given it, but I think we can show that, though questions about whether other things are equal frequently involve evaluative considerations, it is not logically necessary that they should in every case. I shall postpone discussion of this until after the next step.

What is the relation between (4) and (5)? Analogous to the tautology which explicates the relation of (3) and (4) there is here the tautology that, other things being equal, one ought to do what one is under an obligation to do. And here, just as in the previous case, we need some premise of the form:

(4a) Other things are equal.

We need the *ceteris paribus* clause to eliminate the possibility that something extraneous to the relation of 'obligation' to 'ought' might interfere.[1] Here, as in the previous two steps, we eliminate the appear-

---

[1] The *ceteris paribus* clause in this step excludes somewhat different sorts of cases from those excluded in the previous step. In general we say, 'He undertook an obligation, but nonetheless he is not (now) under an obligation' when the obligation has been *removed*, e.g., if the promisee says, 'I release you from your obligation'. But we say, 'He is under an obligation, but nonetheless ought not to fulfil it' in cases where the obligation is *overridden* by some other considerations, e.g., a prior obligation.

ance of enthymeme by pointing out that the apparently suppressed premise is tautological and hence, though formally neat, it is redundant. If, however, we wish to state it formally, this argument is of the same form as the move from (3) to (4): If E then (if UO then O); E for other things are equal, UO for under obligation, O for ought. Adding the premises E and UO we derive O.

Now a word about the phrase 'other things being equal' and how it functions in my attempted derivation. This topic and the closely related topic of defeasibility are extremely difficult and I shall not try to do more than justify my claim that the satisfaction of the condition does not necessarily involve anything evaluative. The force of the expression 'other things being equal' in the present instance is roughly this. Unless we have some reason (that is, unless we are actually prepared to give some reason) for supposing the obligation is void (Step 4) or the agent ought not to keep the promise (step 5), then the obligation holds and he ought to keep the promise. It is not part of the force of the phrase 'other things being equal' that in order to satisfy it we need to establish a universal negative proposition to the effect that no reason could ever be given by anyone for supposing the agent is not under an obligation or ought not to keep the promise. That would be impossible and would render the phrase useless. It is sufficient to satisfy the condition that no reason to the contrary can in fact be given.

If a reason is given for supposing the obligation is void or that the promiser ought not to keep a promise, then characteristically a situation calling for an evaluation arises. Suppose, for example, we consider a promised act wrong, but we grant that the promiser did undertake an obligation. Ought he to keep the promise? There is no established procedure for objectively deciding such cases in advance, and an evaluation (if that is really the right word) is in order. But unless we have some reason to the contrary, the *ceteris paribus* condition is satisfied, no evaluation is necessary, and the question whether he ought to do it is settled by saying 'he promised'. It is always an open possibility that we may have to make an evaluation in order to derive 'he ought' from 'he promised', for we may have to evaluate a counterargument. But an evaluation is not logically necessary in every case, for there may as a matter of fact be no counterarguments. I am therefore inclined to think that there is nothing necessarily evaluative about the *ceteris paribus* condition, even though deciding whether it is satisfied will frequently involve evaluations.

But suppose I am wrong about this: would that salvage the belief in an unbridgeable logical gulf between 'is' and 'ought'? I think not, for we can always rewrite my steps (4) and (5) so that they include the *ceteris paribus* clause as part of the conclusion. Thus from our premises we would then have derived 'Other things being equal Jones ought to pay Smith five dollars', and that would still be sufficient to refute the tradition, for we would still have shown a relation of entailment between descriptive and evaluative statements. It was not the fact that extenuating circumstances can void obligations that drove philosophers to the naturalistic fallacy fallacy; it was rather a theory of language, as we shall see later on.

We have thus derived (in as strict a sense of 'derive' as natural languages will admit of) an 'ought' from an 'is'. And the extra premises which were needed to make the derivation work were in no cause moral or evaluative in nature. They consisted of empirical assumptions, tautologies, and descriptions of word usage. It must be pointed out also that the 'ought' is a 'categorical' not a 'hypothetical' ought. (5) does not say that Jones ought to pay up if he wants such and such. It says he ought to pay up, period. Note also that the steps of the derivation are carried on in the third person. We are not concluding 'I ought' from 'I said "I promise"', but 'he ought' from 'he said "I promise"'.

The proof unfolds the connexion between the utterance of certain words and the speech act of promising and then in turn unfolds promising into obligation and moves from obligation to 'ought'. The step from (1) to (2) is radically different from the others and requires special comment. In (1) we construe 'I hereby promise . . .' as an English phrase having a certain meaning. It is a consequence of that meaning that the utterance of that phrase under certain conditions is the act of promising. Thus by presenting the quoted expressions in (1) and by describing their use in (1a) we have as it were already invoked the institution of promising. We might have started with an even more ground-floor premise than (1) by saying:

(1b) Jones uttered the phonetic sequence: /ai + hirbai + pramis + təpei + yu + smiθ + faiv + dalərz/

We would then have needed extra empirical premises stating that this phonetic sequence was associated in certain ways with certain meaningful units relative to certain dialects.

The moves from (2) to (5) are relatively easy. We rely on definitional connexions between 'promise', 'obligate', and 'ought', and the only problem which arises is that obligations can be overridden or removed in a variety of ways and we need to take account of that fact. We solve our difficulty by adding further premises to the effect that there are no contrary considerations, that other things are equal.

II

In this section I intend to discuss three possible objections to the derivation.

First Objection

Since the first premise is descriptive and the conclusion evaluative, there must be a concealed evaluative premise in the description of the conditions in (1b).

So far, this argument merely begs the question by assuming the logical gulf between descriptive and evaluative which the derivation is designed to challenge. To make the objection stick, the defender of the distinction would have to show how exactly (1b) must contain an evaluative premise and what sort of premise it might be. Uttering certain words in certain conditions just *is* promising and the description of these conditions needs no evaluative element. The essential thing is that in the transition from (1) to (2) we move from the specification of a certain utterance of words to the specification of a certain speech act. The move is achieved because the speech act is a conventional act; and the utterance of the words, according to the conventions, constitutes the performance of just that speech act.

A variant of this first objection is to say: all you have shown is that 'promise' is an evaluative, not a descriptive, concept. But this objection again begs the question and in the end will prove disastrous to the original distinction between descriptive and evaluative. For that a man uttered certain words and that these words have the meaning they do are surely objective facts. And if the statement of these two objective facts plus a description of the conditions of the utterance is sufficient to entail the statement (2) which the objector alleges to be an evaluative statement (Jones promised to pay Smith five dollars), then an evaluative conclusion is derived from descriptive premises without even going through steps (3), (4), and (5).

Second Objection

Utimately the derivation rests on the principle that one ought to keep one's promises and that is a moral principle, hence evaluative. I don't know whether 'one ought to keep one's promises' is a 'moral' principle, but whether or not it is, it is also tautological; for it is nothing more than a derivation from the two tautologies:

All promises are (create, are undertakings of, are acceptances of) obligations,

and

One ought to keep (fulfil) one's obligations.

What needs to be explained is why so many philosophers have failed to see the tautological character of this principle. Three things I think have concealed its character from them.

The first is a failure to distinguish external questions about the institution of promising from internal questions asked within the framework of the institution. The questions 'Why do we have such an institution as promising?' and 'Ought we to have such institutionalized forms of obligation as promising?' are external questions asked about and not within the institution of promising. And the question 'Ought one to keep one's promises?' can be confused with or can be taken as (and I think has often been taken as) an external question roughly expressible as 'Ought one to accept the institution of promising?' But taken literally, as an internal question, as a question about promises and not about the institution of promising, the question 'Ought one to keep one's promises?' is as empty as the question 'Are triangles three-sided?' To recognize something as a promise is to grant that, other things being equal, it ought to be kept.

A second fact which has clouded the issue is this. There are many situations, both real and imaginable, where one ought not to keep a promise, where the obligation to keep a promise is overridden by some further considerations, and it was for this reason that we needed those clumsy *ceteris paribus* clauses in our derivation. But the fact that obligations can be overridden does not show that there were no obligations in the first place. On the contrary. And these original obligations are all that is needed to make the proof work.

Yet a third factor is the following. Many philosophers still fail to realize the full force of saying that 'I hereby promise' is a performative expression. In uttering it one performs but does not describe the act of promising. Once promising is seen as a speech act of a kind different from describing, then it is easier to see that one of the features of the act is the undertaking of an obligation. But if one thinks the utterance of 'I promise' or 'I hereby promise' is a peculiar kind of description—for example, of one's mental state—then the relation between promising and obligation is going to seem very mysterious.

Third Objection

The derivation uses only a factual or inverted-commas sense of the evaluative terms employed. For example, an anthropologist observing the behaviour and attitudes of the Anglo-Saxons might well go through these derivations, but nothing evaluative would be included. Thus step (2) is equivalent to 'He did what they call promising' and step (5) to 'According to them he ought to pay Smith five dollars'. But since all of the steps (2) to (5) are in *oratio obliqua* and hence disguised statements of fact, the fact-value distinction remains unaffected.

This objection fails to damage the derivation, for what it says is only that the steps *can* be reconstructed as in *oratio obliqua*, that we can construe them as a series of external statements, that we can construct a parallel (or at any rate related) proof about reported speech. But what I am arguing is that, taken quite literally, without any *oratio obliqua* additions or interpretations, the derivation is valid. That one can construct a similar argument which would fail to refute the fact-value distinction does not show that this proof fails to refute it. Indeed it is irrelevant.

III

So far I have presented a counterexample to the thesis that one cannot derive an 'ought' from an 'is' and considered three possible objections to it. Even supposing what I have said so far is true, still one feels a certain uneasiness. One feels there must be some trick involved somewhere. We might state our uneasiness thus: How can my granting a mere fact about a man, such as the fact that he uttered certain words or that he made a promise, commit *me* to the view that *he* ought to do something? I now want briefly to discuss what broader philosophic significance my attempted derivation may have, in such a way as to give us the outlines of an answer to this question.

I shall begin by discussing the grounds for supposing that it cannot be answered at all.

The inclination to accept a rigid distinction between 'is' and 'ought', between descriptive and evaluative, rests on a certain picture of the way words relate to the world. It is a very attractive picture, so attractive (to me at least) that it is not entirely clear to what extent the mere presentation of counterexamples can challenge it. What is needed is an explanation of how and why this classical empiricist picture fails to deal with such counterexamples. Briefly, the picture is constructed something like this: first we present examples of so-called descriptive statements ('my car goes eighty miles an hour', 'Jones is six feet tall', 'Smith has brown hair'), and we contrast them with so-called evaluative statements ('my car is a good car', 'Jones ought to pay Smith five dollars', 'Smith is a nasty man'). Anyone can see that they are different. We articulate the difference by pointing out that for the descriptive statements the question of truth or falsity is objectively decidable, because to know the meaning of the descriptive expressions is to know under what objectively ascertainable conditions the statements which contain them are true or false. But in the case of evaluative statements the situation is quite different. To know the meaning of the evaluative expressions is not by itself sufficient for knowing under what conditions the statements containing them are true or false, because the meaning of the expressions is such that the statements are not capable of objective or factual truth or falsity at all. Any justification a speaker can give of one of his evaluative statements essentially involves some appeal to attitudes he holds, to criteria of assessment he has adopted, or to moral principles by which he has chosen to live and judge other people. Descriptive statements are thus objective, evaluative statements subjective, and the difference is a consequence of the different sorts of terms employed.

The underlying reason for these differences is that evaluative statements perform a completely different job from descriptive statements. Their job is not to describe any features of the world but to express the speaker's emotions, to express his attitudes, to praise or condemn, to laud or insult, to commend, to recommend, to advise, and so forth. Once we see the different jobs the two perform, we see that there must be a logical gulf between them. Evaluative statements must be different from descriptive statements in order to do their job, for if they were objective they could no longer function to evaluate. Put metaphysically, values cannot lie in the world, for if they did they would cease to be values and would just be another part of the world. Put in the formal mode, one cannot define an evaluative word in terms of descriptive words, for if one did, one would no longer be able to use the evaluative word to commend, but only to describe. Put yet another way, any effort to derive an 'ought' from an 'is' must be a waste of time, for all it could show even if it succeeded would be that the 'is' was not a real 'is' but only a disguised 'ought' or, alternatively, that the 'ought' was not a real 'ought' but only a disguised 'is'.

This summary of the traditional empirical view has been very brief, but I hope it conveys something of the power of this picture. In the hands of certain modern authors, especially Hare and Nowell-Smith, the picture attains considerable subtlety and sophistication.

What is wrong with this picture? No doubt many things are wrong with it. In the end I am going to say that one of the things wrong with it is that it fails to give us any coherent account of such notions as commitment, responsibility, and obligation.

In order to work toward this conclusion I can begin by saying that the picture fails to account for the *different types* of 'descriptive' statements. Its paradigms of descriptive statements are such utterances as 'my car goes eighty miles an hour', 'Jones is six feet tall', 'Smith has brown hair', and the like. But it is forced by its own rigidity to construe 'Jones got married', 'Smith made a promise', 'Jackson has five dollars', and 'Brown hit a home run' as descriptive statements as well. It is so forced, because whether or not someone got married, made a promise, has five dollars, or hit a home run is as much a matter of objective fact as whether he has red hair or brown eyes. Yet the former kind of statement (statements containing 'married', 'promise', and so forth) seem to be quite different from the simple empirical paradigms of descriptive statements. How are they different? Though both kinds of statements state matters of objective fact, the statements containing words such as 'married', 'promise', 'home run', and 'five dollars' state facts whose existence presupposes certain institutions: a man has five dollars, given the institution of money. Take away the institution and all he has is a rectangular bit of paper with green ink on it. A man hits a home run only given the institution of baseball; without the institution he only hits a sphere with a stick. Similarly, a man gets married or makes a promise only within the institutions of marriage and promising. Without them, all he does is utter words or makes gestures. We might characterize such facts as institutional facts, and contrast them with noninstitutional, or brute, facts: that a man has a bit of paper with green ink on it is a brute fact, that he has five dollars is an institutional fact.[1] The classical picture fails to account for the differences between statements of brute fact and statements of institutional fact.

The word 'institution' sounds artificial here, so let us ask: what sorts of institutions are these? In order to answer that question I need to distinguish between two different kinds of rules or conventions.

[1] For a discussion of this distinction see G. E. M. Anscombe, 'Brute Facts', *Analysis* (1958).

Some rules regulate antecedently existing forms of behaviour. For example, the rules of polite table behaviour regulate eating, but eating exists independently of these rules. Some rules, on the other hand, do not merely regulate but create or define new forms of behaviour: the rules of chess, for example, do not merely regulate an antecedently existing activity called playing chess; they, as it were, create the possibility of or define that activity. The activity of playing chess is constituted by action in accordance with these rules. Chess has no existence apart from these rules. The distinction I am trying to make was foreshadowed by Kant's distinction between regulative and constitutive principles, so let us adopt his terminology and describe our distinction as a distinction between regulative and constitutive rules. Regulative rules regulate activities whose existence is independent of the rules; constitutive rules constitute (and also regulate) forms of activity whose existence is logically dependent on the rules.[1]

Now the institutions that I have been talking about are systems of constitutive rules. The institutions of marriage, money, and promising are like the institutions of baseball or chess in that they are systems of such constitutive rules or conventions. What I have called institutional facts are facts which presuppose such institutions.

Once we recognize the existence of and begin to grasp the nature of such institutional facts, it is but a short step to see that many forms of obligations, commitments, rights, and responsibilities are similarly institutionalized. It is often a matter of fact that one has certain obligations, commitments, rights, and responsibilities, but it is a matter of institutional, not brute, fact. It is one such institutionalized form of obligation, promising, which I invoked above to derive an 'ought' from an 'is'. I started with a brute fact, that a man uttered certain words, and then invoked the institution in such a way as to generate institutional facts by which we arrived at the institutional fact that the man ought to pay another man five dollars. The whole proof rests on an appeal to the constitutive rule that to make a promise is to undertake an obligation.

We are now in a position to see how we can generate an indefinite number of such proofs. Consider the following vastly different example. We are in our half of the seventh inning and I have a big lead off second base. The pitcher whirls, fires to the shortstop covering, and I am tagged out a good ten feet down the line. The umpire shouts, 'Out!' I, however, being a positivist, hold my ground. The umpire

[1] For a discussion of a related distinction see J. Rawls, 'Two Concepts of Rules', *Philosophical Review*, LXIV (1955).

tells me to return to the dugout. I point out to him that you can't derive an 'ought' from an 'is'. No set of descriptive statements describing matters of fact, I say, will entail any evaluative statements to the effect that I should or ought to leave the field. 'You just can't get orders or recommendations from facts alone. What is needed is an evaluative major premise. I therefore return to and stay on second base (until I am carried off the field). I think everyone feels my claims here to be preposterous, and preposterous in the sense of logically absurd. Of course you can derive an 'ought' from an 'is', and though to actually set out the derivation in this case would be vastly more complicated than in the case of promising, it is in principle no different. By undertaking to play baseball I have committed myself to the observation of certain constitutive rules.

We are now also in a position to see that the tautology that one ought to keep one's promises is only one of a class of similar tautologies concerning institutionalized forms of obligation. For example, 'one ought not to steal' can be taken as saying that to recognize something as someone else's property necessarily involves recognizing his right to dispose of it. This is a constitutive rule of the institution of private property.[1] 'One ought not to tell lies' can be taken as saying that to make an assertion necessarily involves undertaking an obligation to speak truthfully. Another constitutive rule. 'One ought to pay one's debts' can be construed as saying that to recognize something as a debt is necessarily to recognize an obligation to pay it. It is easy to see how all these principles will generate counterexamples to the thesis that you cannot derive an 'ought' from an 'is'.

My tentative conclusions, then, are as follows:

1. The classical picture fails to account for institutional facts.
2. Institutional facts exist within systems of constitutive rules.
3. Some systems of constitutive rules involve obligations, commitments, and responsibilities.

---

[1] Proudhon said: 'Property is theft'. If one tries to take this as an internal remark it makes no sense. It was intended as an external remark attacking and rejecting the institution of private property. It gets its air of paradox and its force by using terms which are internal to the institution in order to attack the institution.

Standing on the deck of some institutions one can tinker with constitutive rules and even throw some other institutions overboard. But could one throw all institutions overboard (in order perhaps to avoid ever having to derive an 'ought' from an 'is')? One could not and still engage in those forms of behaviour we consider characteristically human. Suppose Proudhon had added (and tried to live by): 'Truth is a lie, marriage is infidelity, language is uncommunicative, law is a crime', and so on with every possible institution.

4. Within those systems we can derive 'ought's' from 'is's' on the model of the first derivation.

With these conclusions we now return to the question with which I began this section: How can my stating a fact about a man, such as the fact that he made a promise, commit me to a view about what he ought to do? One can begin to answer this question by saying that for me to state such an institutional fact is already to invoke the constitutive rules of the institution. It is those rules that give the word 'promise' its meaning. But those rules are such that to commit myself to the view that Jones made a promise involves committing myself to what he ought to do (other things being equal).

If you like, then, we have shown that 'promise' is an evaluative word, but since it is also purely descriptive, we have really shown that the whole distinction needs to be re-examined. The alleged distinction between descriptive and evaluative statements is really a conflation of at least two distinctions. On the one hand there is a distinction between different kinds of speech acts, one family of speech acts including evaluations, another family including descriptions. This is a distinction between different kinds of illocutionary force.[1] On the other hand there is a distinction between utterances which involve claims objectively decidable as true or false and those which involve claims not objectively decidable, but which are 'matters of personal decision' or 'matters of opinion'. It has been assumed that the former distinction is (must be) a special case of the latter, that if something has the illocutionary force of an evaluation, it cannot be entailed by factual premises. Part of the point of my argument is to show that this contention is false, that factual premises can entail evaluative conclusions. If I am right, then the alleged distinction between descriptive and evaluative utterances is useful only as a distinction between two kinds of illocutionary force, describing and evaluating, and it is not even very useful there, since if we are to use these terms strictly, they are only two among hundreds of kinds of illocutionary force; and utterances of sentences of the form (5)—'Jones ought to pay Smith five dollars'—would not characteristically fall in either class.

---

[1] See J. L. Austin, *How to Do Things with Words* (Cambridge, Mass., 1962), for an explanation of this notion.

VIII

THE PROMISING GAME

R. M. HARE

ONE OF THE MOST fundamental questions about moral judgements is whether they, and other value-judgements, can be logically derived from statements of empirical fact. Like most important philosophical questions, this one has reached the stage at which its discussion is bound to proceed piecemeal, in terms of particular examples, arguments and counterarguments. This article is intended as a contribution to one such controversy. In a recent article, 'How to derive "ought" from "is"'[1], Professor J. R. Searle attempts a feat which many before him have thought to perform. His argument, though it seems to me unsound, is set out with such clarity and elegance as amply to repay examination.

He asks us to consider the following series of statements:

(1) Jones uttered the words 'I hereby promise to pay you, Smith, five dollars'.

(2) Jones promised to pay Smith five dollars.

(3) Jones placed himself under (undertook) an obligation to pay Smith five dollars.

(4) Jones is under an obligation to pay Smith five dollars.

(5) Jones ought to pay Smith five dollars.

He then argues concerning this list that 'the relation between any statement and its successor, while not in every case one of 'entailment', is nonetheless not just a contingent relation; and the additional statements necessary to make the relationship one of entailment do not

From *Revue Internationale de Philosophie*, No. 70 (1964), pp. 398–412. Reprinted by permission of the author and the *Revue Internationale de Philosophie*.

[1] *Philosophical Review*, 1964. I must acknowledge the help I have received from an unpublished paper which Professor A. G. N. Flew kindly lent me, as well as from several enjoyable arguments with Professor Searle himself. Searle's argument, though I cannot accept it, is both more plausible, and sets a higher moral tone, than that recently supplied by Mr. MacIntyre and repeated in an unimportantly different form by Professor Black (*Phil. Rev.*, 1959 and 1964). While Searle seeks to demonstrate logically that we ought to keep our promises, Black and MacIntyre seek to demonstrate that we ought to do whatever is the one and only means to achieving *anything* that we happen to want, or avoiding *anything* that we want to avoid.

need to involve any evaluative statements, moral principles, or any-thing of the sort' (p. 44).[1]

Though there may be other steps in the argument that are open to question, I shall concentrate on those from (1) to (2) and from (2) to (3). One of the 'additional statements' which Searle supplies between (1) and (2) is

(1a) Under certain conditions C anyone who utters the words (sen-tence) 'I hereby promise to pay you, Smith, five dollars' promises to pay Smith five dollars.

This, he says, in conjunction with the further premise,

(1b) Conditions C obtain,
turns the step from (1) to (2) into an entailment (pp. 44 f.). Next, he similarly inserts between (2) and (3), in order to show that that step is an entailment, what he calls the 'tautological'[2] premise,

(2a) All promises are acts of placing oneself under (undertaking) an obligation to do the thing promised.

This premise is 'tautological' because 'No analysis of the concept of promising will be complete which does not include the feature of the promiser placing himself under an obligation' (p. 45).[3]

Later, Searle puts what appears to be the same point in terms of what he calls 'constitutive rules'. There are some institutions which are not merely regulated but constituted by the rules governing them. Thus 'the rules of chess, for example, do not merely regulate an antecedently existing activity called playing chess; they, as it were, create the possibility of or define that activity' (p. 55).[4] The rules of chess and baseball are examples of constitutive rules, and so is 'the constitutive rule that to make a promise is to undertake an obligation' (p. 56).[5]

I wish to consider the relations between (1a) and (2a). In order to clarify them, I shall appeal to the 'baseball' analogy with which Searle has helpfully provided us (p. 56). He describes a set of em-pirical conditions such that, if they obtain, a baseball-player is out, and is obliged to leave the field. I will call these conditions 'E',

---

[1] p. 102 of this volume. [Ed.]
[2] 'Analytic' seems to me preferable; but I will use Searle's term.
[3] [p. 103 Ed.]
[4] [p. 112 Ed.]
[5] [p. 112 Ed.]

in order to conceal my ignorance of the rules of baseball in which they are specified. What correspond, in the 'promising' case, to conditions E in the baseball case, are conditions C *together with* the condition that the person in question should have uttered the words 'I promise, etc.'. Let us number the propositions in the 'baseball' case to correspond with Searle's numbering in the 'promising' case, distinguishing them by the addition of a 'prime'. There will then be a constitutive rule of baseball to the effect that

(1a′) Whenever a player satisfies conditions E, he is out. And, since no analysis of the concept *out* will be complete which does not include the feature of the player who is out being obliged to leave the field, we can add the 'tautological' premise,

(2a′) All players who are out are obliged to leave the field.

We can simplify the argument by combining (1a′) and (2a′) into the single constitutive rule,

(1a′*) Whenever a player satisfies conditions E, he is obliged to leave the field.

For, if the definition in virtue of which (2a′) is a tautology is applied direct to (1a′), it turns into (1a′*). And similarly in the 'promising' case, the argument will be simplified if we combine (1a) and (2a) into the single constitutive rule,

(1a*) Under certain conditions C anyone who utters the words (sentence) 'I hereby promise to pay you, Smith, five dollars' places himself under (undertakes) an obligation to pay Smith five dollars.

The rule could be put in a general form, leaving out the reference to Smith; but we need not trouble with this.

What then is the status of (1a*)? Five answers seem plausible enough to merit discussion:

(a) It is a tautology;
(b) It is a synthetic empirical statement about English word-usage;
(c) It is a synthetic prescription about word-usage in English;
(d) It is a synthetic empirical statement about something other than word-usage;
(e) It is, or implicitly contains, a synthetic evaluation or prescription, not merely about word-usage.

Searle would appear to maintain (b). I shall argue for (e). Since the arguments which I shall use against (a), (b) and (c) are all the same,

I shall not need to detail them separately for the three answers; (d) will require to be rebutted independently, but this will not take long.

Let us start by discussing the status of the analogous statement (1a′*). Is it a tautology? There certainly is a tautology with which it can be easily confused, namely

(1a′*⁺) *In (i.e. according to the rules of) baseball*, whenever a player satisfies conditions E, he is obliged to leave the field.

This is a tautology because a definition of 'baseball' would have to run 'a game with the following rules, viz. ...' followed by a list of rules, including (1a′*) or its equivalent. But this does not make (1a′*) itself, in which the italicized part is omitted, into a tautology. (1a′*) is a summary of part of the rules of baseball; and, although it may be that some of the rules of a game are tautologies, it is impossible that they should all be. For if they were, what we should have would be, not the rules for playing a game, but rules (or, more strictly, exemplifications of rules) for speaking correctly about the game. To conform to the rules of a game it is necessary to act, not merely speak, in certain ways. Therefore the rules are not tautologies.

For the same reasons, as we shall see, the rules of baseball (and in particular (1a′) and (1a′*)) cannot be treated as synthetic statements, or even as synthetic prescriptions, about word-usage. They are about how a game is, or is to be, played.

Let us now apply all this to the 'promising' case. By parity of reasoning it is clear that (1a*) is not a tautology, although it is easy to confuse it with another proposition (1a*⁺), which *is* a tautology. (1a*⁺) will consist of (1a*), preceded by the words 'In the institution of promising'—we might say, if it were not liable to misinterpretation, 'In the promising game'. This is a tautology, because it is expansible into 'According to the rules of an institution whose rules say "Under conditions C anyone who utters the words ... (etc., as in (1a*))", under conditions C anyone who utters the words ... (etc., as in (1a*))'. But (1a*) itself is not a tautology. As before, the constitutive rules of an institution may contain some tautologies, but they cannot all be tautologies, if they are going to prescribe that people *act* in certain ways and not in others. And, as before, we must not be misled into thinking that, because it is a tautology that promising is an institution of which (1a*) is a constitutive rule, (1a*) itself is a tautology.

As before, and for analogous reasons, (1a*) is neither a synthetic statement nor a synthetic prescription about how English is, or is or ought to be, spoken. Just because it has the consequences which Searle claims for it, it is more than this.

There is one apparent disparity between the 'promising' and 'baseball' cases which might be a source of confusion. In the 'baseball' case the word 'baseball' does not occur in (1a′*); and therefore, though (1a′*) is in a sense definitive of 'baseball', it is not thereby made tautologous. But in the 'promising' case, (1a*) does contain the word 'promise'; and this makes it much more plausible to suggest that (1a*), since it is in a sense explicative of the notion of promising, is a tautology. This plausibility is even stronger in the case of (1a). The answer to this objection may help to clarify the whole procedure of introducing a word like 'promise' into the language. The word is introduced by means of such a proposition as (1a*). But we must not be misled into thinking that this makes (1a*) a tautology, or a mere statement about word-usage. For, as we shall see, it is a characteristic of words like 'promise', which have meaning only within institutions, that they can be introduced into language only when certain synthetic propositions about how we should *act* are assented to. (1a*) is such a proposition. The word 'promise' depends for its meaning upon the proposition, but the proposition is not true solely in virtue of the meaning of 'promise'. Similarly, a word like 'out' is dependent for its meaning upon the rules of baseball or cricket; but those rules are not tautologies in virtue of the meaning of 'out' and other such words.

However, this may not seem to go to the root of the objection. For Searle's argument could be stated without mentioning the word 'promise' at all. He could simply, in (1a), substitute the words 'place upon himself an obligation' for the word 'promise' throughout. The proposition then becomes

> Under certain conditions C anyone who utters the words (sentence) 'I hereby place upon myself an obligation to pay you, Smith, five dollars' places upon himself an obligation to pay Smith five dollars.

Surely, it might be said, I cannot deny that *this* is a tautology, or, alternatively, a statement about word-usage. But this is just what I do wish to deny. For, to begin with, if the mere repetition of the words 'place . . . an obligation' in the proposition made it into a tautology, it is hard to see what the words 'Under certain conditions C' are doing; one might think that under any conditions whatever a person who says 'I hereby place upon myself an obligation, etc.' must necessarily

have thereby placed upon himself an obligation, etc. But once we have
seen that this is not so (for example, the man might be under duress
or mad), we see that the appearance of tautology is deceptive. It is
not in general true (let alone tautologous) that the man who says 'p'
makes it the case that p. Something like this does happen in the case
of what used to be called performative verbs; it happens in our present
case with the verb 'promise'. The man who says 'I promise', promises
(under certain conditions). But it is not a tautology that he does so,
nor is it a tautology that the man who says 'I hereby place myself under
an obligation' places himself under an obligation, even under certain
(empirical) conditions. Nor are either of these merely remarks about
word-usage. For it is a necessary condition for the adoption of these
performative expressions that certain synthetic constitutive (and not
merely linguistic) rules be also adopted, thus creating the institution
within which the expressions have meaning.

To make this clearer, let us suppose that we have already in our
language the word 'obligation' (and kindred words like 'ought'),
but that none of our obligations has been, as Searle puts it, 'institutionalized' (p. 56).[1] That is to say, we can speak of our having obligations (e.g. to feed our children) and even of our placing upon ourselves
obligations (e.g., by having children we place upon ourselves the
obligation to feed them); but we cannot yet speak of placing upon
ourselves an obligation just by saying, merely, 'I place upon myself
the obligation, etc.'. Then suppose that some inventive person suggests the adoption of this useful expression (or rather its conversion to
this new use). The other members of society may well stare at him and
say 'But we don't see how you can place upon yourself an obligation
just by saying these words'. What he will then have to say, in order
to sell this device to them, and therewith the institution of which it
is a part, is something like this: 'You have to adopt the constitutive
rule or moral principle that one has an obligation to do those things
of which one has said "I (hereby) place upon myself an obligation to
do them".' When they have adopted this principle, or in adopting it,
they can introduce the new use for the expression. And the principle
is a synthetic one. It is a new synthetic moral principle, and not merely
a new way of speaking, that is being introduced; this shows up in the
fact that, if they adopt the principle, they will have acquired obligations to do things that they have not done before, not merely to speak
in ways that they have not spoken before.

There may be, indeed, an interpretation on which (1a), (1a*) and

[1] [p. 112 of this volume. Ed.]

their analogues could be said to be statements 'about' the English language. They could be treated as statements which say, or imply, that the English have in their language the performative expression 'I promise', or the performative expression 'I place myself under an obligation', whose use is tied to the institution of promising (or undertaking obligations); and which therefore imply also that the English (or sufficient of them) subscribe to the rules of this institution. The latter half of this would be an anthropological statement about the English. But it is obvious that such a statement cannot generate the entailments which Searle requires. For the conclusions which will then follow will be, at most, of the type: 'The English subscribe to the view that Jones is under an obligation'; 'The English subscribe to the view that Jones ought', etc. For the required non-anthropological, moral (or at least prescriptive) conclusions to follow, (1a) must, interpreted in the light of (2a), be taken as expressing the speaker's own subscription to the rules of the institution of promising, i.e. to moral principles. I do not wish to argue which is the most natural way to take these statements; all I need to say is that *unless* they are taken in this way, the derivation will not work.

It is often the case that performative expressions cannot be introduced without the adoption of synthetic constitutive rules. Thus it would be impossible to introduce the expression 'I stake a claim to this land' unless there were adopted, at the same time, a principle that by saying this, under the appropriate conditions, if the claimant has not been forestalled by somebody else, he acquires at least some claim to the land. In pioneering days in America one could do this; but try doing it in modern Siberia, where they do not have that principle.

Another way of showing that (1a*) is not a tautology, and is not made so by the fact that it is used for introducing the word 'promise' into the language, is the following. If (1a*) were true in virtue of the meaning of the word 'promise', and therefore tautologous, then both (1a) and (2a) would have to be tautologous. For (1a*) was arrived at by applying to (1a) the definition which made (2a) tautologous; and it is impossible to get a tautology out of a synthetic proposition by definitional substitution. But (1a) and (2a) cannot both be made tautologous without an equivocation on the word 'promise'. For (2a) is tautologous, if it is, in virtue of *one* definition of 'promise', and (1a) is tautologous, if it is, in virtue of *another* definition of 'promise' (or, on the alternative suggestion that (1a) is a statement about language, it can be so only in virtue of *another* definition of 'promise'). If we take

(1a) as tautologous, or as a usage-statement, it will have to be in virtue of some such definition as the following:

(D1) Promising is saying, under certain conditions C, 'I hereby promise, etc.'.

But (2a), if it is tautologous, is so in virtue of a *different* definition, namely

Promising is placing oneself under an obligation.... How the definition is completed does not matter; it has at any rate to start like this. To make (1a*) tautologous, or a usage-statement, we have to take 'promise' simultaneously in these two different senses. And the trouble cannot be escaped by completing the last definition thus:

(D2) Promising is placing oneself under an obligation by saying, under certain conditions C, 'I hereby promise, etc.'.

This definition sounds attractive, and may be more or less correct; but it does not make (1a) a tautology, and would make it into more than a statement about word-usage. According to (D2), a man who says 'I hereby promise, etc.' has satisfied only one of the conditions of promising, but may not have satisfied the other; he may have said the words, but may not have thereby placed upon himself any obligation. We can only say that he has succeeded in doing this if we assent to the *synthetic* principle (1*). The necessity of assenting to this synthetic principle before the trick works may be concealed by taking (D2), not as a verbal definition of the modern type, but as that old device of synthetic-a-priorists, an 'essential' or 'real' definition of promising. But then it will be synthetic.

I conclude, for these reasons, that (1*) cannot be tautologous or a statement about word-usage, but must be a synthetic constitutive rule of the institution of promising. If the constitutive rules of the institution of promising are moral principles, as I think they are, then (1a*) is a synthetic moral principle. It follows that, if Searle sticks to it that (2a) is tautologous, he must allow that (1a) either is or implicitly contains a synthetic moral principle. But this would destroy his argument; and indeed he says that it is not; for, after introducing it, he says 'As far as I can see, no moral premises are lurking in the logical woodpile' (p. 43).[1] He says this, in spite of the fact that he is going on immediately to make (1a) by definition equivalent to (1a*), which we have seen to be a synthetic moral principle.

It might be suggested that (1a) is an empirical statement of some non-linguistic sort. I am assured by Searle that he does not think this;

[1] [p. 103 of this volume. Ed.]

but the suggestion is worth examining. If it were true, it might save his argument, which is, essentially, that no moral or other non-empirical, non-tautological, premises have to be included. He spends some effort in showing that conditions C, to which (1a) alludes, are empirical conditions—and this may be granted for the sake of argument. But, although this would make the proposition (1b), 'Conditions C obtain', into an empirical statement, it by no means makes (1a) into one. For however empirical these conditions C may be, it is possible to construct non-empirical propositions, and even imperatives, of the form 'Under conditions C, p'—e.g. 'Under conditions C, switch off (or you ought to switch off) the motor'. Nevertheless, it is easy to be misled into thinking that, if the conditions under which a man who utters 'I hereby promise' can correctly be said to have made a promise are empirical conditions, this proves that (1a) is not a moral statement.

I said that I would concentrate my attack on steps (1) to (3) of Searle's argument. But I may mention here that an analogous attack could be made against steps (3) to (5). These too depend on a non-tautologous rule of the institution of promising, or in general of (performatively) placing oneself under obligations. This non-tautologous rule is as follows:

(3a) If anybody has placed himself under an obligation (in the past) he is (still) under an obligation, unless he has done already what he was obliged to do.

To find out whether this is a tautology, we should have, as before, to rewrite it with the aid of the definition or tautology which is required to make the step from (4) to (5) into an entailment, viz. the definition

(D3) For one to be under an obligation to do a thing is for it to be the case that one ought to do that thing

(I shall not enquire whether this definition is a sufficient one; it is probably not); or the tautology

(4a) All people who are under obligations to do things ought to do them.

(3a) then turns into

(3a*) If anybody has placed himself under an obligation (in the past), it is (still) the case that he ought to do the thing that he placed himself under an obligation to do, unless he has already done it. That this is not a tautology (or for that matter a statement about word-usage) could be shown, if it is not plain already, by an argument analogous to the preceding.

I will conclude with some general remarks about the nature of the mistake that Searle seems to me to have made in this paper. There are many words which could not have a use unless certain propositions were assented to by the users or a sufficient number of them. The possibility of using a word can depend on assent to synthetic propositions. This will apply especially to many words whose use is dependent upon the existence of institutions, though not only to them.[1] Unless there were laws of property, we could not speak of 'mine' and 'thine'; yet the laws of property are not tautologies. Unless there were a readiness to accept currency in exchange for goods, words like 'dollar' and 'pound' would pass out of use; yet to be ready to accept currency in exchange for goods is not to assent to a tautology or to a statement about language. In a community which did not play, or accept the rules of, baseball, the word 'out', as it is used by umpires, would lack a use (though not as used by anthropologists, if they were discussing the ways of a community which did have the game); but this does not make the rules of baseball into tautologies or statements about word-usage.

In the case of promising we have a similar phenomenon. Unless a sufficient number of people were prepared to assent to the moral principles which are the constitutive rules of the institution of promising, the word 'promise' could not have a use. To take the extreme case: suppose that nobody thought that one ought to keep promises. It would then be impossible to make a promise; the word 'promise' would become a mere noise (except, as before, in the mouths of anthropologists), unless it acquired some new use. But it does not follow from this that the moral principles, assent to which by a sufficient number of people is a condition for the remaining in use of the word 'promise', are themselves analytic.

It is necessary, moreover, only that a sufficiently large number of people should assent to the constitutive rule. If they do so, and if the word in question comes into use, it is possible for people who do not assent to the rules to use the word comprehensibly. Thus an anarchist can use the word 'property'; a man who for reasons of his own has no confidence in paper money, and is therefore not prepared to exchange goods for it, can still use the word 'pound'; and a Macchiavellian politician who recognizes no duty to keep promises

---

[1] What Kant was driving at, without the synthetic-a-priorism, might possibly be hinted at by pointing out that many words that we use in physics and in everyday life, such as 'table', and in general 'material object', would lack a use unless we made certain assumptions about the regularity of the universe.

can still use the word 'promise'. He can even use it to make promises, always provided that his moral opinions are not too well known.

Such people are, admittedly, parasites; but not all parasites are reprehensible. Let us suppose that somebody is opposed to fox-hunting. This does not stop him engaging in fox-hunting, in the sense of going to meets, following hounds, etc., and using all the terminology of the chase. He may think it his duty, whenever he can get away with it, to help the fox to escape (that may be why he goes fox-hunting); but this does not involve him in any self-contradiction. It may be that to try to help foxes to escape is contrary to the constitutive rules for fox-hunting[1]; for unless there were among these rules one which said that the object of the game was to kill the fox, it would not be fox-*hunting*. But this does not stop our opponent of blood sports masquerading as a person who accepts this rule; nor does it mean that, by so masquerading, he lays upon himself any obligation to abide by it. And in just the same way the Macchiavellian politician can, without self-contradiction, think it his duty to break some of the promises he makes (and think this even while he is making them). He could not have made them unless the word 'promise' were in use; and it could not be in use unless a sufficient number of people assented to the moral principles governing promising; but this does not mean that a person who, while making promises, dissents, silently, from the principles contradicts himself. In using the word 'promise' indeed, he is masquerading as one who thinks that one ought to keep promises, just as one who lies is masquerading as one who thinks that p, when he does not. But neither the liar nor the man who makes lying promises is contradicting himself. And when the lying promiser comes to break his promise, he is still not contradicting himself; he can say 'I pretended to think, when I made the promise, that one ought to keep promises; but I don't really think this and never have'.

Talking about 'institutional facts', though it can be illuminating, can also be a peculiarly insidious way of committing the 'naturalistic fallacy'. I do not think that Searle actually falls into this particular trap; but others perhaps have. There are moral and other principles, accepted by most of us, such that, if they were not generally accepted, certain institutions like property and promising could not exist. And

---

[1]It might be objected that the rules of fox-hunting are not constitutive but regulative. This would depend on establishing some relevant difference between the chasing of foxes and the chasing of cricket balls—a question into which I shall not go, but whose investigation might cast doubt on this distinction.

E

if the institutions do exist, we are in a position to affirm certain 'institutional facts' (for example, that a certain piece of land is my property), on the ground that certain 'brute facts' are the case (for example, that my ancestors have occupied it from time immemorial). But from the 'institutional facts', certain obviously prescriptive conclusions can be drawn (for example, that nobody ought to deprive me of the land). Thus it looks as if there could be a straight deduction, in two steps, from brute facts to prescriptive conclusions *via* institutional facts. But the deduction is a fraud. For the brute fact is a ground for the prescriptive conclusion only if the prescriptive principle which is the constitutive rule of the institution be accepted; and this prescriptive principle is not a tautology. For someone (a communist for example) who does not accept this non-tautologous prescriptive principle, the deduction collapses like a house of cards—though this does not prevent him from continuing to use the word 'property' (with his tongue in his cheek).

Similarly with promising. It may seem as if the 'brute fact' that a person has uttered a certain phonetic sequence entails the 'institutional fact' that he has promised, and that this in turn entails that he ought to do a certain thing. But this conclusion can be drawn only by one who accepts, in addition, the non-tautologous principle that one ought to keep one's promises. For unless one accepts this principle, one is not a subscribing member of the institution which it constitutes, and therefore cannot be compelled logically to accept the institutional facts which it generates in such a sense that they entail the conclusion, though of course one must admit their truth, regarded purely as pieces of anthropology.

If I do not agree with Searle's reasons for maintaining that we ought to keep our promises, what are my own reasons? They are of a fundamentally different character, although they take in parts of Searle's argument in passing. To break a promise is, normally, a particularly gross form of deception. It is grosser than the failure to fulfil a declaration of intention, just because (if you wish) our society has, *pari passu* with the introduction of the word 'promise', adopted the moral principle that one ought to keep promises, thus constituting the institution called 'promising'. My reason for thinking that I ought not to take parasitic advantage of this institution, but ought to obey its rules, is the following. If I ask myself whether I am willing that I myself should be deceived in this way, I answer unhesitatingly that I am not. I therefore cannot subscribe to any moral principle which permits people to deceive other people in this way (any general principle which says 'It is all right to break promises'). There may be more specific principles which I could accept, of the form 'It is all right to break promises in situations of type S'. Most people accept some specific principles of this form. What anybody can here substitute for 'S' he will determine, if he follows my sort of reasoning, by asking himself, for any proposed value of 'S', whether he can subscribe to the principle when applied to all cases, including cases in which he is the person to whom the promise is made. Thus the morality of promise-keeping is a fairly standard application of what I have called elsewhere[1] the 'golden-rule' type of moral argument; it needs no 'is'-'ought' derivations to support it—derivations whose validity will be believed in only by those who have ruled out a priori any questioning of the existing institutions on whose rules they are based.

[1] *Freedom and Reason*, esp. pp. 86–125.

IX

THE INTERPRETATION OF THE MORAL PHILOSOPHY OF J. S. MILL[1]

J. O. URMSON

IT IS A MATTER which should be of great interest to those who study the psychology of philosophers that the theories of some great philosophers of the past are studied with the most patient and accurate scholarship, while those of others are so burlesqued and travestied by critics and commentators that it is hard to believe that their works are ever seriously read with a sympathetic interest, or even that they are read at all. Amongst those who suffer most in this way John Stuart Mill is an outstanding example. With the exception of a short book by Reginald Jackson,[2] there is no remotely accurate account of his views on deductive logic, so that, for example, the absurd view that the syllogism involves *petitio principii* is almost invariably fathered on him; and, as Von Wright says, 'A good systematic and critical monograph on Mill's Logic of Induction still remains to be written'.[3] But even more perplexing is the almost universal misconstruction placed upon Mill's ethical doctrines; for his *Utilitarianism* is a work which every undergraduate is set to read and which one would therefore expect Mill's critics to have read at least once. But this, apparently, is not so; and instead of Mill's own doctrines a travesty is discussed, so that the most common criticisms of him are simply irrelevant. It will not be the thesis of this paper that Mill's views are immune to criticism, or that they are of impeccable clarity and verbal consistency; it will be maintained that, if interpreted with, say, half the sympathy automatically accorded to Plato, Leibniz, and Kant, an essentially consistent thesis can be discovered which is very superior to that usually attributed to Mill and immune to the common run of criticisms.

One further note must be made on the scope of this paper. Mill in his *Utilitarianism* attempts to do two things; first, he attempts to

From *Philosophical Quarterly*, Vol. 3 (1953), pp. 33–39. Reprinted by permission of the author and the *Philosophical Quarterly*.

[1] [This article is discussed by H. J. McCloskey in 'An Examination of Restricted Utilitarianism', *Philosophical Review*, (1957). Ed.]

[2] *An Examination of the Deductive Logic of J. S. Mill* (1941).

[3] *A Treatise on Induction and Probability* (1951), p. 164.

state the place of the conception of a *summum bonum* in ethics, secondly, he attempts to give an account of the nature of this ultimate end. We shall be concerned only with the first of these two parts of Mill's ethical theory; we shall not ask what Mill thought the ultimate end was, and how he thought that his view on this point could be substantiated, but only what part Mill considered that the notion of an ultimate end, whatever it be, must play in a sound ethical theory. This part of Mill's doctrine is logically independent of his account of happiness.

Two Mistaken Interpretations of Mill

Some of Mill's expositors and critics have thought that Mill was attempting to analyse or define the notion of right in terms of the *summum bonum*. Thus Mill is commonly adduced as an example of an ethical naturalist by those who interpret his account of happiness naturalistically, as being one who defined rightness in terms of the natural consequences of actions. Moore, for example, while criticising Mill's account of the ultimate end says: 'In thus insisting that what is right must mean what produces the best possible results Utilitarianism is fully justified'.[1] Others have been less favourable in their estimation of this alleged view of Mill's. But right or wrong, it seems clear to me that Mill did not hold it. Mill's only reference to this analytic problem is on page 27 (of the Everyman edition, to which all references will be made), where he refers to a person 'who sees in moral obligation a transcendent fact, an objective reality belonging to the province of "Things in themselves"', and goes on to speak of this view as an irrelevant opinion 'on this point of Ontology', as though the analysis of ethical terms was not part of ethical philosophy at all as he conceived it, but part of ontology. It seems clear that when Mill speaks of his quest being for the 'criterion of right and wrong' (p. 1), 'concerning the foundation of morality' (p. 1) for a 'test of right and wrong' (p. 2), he is looking for a 'means of ascertaining what is right or wrong' (p. 2), not for a definition of these terms. We shall not, therefore, deal further with this interpretation of Mill; if a further refutation of it is required it should be sought in the agreement of the text with the alternative exposition shortly to be given.

The other mistaken view avoids the error of this first view, and indeed is incompatible with it. It is, probably, the received view. On this interpretation Mill is looking for a test of right or wrong as the

---

[1] *Principia Ethica*, reprinted 1948, p. 106.

ultimate test by which one can justify the ascription of rightness or wrongness to courses of action, rightness and wrongness being taken to be words which we understand. This test is taken to be whether the course of action does or does not tend to promote the ultimate end (which Mill no doubt says is the general happiness). So far there is no cause to quarrel with the received view, for it is surely correct. But in detail the view is wrong. For it is further suggested that for Mill this ultimate test is also the immediate test; the rightness or wrongness of any particular action is to be decided by considering whether it promotes the ultimate end. We may, it might be admitted, on Mill's view sometimes act, by rule of thumb or in a hurry, without actually raising this question; but the actual justification, if there is one, must be directly in terms of consequences, including the consequences of the example that we have set. On this view, then, Mill holds that an action, a particular action, is right if it promotes the ultimate end better than any alternative, and otherwise it is wrong. However we in fact make up our minds in moral situations, so far as justification goes no other factor enters into the matter. It is clear that on this interpretation Mill is immediately open to two shattering objections; first, it is obviously and correctly urged, if one has, for example, promised to do something it is one's duty to do it at least partly because one has promised to do it and not merely because of consequences, even if these consequences are taken to include one's example in promise-breaking. Secondly, it is correctly pointed out that on this view a man who, *ceteris paribus*, chooses the inferior of two musical comedies for an evening's entertainment has done a moral wrong, and this is preposterous.[1] If this were in fact the view of Mill, he would indeed be fit for little more than the halting eristic of philosophical infants.

A Revised Interpretation of Mill

I shall now set out in a set of propositions what I take to be in fact Mill's view and substantiate them afterwards from the text. This will obscure the subtleties but will make clearer the main lines of interpretation.

A. A particular action is justified as being right by showing that it is in accord with some moral rule. It is shown to be wrong by showing that it transgresses some moral rule.

B. A moral rule is shown to be correct by showing that the recognition of that rule promotes the ultimate end.

[1] For one example of this interpretation of Mill and the first and more important objection, see Carritt, *The Theory of Morals*, ch. iv.

C. Moral rules can be justified only in regard to matters in which the general welfare is more than negligibly affected.

D. Where no moral rule is applicable the question of the rightness or wrongness of particular acts does not arise, though the worth of the actions can be estimated in other ways.

As a terminological point it should be mentioned that where the phrase 'moral rule' occurs above Mill uses the phrase 'secondary principle' more generally, though he sometimes says 'moral law'. By these terms, whichever is preferred, Mill is referring to such precepts as 'Keep promises', 'Do no murder', or 'Tell no lies'. A list of which Mill approves is to be found in *On Liberty* (p. 135).

There is, no doubt, need of further explanation of these propositions; but that, and some caveats, can best be given in the process of establishing that these are in fact Mill's views. First, then, to establish from the text that in Mill's view particular actions are shown to be right or wrong by showing that they are or are not in accord with some moral rule. (i) He says with evident approbation on p. 2: 'The intuitive, no less than what may be termed the inductive, school of ethics, insists on the necessity of general laws. They both agree that the morality of an individual action is not a question of direct perception, but of the application of a law to an individual case. They recognise also, to a great extent, the same moral laws'. Mill reproaches these schools only with being unable to give a unifying rationale of these laws (as he will do in proposition B). (ii) He says on page 22: 'But to consider the rules of morality as improvable is one thing; to pass over the intermediate generalisations entirely, and endeavour to test each individual action directly by the first principle, is another. It is a strange notion that the acknowledgement of a first principle is inconsistent with the admission of secondary ones'. He adds, with feeling: 'Men really ought to leave off talking a kind of nonsense on this subject which they would neither talk nor listen to on other matters of practical concernment'. (iii) Having admitted on p. 23 that 'rules of conduct cannot be so framed as to require no exceptions', he adds (p. 24) 'We must remember that only in these cases of conflict between secondary principles is it requisite that first principles should be appealed to. There is no case of moral obligation in which some secondary principle is not involved; and if only one, there can seldom be any real doubt which one it is, in the mind of any person by whom the principle itself is recognised'. This quotation supports both propositions A and D. It shows that for Mill moral rules are not merely rules of thumb which aid the unreflective man in making up his mind, but an essential part of moral reasoning. The relevance of a moral rule is the criterion of whether we are dealing with a case of right or wrong or some other moral or prudential situation. (iv) The last passage which we shall select to establish this interpretation of Mill (it would be easy to find more) is also a joint confirmation of propositions A and D, showing that our last was not an *obiter dictum* on which we have placed too much weight. In the chapter entitled 'On the connection between justice and utility', Mill has maintained that it is a distinguishing mark of a just act that it is one required by a specific rule or law, positive or moral, carrying also liability to penal sanctions. He then writes this important paragraph (p. 45), which in view of its importance and the neglect that it has suffered must be quoted at length: 'The above is, I think, a true account, as far as it goes, of the origin and progressive growth of the idea of justice. But we must observe, that it contains, as yet, nothing to distinguish that obligation from moral obligation in general. For the truth is, that the idea of penal sanction, which is the essence of law, enters not only into the conception of injustice, but into that of any kind of wrong. We do not call anything wrong, unless we mean to imply that a person ought to be punished in some way or other for doing it; if not by law, by the opinion of his fellow-creatures; if not by opinion, by the reproaches of his own conscience. This seems to be the real turning point of the distinction between morality and simple expediency. It is a part of the notion of Duty in every one of its forms, that a person may rightfully be compelled to fulfil it. Duty is a thing which may be exacted from a person, as one exacts a debt. Unless we think that it may be exacted from him, we do not call it his duty. . . . There are other things, on the contrary, which we wish that people should do, which we like or admire them for doing, perhaps dislike or despise them for not doing, but yet admit that they are not bound to do; it is not a case of moral obligation; we do not blame them, that is, we do not think that they are proper objects of punishment. . . . I think there is no doubt that this distinction lies at the bottom of the notions of right and wrong; that we call any conduct wrong, or employ, instead, some other term of dislike or disparagement, according as we think that the person ought, or ought not, to be punished for it; and we say, it would be right to do so and so, or merely that it would be desirable or laudable, according as we would wish to see the person whom it concerns, compelled, or only persuaded and exhorted, to act in that manner'. How supporters of the received view have squared it with this passage I do not know; they do not mention it. If they have noticed it at all it is, presumably, regarded as an example of Mill's inconsistent eclecticism. Mill here makes it quite clear that in his view right and wrong are derived from moral rules; in other cases where the ultimate end is no doubt affected appraisal of conduct must be made in other ways. For example, if one's own participation in the ultimate end is impaired without breach of moral law, it is (*Liberty*, p. 135) imprudence or lack of self respect, it is not wrongdoing. So much for the establishment of this interpretation of Mill, in a positive way, as regards points A and D. We must now ask whether there is anything in Mill which is inconsistent with it and in favour of the received view.

It is impossible to show positively that there is nothing in Mill which favours the received view against the interpretation here given, for it would require a complete review of everything that Mill says. We shall have to be content with examining two points which might be thought to tell in favour of the received view.

(*a*) On p. 6 Mill says: 'The creed which accepts as the foundation of morals, Utility, or the Greatest Happiness Principle, holds that actions are right in proportion as they tend to promote happiness, wrong as they tend to promote the reverse of Happiness'. This seems to be the well-known sentence which is at the bottom of the received interpretation. Of course, it could be taken as a loose and inaccurate statement of the received view, if the general argument required it. But note that strictly one can say that a certain action tends to produce a certain result only if one is speaking of type- rather than token-actions. Drinking alcohol may tend to promote exhilaration, but my drinking this particular glass either does or does not produce it. It seems, then, that Mill can well be interpreted here as regarding moral rules as forbidding or enjoining types of action, in fact as making the point that the right moral rules are the ones which promote the ultimate end (my proposition B), not as saying something contrary to proposition A. And this, or something like it, is the interpretation which consistency requires. Mill's reference to 'tendencies of actions' at the top of p. 22 supports the stress here laid on the word 'tend', and that context should be examined by those who require further conviction.

(*b*) Mill sometimes refers to moral rules as 'intermediate generalisations' (e.g., p. 22) from the supreme principle, or as 'corollaries' of it (also p. 22). These are probably the sort of phrases which lead people to think that they play a purely heuristic rôle in ethical thinking for Mill. As for the expression 'intermediate generalisation', Mill undoubtedly thinks that we should, and to some extent do, arrive at and improve our moral rules by such methods as observing that a certain type of action has had bad results of a social kind in such an overwhelming majority of cases that it ought to be banned. (But this is an over-simplification; see the note on p. 58 on how we ought to arrive at moral rules, and the pessimistic account of how we in fact arrive at them in *Liberty*, p. 69–70). But this account of the genesis of moral rules does not require us to interpret them as being anything but rules when once made. It really seems unnecessary to say much of the expression 'corollary'; Mill obviously cannot wish it to be taken literally; in fact it is hard to state the relation of moral rules to a justifying principle with exactitude and Mill, in a popular article in *Fraser*, did not try very hard to do so.

Moral Rules and the Ultimate End

We have already been led in our examination of possible objections to proposition A to say something in defence of the view that Mill thought that a moral rule is shown to be correct by showing that the recognition of that rule promotes the ultimate end (proposition B). A little more may be added on this point, though it seems fairly obvious that if we are right in saying that the supreme principle is not to be evoked, in Mill's view, in the direct justification of particular right acts, it must thus come in in an indirect way in view of the importance that Mill attached to it. And it is hard to think what the indirect way is if not this. (i) On p. 3 Mill reproaches other moral philosophers with not giving a satisfactory account of moral rules in terms of a fundamental principle, though they have correctly placed moral rules as governing particular actions. It would be indeed the mark of an inconsistent philosopher if he did not try to repair the one serious omission which he ascribes to others. (ii) Mill ascribes to Kant (p. 4) the use of utilitarian arguments because, Mill alleges, he in fact supports the rules of morality by showing the evil consequences of not adopting them or adopting alternatives. Thus Mill is here regarding as distinctively utilitarian the justification or rejection of moral rules on the ground of consequences. He could hardly have wished to suggest that Kant would directly justify, even inadvertently, particular actions on such grounds. But it is perhaps not to the point to argue this matter more elaborately. If anyone has been convinced by what has gone before, he will not need much argument on this point; with others it is superfluous to make the attempt.

In what Fields are Moral Rules of Right and Wrong Applicable?

The applicability of moral rules is, says Mill, 'the characteristic difference which marks off, not justice, but morality in general, from the remaining provinces of Expediency and Worthiness' (p. 46). Mill says little or nothing in *Utilitarianism* about the boundary between morality and worthiness (surely it would be better to have said the boundary between right and wrong on the one hand and other forms of both moral and non-moral appraisal on the other?). It seems reasonable to suppose that he would have recognised that the use of moral rules must be confined to matters in which the kind of consequence is sufficiently invariable for there not to be too many exceptions. But this is a pragmatic limitation; Mill does have something to say about a limitation in principle in *Liberty* which I have crudely summarised in my proposition C—moral rules can be justifiably maintained in regard only to matters in which the general welfare is more than negligibly affected.

It is important to note that Mill in *Liberty* is concerned with freedom from moral sanctions as well as the sanctions of positive law. The distinction between self-regarding and other actions is regarded by him as relevant to moral as well as to political philosophy. The most noteworthy passage which bears on the scope of moral rules is on page 135. Here he mentions such things as encroachment on the rights of others as being 'fit objects of moral reprobation, and, in grave cases, of moral retribution and punishment'. But self-regarding faults (low tastes and the like) are 'not properly immoralities and to whatever pitch they are carried, do not constitute wickedness . . . The term duty to oneself, when it means anything more than prudence, means self-respect or self-development'. Self-regarding faults render the culprit 'necessarily and properly a subject of distaste, or, in extreme cases, even of contempt', but this is in the sphere of worthiness not of right and wrong.

So much then for Mill's account of the logic of moral reasoning. It must be emphasised that no more has been attempted than a skeleton plan of Mill's answer, and that Mill puts the matter more richly and more subtly in his book. Even on the question of general interpretation more store must be laid on the effect of a continuous reading in the light of the skeleton plan than on the effect of the few leading quotations introduced in this paper. It is emphatically not the contention of this paper that Mill has given a finally correct account of these matters which is immune to all criticism; an attempt has been made only to give a sympathetic account without any criticism favourable or unfavourable. But I certainly do maintain that the current interpretations of Mill's *Utilitarianism* are so unsympathetic and so incorrect that the majority of criticisms which have in fact been based on them are irrelevant and worthless.

X

INTERPRETATIONS OF MILL'S 'UTILITARIANISM'

J. D. MABBOTT

PROFESSOR URMSON'S article 'The Interpretation of the Moral Philosophy of J. S. Mill' in *The Philosophical Quarterly* for January 1953 (Vol. 3, No. 10) is a most interesting and stimulating piece of work. The main point Urmson makes is that previous critics have interpreted Mill to hold, as G. E. Moore certainly did hold, that 'it is always the duty of every agent to do that one, among all the actions which he *can* do on any given occasion, whose *total consequence* will have the greatest intrinsic value' (Moore, *Ethics*, p. 232). But, on Urmson's view, Mill's real position was as follows. 'A. A particular action is justified as being right by showing that it is in accord with some moral rule. It is shown to be wrong by showing that it transgresses some moral rule. B. A moral rule is shown to be correct by showing that the recognition of that rule promotes the ultimate end (sc. the greatest happiness of the greatest number)' (p. 35).[1] I think in the second clause there are two slight amendments to be made. 'Recognition' is not enough; practice according to the rule is required. And 'promotes' suggests that all defensible moral rules are in fact recognized or obeyed; I should prefer 'would promote' (at least as an elucidation of Mill).

Now from these two principles there follow two crucial differences between the orthodox interpretation of utilitarianism and that of Urmson. (1) On the orthodox interpretation it is never right to do an action when some alternative action would produce more good (cf. the Moore quotation above). But on Urmson's view it may be right to do an action which is in accord with a moral rule, even if that particular action does less good than some alternative action—on the ground that the general practice of the rule does more good than the omission of such practice or the practice of an alternative rule. (2) On the orthodox interpretation (again compare G. E. Moore) the rightness of an action is determined by its *actual* consequences; on Urmson's

From *Philosophical Quarterly*, Vol. 6 (1956), pp. 115–20. Reprinted by permission of the author and the *Philosophical Quarterly*.

[1] [p. 130–131 of this volume. Ed.]

interpretation by *hypothetical* consequences, by what *would happen if* the rule which the action follows were generally practised.

Now there is one passage in 'Utilitarianism' (Everyman Edition—to which all other references will be given—pp. 17–18) in which Mill explicitly accepts both these important corollaries; though Urmson does not quote it, it is one of the most striking pieces of evidence in favour of his interpretation. 'In the case of abstinences indeed—of things which people forbear to do from moral considerations, *though the consequences in the particular case might be beneficial*—it would be unworthy of an intelligent agent not to be consciously aware that the action is of a kind which, *if practised generally, would be generally injurious*, and that this is the ground of the obligation to abstain from it.

Re-reading Mill in the light of Urmson's comments reveals many passages such as this in his support, passages whose significance certainly seems to have escaped previous critics. But it seems to me doubtful whether Mill is as clearly and consistently committed to the Urmson view as he suggests. Many passages fit the old orthodox interpretation and I doubt whether Mill himself realized the fundamental differences between the two views. The remainder of this paper is intended not only to show the difficulties which some passages in Mill present to Urmson's thesis but also to use these difficulties to bring out more sharply the differences between the two views.

The main point of the new interpretation is that the first principle is not relevant to determine the rightness of any particular act. Mill says there is only one exception to this, namely the case in which two rules conflict. 'We must remember that only in these cases of conflict between secondary principles is it requisite that first principles should be appealed to. There is no case of moral obligation in which some secondary principle is not involved; and, if only one, there can seldom by any doubt which one it is' (p. 24). But when two rules conflict what question do I ask? How do I apply the first principle to escape my dilemma? Do I ask whether keeping the one rule would *in general* do more good than keeping the other? This would seem, on Urmson's interpretation, to be the right question, but it would be very difficult to answer. Or do I ask whether keeping the one rule *on this particular occasion* will do more good than keeping the other? But then I might as well have left out all reference to the rules and just asked whether act A which happens to accord with rule X will do more good than act B which happens to accord with rule Y. Mill gives no guidance to the question which he would approve.

The passage quoted above maintains that the *only* exception to the

ban on deciding particular actions by reference to the first principle
is that of conflict of secondary principles. But there is another
exception which Mill elsewhere allows. The 'chief exception' to the
rule against lying is said to be where withholding the truth 'would
save an individual from great and unmerited evil' (p. 21). The word
'unmerited' may seem to import a conflicting secondary principle—
'to each his due'; but I do not think this is the main point. Mill is
admitting what all would admit, that when the consequences of
keeping a secondary rule are very bad indeed (or of breaking it very
good) an exception may be made. Now this other exception (and it is
called the 'chief exception') also produces a further difficulty in
Urmson's interpretation. Mill also says, in the passage quoted above
from p. 24, that there is no case of moral obligation in which a
secondary principle is not involved. What of the case where no
secondary principle is involved and yet some act open to me can
produce very good results or avert very bad ones? Would not such
an act be moral, right, my duty? Yet the only principle here is the first
principle. It may be recalled that alongside his prima facie duties
of keeping faith, etc., which correspond to Mill's secondary principles,
Sir David Ross lists prima facie duties of beneficence and non-male-
ficence. One way of putting the two present difficulties is that on
Urmson's interpretation of Mill the production of the greatest
happiness would have to be (*a*) a prima facie obligation (i.e. relevant
to determine the rightness of particular acts), (*b*) the basis of every
other prima facie obligation (or secondary principle), (*c*) the arbiter
between conflicting prima facie obligations.

The third difficulty, and one admitted by Urmson, is that Mill calls
the secondary principles 'corollaries' of the first principle (p. 22).
But they can hardly be corollaries if in a particular case they contradict
the first principle when I abstain from a particular act in order to obey
a rule 'though the consequences in the particular case might be beneficial' (p. 18, cited above). The term 'corollary' suggests, as Urmson
agrees, that the value of secondary principles is purely heuristic; and
this is borne out by Mill's metaphors. 'It is a strange notion that the
acknowledgement of a first principle is inconsistent with the admission
of secondary ones . . . . To inform the traveller of a destination is not to
forbid the use of landmarks and direction-posts on the way' (pp.
22-3). But a land-mark or signpost may on a particular occasion fail
to point the best way to a destination. I may be on foot and there is
an obvious short-cut across the fields; or the sign-posted road may be
visibly blocked by floods or drifts. We should then say 'neglect the

signpost'. But what happens when we cash the metaphor? The destination is the greatest happiness of the greatest number; the signpost the secondary rule. What happens when a signpost visibly fails to point the best route? Shall we neglect it? On Urmson's interpretation Mill must say 'No, there are occasions when, though you see another route leads to the general happiness, you must follow the signpost— the secondary rule'. Similarly with the comparison (p. 23) with an almanack (which saves the navigator from having to calculate on each occasion what course to set). No problem arises if the almanack is held to be infallible. But the almanack of secondary principles does not in every case provide sailing directions leading to the maximum happiness. Yet even when it does not, Mill must maintain (on Urmson's interpretation) that we should follow it.

It might be suggested to meet that difficulty, as it is by Burke and by G. E. Moore (*Principia Ethica*, p. 162), that the reason why we should follow a rule even when breaking it will visibly produce better consequences is that the rule enshrines the stored wisdom of generations of men with their experience and traditions and that the individual is therefore likely to be mistaken in his judgement that better consequences will result from breaking it, especially as bias or prejudice may influence his judgement. But it is easy to find cases where bias and prejudice are excluded, and such a view as Moore's would prescribe a rigid adherence to rules, which no one would defend.

A further difficulty closely related to the preceding one arises when Mill tries to explain away the case where we have a duty to follow a rule when more good would be done by some alternative action. 'It may be held that it is expedient for some immediate object, some temporary purpose, to violate a rule whose observation is expedient in a much higher degree'. Thus 'it would often be expedient to obtain some object useful to ourselves or others to tell a lie' (p. 21). But Mill then goes on to argue that in fact telling the lie in such a case would not have better results than telling the truth. He has already foreshadowed his argument by calling the good results of telling the lie 'temporary' and 'immediate'. He says telling the truth will do more good in the long run for two reasons 'inasmuch as the cultivation in ourselves of a sensitive feeling on the subject of veracity is one of the most useful, and the enfeeblement of that feeling one of the most hurtful, things to which our conduct can be instrumental; and inasmuch as any, even unintentional, deviation from truth does that much towards weakening the trustworthiness of human assertion' (p. 21). Now the crucial point to notice is that Mill is here relying on the consequences of telling this particular truth now and not on the consequences of truth-telling in general.

It is perhaps worth noticing that the two arguments themselves are inconclusive, since they are the arguments usually used by utilitarians of the orthodox or non-Urmson type to explain why a rule should be kept on some occasions when more good would be done to those directly concerned by breaking it. Keeping the rule will do indirect or long-term good in two ways: (1) by strengthening in the agent the habit of keeping the rule; (2) by fostering the reliance others will place in the keeping of it. I shall discuss these arguments in the reverse order for reasons which will appear in the discussion.

Ross raised the vital difficulty for the 'fostering-reliance' argument. If my breaking of the rule is not known to anyone else, general reliance on the rule will be unaffected. In *The Right and the Good* Ross illustrated this point by what Mr. Nowell-Smith has called an instance of 'desert-island morality' (*Ethics*, p. 240). This is unfair, for Ross in his later book, *Foundations of Ethics*, gives a simple real life example. It is important to see that real life examples are frequent and easy to find. I quoted two from my own experience in my article on 'Punishment' in *Mind* (April 1939), which turns throughout on this very distinction between orthodox and Urmson-type utilitarianism with which we are here concerned, and a third in 'Moral Rules' (*Proceedings of the British Academy*, 1953). As the point is vital, I offer yet another. An ex-pupil of mine was secretary to a very rich man. His employer had ordered him to put all begging letters in the wastepaper basket unanswered. He was liberal to his chosen causes and life was too short to verify the bona fides of every begging letter. His employer also had a habit of leaving bundles of notes in the pockets of his suits. These the secretary regularly extracted before sending suits to be cleaned, and returned them to his employer who at once put them into another pocket uncounted. One slack morning the secretary read the begging letters out of curiosity and found among them one which made a good case. A few minutes earlier he had found a bundle of notes in a blazer pocket. He told me that he had wondered whether to pick off five of the notes and send them to the writer of the letter. 'My boss would never have known'. I asked him whether he did, and he replied 'No, it wasn't my money'. This is not a utilitarian reason; and, in particular the fact that his boss would never have known removes the 'fostering-reliance' argument. But, it may be said, there is one person who would know and that is the secretary himself, and here the utilitarian will fall back on the other argument. The secretary, if he sent the money, would enfeeble his tendency not to take other people's property and on other occasions this enfeeblement would have bad results. But this argument also is no good. For a utilitarian secondary rules are not to be applied without exception and therefore rigid habits should not be acquired. The following dialogue at a bridge table will illustrate the fallacy. I am third player on the first trick; the second player has played the ace; I hold the King. I remember I have been told that third player should play high. I whisper to my mentor standing behind me 'What do I play?' He says 'The King'. 'But it will do no good; the ace has been played'. 'Never mind that. You must play your King; otherwise you will enfeeble your tendency to play high as third player'. 'But is this rule an absolute rule?' 'No, there are exceptions'. 'What are they?' 'When it will do no good to play high?' 'But this is such a case'. 'Never mind. You must not weaken your good habits'.

There is an interesting parallel to this last point in Mill's treatment of rights. In his essay 'On Liberty' he argues that a man should not be prevented from publishing his scientific opinions. He argues this on the grounds that his opinion may be true or part of the truth, in which case it will be useful for it to become known. Even if it is false it will serve the useful purpose of keeping the holders of the true opinion alert and preventing the true opinion from becoming a dead dogma. The point of special interest here is that he recognizes that some might say that a man has a right to publish his scientific opinions even if publishing them will have none of these beneficial results. His comment is 'It is proper to state that I forego any advantage which could be derived to my argument from the idea of abstract right as a thing independent of utility'. It might be supposed that he is admitting there is such an advantage. But he goes on 'I regard utility as the ultimate appeal in all ethical questions, but it must be utility in the largest sense grounded in the permanent interests of man as an intelligent being' (Everyman Edition, p. 74). He is appealing here, as in the case of truth-telling, to the long-term results of publication in the particular case. Now I have come across a little periodical devoted to maintaining that the earth is flat. It can hardly be held that this is the whole truth. That part of the truth which it might be said to enshrine (that a small part of the earth's surface is very nearly flat) has already been included in the orthodox view. And it is difficult to believe that the publication of this little periodical keeps the Astronomer Royal on his toes. Yet most of us would reject the suppression of the periodical. But we need not call this an abstract right (or a self-evident or natural right). We can say that it is *generally* useful to have this rule and to apply it in all cases, even though in some cases no good will accrue from its application. This would be the Urmson interpretation, but it does not seem to be Mill's argument.

This paper is not concerned with the rival merits of the two types of utilitarianism. I argued that issue in my papers on 'Punishment' (1939) and 'Moral Rules' (1953) cited above. I have taken Mill's text as a means of sharpening the distinctions between them.

It is interesting that in an article entitled 'Two Concepts of Rules' (*Philosophical Review*, Vol. LXIV, Jan. 1955) Mr. J. B. Rawls discusses the same issue and illustrates his points by reference to another great utilitarian, John Austin. He shows convincingly that Austin in his *Lectures on Jurisprudence* (Vol. I, p. 116) states very clearly the Urmson interpretation of utilitarianism. But when he goes on to discuss and defend it he slides away from it into the orthodox interpretation, just as I have tried to show Mill does in his essay.

XI

TWO CONCEPTS OF RULES[1]

JOHN RAWLS

IN THIS PAPER I want to show the importance of the distinction between justifying a practice[2] and justifying a particular action falling under it, and I want to explain the logical basis of this distinction and how it is possible to miss its significance. While the distinction has frequently been made,[3] and is now becoming commonplace, there remains the task of explaining the tendency either to overlook it altogether, or to fail to appreciate its importance.

To show the importance of the distinction I am going to defend utilitarianism against those objections which have traditionally been

From *Philosophical Review*, Vol. 64 (1955), pp. 3–32. Reprinted by permission of the author and the *Philosophical Review*.

[1] This is a revision of a paper given at the Harvard Philosophy Club on April 30, 1954. [It is discussed by H. J. McCloskey in 'An Examination of Restricted Utilitarianism'. *Philosophical Review* (1957), and by D. Lyons, *Forms and Limits of Utilitarianism* (Clarendon Press, Oxford 1965). Rawls himself explains his position in 'Justice as Fairness', *Philosophical Review* (1958), footnote to p. 168. Ed.]

[2] I use the word 'practice' throughout as a sort of technical term meaning any form of activity specified by a system of rules which defines offices, roles, moves, penalties, defences, and so on, and which gives the activity its structure. As examples one may think of games and rituals, trials and parliaments.

[3] The distinction is central to Hume's discussion of justice in *A Treatise of Human Nature*, Bk. III, pt. II, esp. secs. 2–4. It is clearly stated by John Austin in the second lecture of *Lectures on Jurisprudence* (4th ed.; London, 1873), i, 116ff. (1st ed., 1832). Also it may be argued that J. S. Mill took it for granted in *Utilitarianism*; on this point cf. J. O. Urmson, 'The Interpretation of the Moral Philosophy of J. S. Mill', *Philosophical Quarterly*, vol. iii (1953). In addition to the arguments given by Urmson there are several clear statements of the distinction in *A System of Logic* (8th ed.; London, 1872), Bk. VI, ch. xii pars. 2, 3, 7. The distinction is fundamental to J. D. Mabbott's important paper, 'Punishment', *Mind*, n.s., vol. xlviii (April, 1939). More recently the distinction has been stated with particular emphasis by S. E. Toulmin in *The Place of Reason in Ethics* (Cambridge, 1950), see esp. ch. xi, where it plays a major part in his account of moral reasoning. Toulmin doesn't explain the basis of the distinction, nor how one might overlook its importance, as I try to in this paper, and in my review of his book (*Philosophical Review*, vol. lx [October, 1951]) as some of my criticisms show, I failed to understand the force of it. See also H. D. Aiken, 'The Levels of Moral Discourse', *Ethics*, vol. lxii (1952), A. M. Quinton, 'Punishment', *Analysis*, vol. xiv (June, 1954); and P. H. Nowell-Smith, *Ethics* (London, 1954), pp. 236–239, 271–273.

made against it in connexion with punishment and the obligation to keep promises. I hope to show that if one uses the distinction in question then one can state utilitarianism in a way which makes it a much better explication of our considered moral judgements than traditional objections would seem to admit.[1] Thus the importance of the distinction is shown by the way it strengthens the utilitarian view regardless of whether that view is completely defensible or not.

To explain how the significance of the distinction may be overlooked, I am going to discuss two conceptions of rules. One of these conceptions conceals the importance of distinguishing between the justification of a rule or practice and the justification of a particular action falling under it. The other conception makes it clear why this distinction must be made and what is its logical basis.

I

The subject of punishment, in the sense of attaching legal penalties to the violation of legal rules, has always been a troubling moral question.[2] The trouble about it has not been that people disagree as to whether or not punishment is justifiable. Most people have held that, freed from certain abuses, it is an acceptable institution. Only a few have rejected punishment entirely, which is rather surprising when one considers all that can be said against it. The difficulty is with the justification of punishment: various arguments for it have been given by moral philosophers, but so far none of them has won any sort of general acceptance; no justification is without those who detest it. I hope to show that the use of the aforementioned distinction enables one to state the utilitarian view in a way which allows for the sound points of its critics.

For our purposes we may say that there are two justifications of punishment. What we may call the retributive view is that punishment is justified on the grounds that wrongdoing merits punishment. It is morally fitting that a person who does wrong should suffer in proportion to his wrongdoing. That a criminal should be punished follows from his guilt, and the severity of the appropriate punishment

---

[1] On the concept of explication see the author's paper, *Philosophical Review*, vol. lx (April, 1951).

[2] While this paper was being revised, Quinton's appeared; footnote 2 supra [Footnote 3, p. 144 of this volume. Ed.] There are several respects in which my remarks are similar to his. Yet as I consider some further questions and rely on somewhat different arguments, I have retained the discussion of punishment and promises together as two test cases for utilitarianism.

depends on the depravity of his act. The state of affairs where a wrongdoer suffers punishment is morally better than the state of affairs where he does not; and it is better irrespective of any of the consequences of punishing him.

What we may call the utilitarian view holds that on the principle that bygones are bygones and that only future consequences are material to present decisions, punishment is justifiable only by reference to the probable consequences of maintaining it as one of the devices of the social order. Wrongs committed in the past are, as such, not relevant considerations for deciding what to do. If punishment can be shown to promote effectively the interest of society it is justifiable, otherwise it is not.

I have stated these two competing views very roughly to make one feel the conflict between them: one feels the force of *both* arguments and one wonders how they can be reconciled. From my introductory remarks it is obvious that the resolution which I am going to propose is that in this case one must distinguish between justifying a practice as a system of rules to be applied and enforced, and justifying a particular action which falls under these rules; utilitarian arguments are appropriate with regard to questions about practices, while retributive arguments fit the application of particular rules to particular cases.

We might try to get clear about this distinction by imagining how a father might answer the question of his son. Suppose the son asks, 'Why was *J* put in jail yesterday?' The father answers, 'Because he robbed the bank at *B*. He was duly tried and found guilty. That's why he was put in jail yesterday'. But suppose the son had asked a different question, namely, 'Why do people put other people in jail?' Then the father might answer, 'To protect good people from bad people' or 'To stop people from doing things that would make it uneasy for all of us; for otherwise we wouldn't be able to go to bed at night and sleep in peace'. There are two very different questions here. One question emphasizes the proper name: it asks why *J* was punished rather than someone else, or it asks what he was punished for. The other question asks why we have the institution of punishment: why do people punish one another rather than, say, always forgiving one another?

Thus the father says in effect that a particular man is punished, rather than some other man, because he is guilty, and he is guilty because he broke the law (past tense). In his case the law looks back, the judge looks back, the jury looks back, and a penalty is visited upon him for something he did. That a man is to be punished, and what his punishment is to be, is settled by its being shown that he broke the law and that the law assigns that penalty for the violation of it.

On the other hand we have the institution of punishment itself, and recommend and accept various changes in it, because it is thought by the (ideal) legislator and by those to whom the law applies that, as a part of a system of law impartially applied from case to case arising under it, it will have the consequence, in the long run, of furthering the interests of society.

One can say, then, that the judge and the legislator stand in different positions and look in different directions: one to the past, the other to the future. The justification of what the judge does, *qua* judge, sounds like the retributive view; the justification of what the (ideal) legislator does, *qua* legislator, sounds like the utilitarian view. Thus both views have a point (this is as it should be since intelligent and sensitive persons have been on both sides of the argument); and one's initial confusion disappears once one sees that these views apply to persons holding different offices with different duties, and situated differently with respect to the system of rules that make up the criminal law.[1]

One might say, however, that the utilitarian view is more fundamental since it applies to a more fundamental office, for the judge carries out the legislator's will so far as he can determine it. Once the legislator decides to have laws and to assign penalties for their violation (as things are there must be both the law and the penalty) an institution is set up which involves a retributive conception of particular cases. It is part of the concept of the criminal law as a system of rules that the application and enforcement of these rules in particular cases should be justifiable by arguments of a retributive character. The decision whether or not to use law rather than some other mechanism of social control, and the decision as to what laws to have and what penalties to assign, may be settled by utilitarian arguments; but if one decides to have laws then one has decided on something whose working in particular cases is retributive in form.[2]

The answer, then, to the confusion engendered by the two views of punishment is quite simple: one distinguishes two offices, that of the judge and that of the legislator, and one distinguishes their different stations with respect to the system of rules which make up the law;

[1] Note the fact that different sorts of arguments are suited to different offices. One way of taking the differences between ethical theories is to regard them as accounts of the reasons expected in different offices.

[2] In this connexion see Mabbott, op. cit., pp. 163–164.

and then one notes that the different sorts of considerations which would usually be offered as reasons for what is done under the cover of these offices can be paired off with the competing justifications of punishment. One reconciles the two views by the time-honoured device of making them apply to different situations.

But can it really be this simple? Well, this answer allows for the apparent intent of each side. Does a person who advocates the retributive view necessarily advocate, as an *institution*, legal machinery whose essential purpose is to set up and preserve a correspondence between moral turpitude and suffering? Surely not.[1] What retributionists have rightly insisted upon is that no man can be punished unless he is guilty, that is, unless he has broken the law. Their fundamental criticism of the utilitarian account is that, as they interpret it, it sanctions an innocent person's being punished (if one may call it that) for the benefit of society.

On the other hand, utilitarians agree that punishment is to be inflicted only for the violation of law. They regard this much as understood from the concept of punishment itself.[2] The point of the utilitarian account concerns the institution as a system of rules: utilitarianism seeks to limit its use by declaring it justifiable only if it can be shown to foster effectively the good of society. Historically it is a protest against the indiscriminate and ineffective use of the criminal law.[3] It seeks to dissuade us from assigning to penal institutions the improper, if not sacrilegious, task of matching suffering with moral turpitude. Like others, utilitarians want penal institutions designed so that, as far as humanly possible, only those who break the law run afoul of it. They hold that no official should have discretionary power to inflict penalties whenever he thinks it for the benefit of

---

[1] On this point see Sir David Ross, *The Right and the Good* (Oxford, 1930), pp. 57–60.

[2] See Hobbes's definition of punishment in *Leviathan*, ch. xxviii; and Bentham's definition in *The Principle of Morals and Legislation*, ch. xii, par. 36, ch. xv, par. 28, and in *The Rationale of Punishment*, (London, 1830), Bk. I, ch. i. They could agree with Bradley that: 'Punishment is punishment only when it is deserved. We pay the penalty, because we owe it, and for no other reason; and if punishment is inflicted for any other reason whatever than because it is merited by wrong, it is a gross immorality, a crying injustice, an abominable crime, and not what it pretends to be.' *Ethical Studies* (2nd ed.; Oxford, 1927), pp. 26–27. Certainly by definition it isn't what it pretends to be. The innocent can only be punished by mistake; deliberate 'punishment' of the innocent necessarily involves fraud.

[3] Cf. Leon Radzinowicz, *A History of English Criminal Law: The Movement for Reform 1750–1833* (London, 1948), esp. ch. xi on Bentham.

society; for on utilitarian grounds an institution granting such power could not be justified.[1]

The suggested way of reconciling the retributive and the utilitarian justifications of punishment seems to account for what both sides have wanted to say. There are, however, two further questions which arise, and I shall devote the remainder of this section to them.

First, will not a difference of opinion as to the proper criterion of just law make the proposed reconciliation unacceptable to retributionists? Will they not question whether, if the utilitarian principle is used as the criterion, it follows that those who have broken the law are guilty in a way which satisfies their demand that those punished deserve to be punished? To answer this difficulty, suppose that the rules of the criminal law are justified on utilitarian grounds (it is only for laws that meet his criterion that the utilitarian can be held responsible). Then it follows that the actions which the criminal law specifies as offences are such that, if they were tolerated, terror and alarm would spread in society. Consequently, retributionists can only deny that those who are punished deserve to be punished if they deny that such actions are wrong. This they will not want to do.

The second question is whether utilitarianism doesn't justify too much. One pictures it as an engine of justification which, if consistently adopted, could be used to justify cruel · and arbitrary institutions. Retributionists may be supposed to concede that utilitarians *intend* to reform the law and to make it more humane; that utilitarians do not *wish* to justify any such thing as punishment of the innocent; and that utilitarians may appeal to the fact that punishment presupposes guilt in the sense that by punishment one understands an institution attaching penalties to the infraction of legal rules, and therefore that it is logically absurd to suppose that utilitarians in justifying *punishment* might also have justified punishment (if we may call it that) of the innocent. The real question, however, is whether the utilitarian, in justifying punishment, hasn't used arguments which

[1] Bentham discusses how corresponding to a punitory provision of a criminal law there is another provision which stands to it as an antagonist and which needs a name as much as the punitory. He calls it, as one might expect, the *anaetiosostic*, and of it he says: 'The punishment of guilt is the object of the former one: the preservation of innocence that of the latter.' In the same connexion he asserts that it is never thought fit to give the judge the option of deciding whether a thief (that is, a person whom he believes to be a thief, for the judge's belief is what the question must always turn upon) should hang or not, and so the law writes the provision: 'The judge shall not cause a thief to be hanged unless he have been duly convicted and sentenced in course of law' (*The Limits of Jurisprudence Defined*. ed. C. W. Everett [New York, 1945], pp. 238–239).

commit him to accepting the infliction of suffering on innocent persons if it is for the good of society (whether or not one calls this punishment). More generally, isn't the utilitarian committed in principle to accepting many practices which he, as a morally sensitive person, wouldn't want to accept? Retributionists are inclined to hold that there is no way to stop the utilitarian principle from justifying too much except by adding to it a principle which distributes certain rights to individuals. Then the amended criterion is not the greatest benefit of society *simpliciter*, but the greatest benefit of society subject to the constraint that no one's rights may be violated. Now while I think that the classical utilitarians proposed a criterion of this more complicated sort, I do not want to argue that point here.[1] What I want to show is that there is *another* way of preventing the utilitarian principle from justifying too much, or at least of making it much less likely to do so: namely, by stating utilitarianism in a way which accounts for the distinction between the justification of an institution and the justification of a particular action falling under it.

I begin by defining the institution of punishment as follows: a person is said to suffer punishment whenever he is legally deprived of some of the normal rights of a citizen on the ground that he has violated a rule of law, the violation having been established by trial according to the due process of law, provided that the deprivation is carried out by the recognized legal authorities of the state, that the rule of law clearly specifies both the offence and the attached penalty, that the courts construe statutes strictly, and that the statute was on the books prior to the time of the offence.[2] This definition specifies what I shall understand by punishment. The question is whether utilitarian arguments may be found to justify institutions widely different from this and such as one would find cruel and arbitrary.

This question is best answered, I think, by taking up a particular accusation. Consider the following from Carritt:

> ... the utilitarian must hold that we are justified in inflicting pain always and only to prevent worse pain or bring about greater happiness. This, then, is all we need to consider in so-called punishment, which must be purely preventive. But if some kind of very cruel crime becomes common, and none of the criminals can be caught, it might be highly expedient, as an example,

---

[1] By the classical utilitarians I understand Hobbes, Hume, Bentham, J. S. Mill, and Sidgwick.

[2] All these features of punishment are mentioned by Hobbes; cf. *Leviathan*, ch. xxviii.

to hang an innocent man, if a charge against him could be so framed that he were universally thought guilty; indeed this would only fail to be an ideal instance of utilitarian 'punishment' because the victim himself would not have been so likely as a real felon to commit such a crime in the future; in all other respects it would be perfectly deterrent and therefore felicific.[1]

Carritt is trying to show that there are occasions when a utilitarian argument would justify taking an action which would be generally condemned; and thus that utilitarianism justifies too much. But the failure of Carritt's argument lies in the fact that he makes no distinction between the justification of the general system of rules which constitutes penal institutions and the justification of particular applications of these rules to particular cases by the various officials whose job it is to administer them. This becomes perfectly clear when one asks who the 'we' are of whom Carritt speaks. Who is this who has a sort of absolute authority on particular occasions to decide that an innocent man shall be 'punished' if everyone can be convinced that he is guilty? Is this person the legislator, or the judge, or the body of private citizens, or what? It is utterly crucial to know who is to decide such matters, and by what authority, for all of this must be written into the rules of the institution. Until one knows these things one doesn't know what the institution is whose justification is being challenged; and as the utilitarian principle applies to the institution one doesn't know whether it is justifiable on utilitarian grounds or not.

Once this is understood it is clear what the countermove to Carritt's argument is. One must describe more carefully what the *institution* is which his example suggests, and then ask oneself whether or not it is likely that having this institution would be for the benefit of society in the long run. One must not content oneself with the vague thought that, when it's a question of *this* case, it would be a good thing if *somebody* did something even if an innocent person were to suffer.

Try to imagine, then, an institution (which we may call 'telishment') which is such that the officials set up by it have authority to arrange a trial for the condemnation of an innocent man whenever they are of the opinion that doing so would be in the best interests of society. The discretion of officials is limited, however, by the rule that they may not condemn an innocent man to undergo such an ordeal unless there is, at the time, a wave of offences similar to that with which they charge him and telish him for. We may imagine that the officials having the discretionary authority are the judges of the higher courts in con-

[1] *Ethical and Political Thinking* (Oxford, 1947), p. 65.

sultation with the chief of police, the minister of justice, and a committee of the legislature.

Once one realizes that one is involved in setting up an *institution*, one sees that the hazards are very great. For example, what check is there on the officials? How is one to tell whether or not their actions are authorized? How is one to limit the risks involved in allowing such systematic deception? How is one to avoid giving anything short of complete discretion to the authorities to telish anyone they like? In addition to these considerations, it is obvious that people will come to have a very different attitude towards their penal system when telishment is adjoined to it. They will be uncertain as to whether a convicted man has been punished or telished. They will wonder whether or not they should feel sorry for him. They will wonder whether the same fate won't at any time fall on them. If one pictures how such an institution would actually work, and the enormous risks involved in it, it seems clear that it would serve no useful purpose. A utilitarian justification for this institution is most unlikely.

It happens in general that as one drops off the defining features of punishment one ends up with an institution whose utilitarian justification is highly doubtful. One reason for this is that punishment works like a kind of price system: by altering the prices one has to pay for the performance of actions it supplies a motive for avoiding some actions and doing others. The defining features are essential if punishment is to work in this way; so that an institution which lacks these features, e.g., an institution which is set up to 'punish' the innocent, is likely to have about as much point as a price system (if one may call it that) where the prices of things change at random from day to day and one learns the price of something after one has agreed to buy it.[1]

---

[1] The analogy with the price system suggests an answer to the question how utilitarian considerations ensure that punishment is proportional to the offence. It is interesting to note that Sir David Ross, after making the distinction between justifying a penal law and justifying a particular application of it, and after stating that utilitarian considerations have a large place in determining the former, still holds back from accepting the utilitarian justification of punishment on the grounds that justice requires that punishment be proportional to the offence, and that utilitarianism is unable to account for this. Cf. *The Right and the Good*, pp. 61–62. I do not claim that utilitarianism can account for this requirement as Sir David might wish, but it happens, nevertheless, that if utilitarian considerations are followed penalties will be proportional to offences in this sense: the order of offences according to seriousness can be paired off with the order of penalties according to severity. Also the absolute level of penalties will be as low as possible. This follows from the assumption that people are rational (i.e., that they are able to take into account the 'prices' the state puts on actions), the utilitarian rule that a penal system should provide a motive for pre-

If one is careful to apply the utilitarian principle to the institution which is to authorize particular actions, then there is *less* danger of its justifying too much. Carritt's example gains plausibility by its indefiniteness and by its concentration on the particular case. His argument will only hold if it can be shown that there are utilitarian arguments which justify an institution whose publicly ascertainable offices and powers are such as to permit officials to exercise that kind of discretion in particular cases. But the requirement of having to build the arbitrary features of the particular decision into the institutional practice makes the justification much less likely to go through.

II

I shall now consider the question of promises. The objection to utilitarianism in connexion with promises seems to be this: it is believed that on the utilitarian view when a person makes a promise the only ground upon which he should keep it, if he should keep it, is that by keeping it he will realize the most good on the whole. So that if one asks the question 'Why should I keep *my* promise?' the utilitarian answer is understood to be that doing so in *this* case will have the best consequences. And this answer is said, quite rightly, to conflict with the way in which the obligation to keep promises is regarded.

Now of course critics of utilitarianism are not unaware that one defence sometimes attributed to utilitarians is the consideration involving the practice of promise-keeping.[1] In this connexion they are supposed to argue something like this: it must be admitted that we feel strictly about keeping promises, more strictly than it might seem our view can account for. But when we consider the matter carefully it is always necessary to take into account the effect which our action will have on the practice of making promises. The promisor must weigh, not only the effects of breaking his promise on the

ferring the less serious offence, and the principle that punishment as such is an evil. All this was carefully worked out by Bentham in *The Principles of Morals and Legislation*, chs. xiii-xv.

[1] Ross, *The Right and the Good*, pp. 37–39, and *Foundations of Ethics* (Oxford, 1939), pp. 92–94. I know of no utilitarian who has used this argument except W. A. Pickard-Cambridge in 'Two Problems about Duty', *Mind*, n.s., xli (April, 1932), 153–157, although the argument goes with G. E. Moore's version of utilitarianism in *Principia Ethica* (Cambridge, 1903). To my knowledge it does not appear in the classical utilitarians; and if one interprets their view correctly this is no accident.

particular case, but also the effect which his breaking his promise will have on the practice itself. Since the practice is of great utilitarian value, and since breaking one's promise always seriously damages it, one will seldom be justified in breaking one's promise. If we view our individual promises in the wider context of the practice of promising itself we can account for the strictness of the obligation to keep promises. There is always one very strong utilitarian consideration in favour of keeping them, and this will ensure that when the question arises as to whether or not to keep a promise it will usually turn out that one should, even where the facts of the particular case taken by itself would seem to justify one's breaking it. In this way the strictness with which we view the obligation to keep promises is accounted for.

Ross has criticized this defence as follows:[1] however great the value of the practice of promising, on utilitarian grounds, there must be some value which is greater, and one can imagine it to be obtainable by breaking a promise. Therefore there might be a case where the promisor could argue that breaking his promise was justified as leading to a better state of affairs on the whole. And the promisor could argue in this way no matter how slight the advantage won by breaking the promise. If one were to challenge the promisor his defence would be that what he did was best on the whole in view of all the utilitarian considerations, which in this case *include* the importance of the practice. Ross feels that such a defence would be unacceptable. I think he is right insofar as he is protesting against the appeal to consequences in general and without further explanation. Yet it is extremely difficult to weigh the force of Ross's argument. The kind of case imagined seems unrealistic and one feels that it needs to be described. One is inclined to think it would either turn out that such a case came under an exception defined by the practice itself, in which case there would not be an appeal to consequences in general on the particular case, or it would happen that the circumstances were so peculiar that the conditions which the practice presupposes no longer obtained. But certainly Ross is right in thinking that it strikes us as wrong for a person to defend breaking a promise by a general appeal to consequences. For a general utilitarian defence is not open to the promisor: it is not one of the defences allowed by the practice of making promises.

---

[1] Ross, *The Right and the Good*, pp. 38–39.

Ross gives two further counterarguments:[1] First, he holds that it overestimates the damage done to the practice of promising by a failure to keep a promise. One who breaks a promise harms his own name certainly, but it isn't clear that a broken promise always damages the practice itself sufficiently to account for the strictness of the obligation. Second, and more important, I think, he raises the question of what one is to say of a promise which isn't known to have been made except to the promisor and the promisee, as in the case of a promise a son makes to his dying father concerning the handling of the estate.[2] In this sort of case the consideration relating to the practice doesn't weigh on the promisor at all, and yet one feels that this sort of promise is as binding as other promises. The question of the effect which breaking it has on the practice seems irrelevant. The only consequence seems to be that one can break the promise without running any risk of being censured; but the obligation itself seems not the least weakened. Hence it is doubtful whether the effect on the practice ever weighs in the particular case; certainly it cannot account for the strictness of the obligation where it fails to obtain. It seems to follow that a utilitarian account of the obligation to keep promises cannot be successfully carried out.

From what I have said in connexion with punishment, one can foresee what I am going to say about these arguments and counterarguments. They fail to make the distinction between the justification of a practice and the justification of a particular action falling under it, and therefore they fall into the mistake of taking it for granted that the promisor, like Carritt's official, is entitled without restriction to bring utilitarian considerations to bear in deciding whether to keep *his* promise. But if one considers what the practice of promising is one will see, I think, that it is such as not to allow this sort of general discretion to the promisor. Indeed, the point of the practice is to abdicate one's title to act in accordance with utilitarian and prudential considerations in order that the future may be tied down and plans

[1] Ross, ibid, p. 39. The case of the nonpublic promise is discussed again in *Foundations of Ethics*, pp. 95–96, 104–105. It occurs also in Mabbott, 'Punishment', op. cit., pp. 155–157, and in A. I. Melden, 'Two Comments on Utilitarianism', *Philosophical Review*, lx (October, 1951), 519–523, which discusses Carritt's example in *Ethical and Political Thinking*, p. 64.

[2] Ross's example is described simply as that of two men dying alone where one makes a promise to the other. Carritt's example (cf. n. 17 supra) [Note 1. Ed] is that of two men at the North Pole. The example in the text is more realistic and is similar to Mabbott's. Another example is that of being told something in confidence by one who subsequenlty dies. Such cases need not be 'desert-island arguments' as Nowell-Smith seems to believe (cf. his *Ethics*, pp. 239–244).

coordinated in advance. There are obvious utilitarian advantages in having a practice which denies to the promisor, as a defence, any general appeal to the utilitarian principle in accordance with which the practice itself may be justified. There is nothing contradictory, or surprising, in this: utilitarian (or aesthetic) reasons might properly be given in arguing that the game of chess, or baseball, is satisfactory just as it is, or in arguing that it should be changed in various respects, but a player in a game cannot properly appeal to such considerations as reasons for his making one move rather than another. It is a mistake to think that if the practice is justified on utilitarian grounds then the promisor must have complete liberty to use utilitarian arguments to decide whether or not to keep his promise. The practice forbids this general defence; and it is a purpose of the practice to do this. Therefore what the above arguments presuppose—the idea that if the utilitarian view is accepted then the promisor is bound if, and only if, the application of the utilitarian principle to his own case shows that keeping it is best on the whole—is false. The promisor is bound because he promised: weighing the case on its merits is not open to him.[1]

Is this to say that in particular cases one cannot deliberate whether or not to keep one's promise? Of course not. But to do so is to deliberate whether the various excuses, exceptions and defences, which are understood by, and which constitute an important part of, the practice, apply to one's own case.[2] Various defences for not keeping one's promise are allowed, but among them there isn't the one that, on general utilitarian grounds, the promisor (truly) thought his action best on the whole, even though there may be the defence that the consequences of keeping one's promise would have been *extremely* severe. While there are too many complexities here to consider all the necessary details, one can see that the general defence isn't allowed if one asks the following question: what would one say of someone who, when asked why he broke his promise, replied simply that breaking it was best on the whole? Assuming that his reply is sincere, and that his belief was reasonable (i.e., one need not consider the possibility that he was mistaken), I think that one would question whether or not he knows what it means to say 'I promise' (in the appropriate circumstances). It would be said of someone who used

[1] What I have said in this paragraph seems to me to coincide with Hume's important discussion in the *Treatise of Human Nature*, Bk. III, pt. 11, sec. 5; and also sec. 6, par. 8.

[2] For a discussion of these, see H. Sidgwick, *The Methods of Ethics* (6th ed.; London, 1901), Bk. III, ch. vi.

this excuse without further explanation that he didn't understand what defences the practice, which defines a promise, allows to him. If a child were to use this excuse one would correct him; for it is part of the way one is taught the concept of a promise to be corrected if one uses this excuse. The point of having the practice would be lost if the practice did allow this excuse.

It is no doubt part of the utilitarian view that every practice should admit the defence that the consequences of abiding by it would have been extremely severe; and utilitarians would be inclined to hold that some reliance on people's good sense and some concession to hard cases is necessary. They would hold that a practice is justified by serving the interests of those who take part in it; and as with any set of rules there is understood a background of circumstances under which it is expected to be applied and which need not—indeed which cannot—be fully stated. Should these circumstances change, then even if there is no rule which provides for the case, it may still be in accordance with the practice that one be released from one's obligation. But this sort of defence allowed by a practice must not be confused with the general option to weigh each particular case on utilitarian grounds which critics of utilitarianism have thought it necessarily to involve.

The concern which utilitarianism raises by its justification of punishment is that it may justify too much. The question in connexion with promises is different: it is how utilitarianism can account for the obligation to keep promises at all. One feels that the recognized obligation to keep one's promise and utilitarianism are incompatible. And to be sure, they are incompatible if one interprets the utilitarian view as necessarily holding that each person has complete liberty to weigh every particular action on general utilitarian grounds. But must one interpret utilitarianism in this way? I hope to show that, in the sorts of cases I have discussed, one cannot interpret it in this way.

III

So far I have tried to show the importance of the distinction between the justification of a practice and the justification of a particular action falling under it by indicating how this distinction might be used to defend utilitarianism against two long-standing objections. One might be tempted to close the discussion at this point by saying that utilitarian considerations should be understood as applying to practices in the first instance and not to particular actions falling under them except insofar as the practices admit of it. One might say that in this modified form it is a better account of our considered moral opinions and let it go at that. But to stop here would be to neglect the interesting question as to how one can fail to appreciate the significance of this rather obvious distinction and can take it for granted that utilitarianism has the consequence that particular cases may always be decided on general utilitarian grounds.[1] I want to argue that this mistake may be connected with misconceiving the logical status of the rules of practices; and to show this I am going to examine two conceptions of rules, two ways of placing them within the utilitarian theory.

The conception which conceals from us the significance of the distinction I am going to call the summary view. It regards rules in the following way: one supposes that each person decides what he shall do in particular cases by applying the utilitarian principle; one supposes further that different people will decide the same particular case in the same way and that there will be recurrences of cases similar to those previously decided. Thus it will happen that in cases of certain kinds the same decision will be made either by the same person at different times or by different persons at the same time. If a case occurs frequently enough one supposes that a rule is formulated to cover that sort of case. I have called this conception the summary view because rules are pictured as summaries of past decisions arrived at by the *direct* application of the utilitarian principle to particular cases. Rules are regarded as reports that cases of a certain sort have been found on *other* grounds to be properly decided in a certain way (although, of course, they do not *say* this).

---

[1] So far as I can see it is not until Moore that the doctrine is expressly stated in this way. See, for example, *Principia Ethica*, p. 147, where it is said that the statement 'I am morally bound to perform this action' is identical with the statement '*This* action will produce the greatest possible amount of good in the Universe' (my italics). It is important to remember that those whom I have called the classical utilitarians were largely interested in social institutions. They were among the leading economists and political theorists of their day, and they were not infrequently reformers interested in practical affairs. Utilitarianism historically goes together with a coherent view of society, and is not simply an ethical theory, much less an attempt at philosophical analysis in the modern sense. The utilitarian principle was quite naturally thought of, and used, as a criterion for judging social institutions (practices) and as a basis for urging reforms. It is not clear, therefore, how far it is necessary to amend utilitarianism in its classical form. For a discussion of utilitarianism as an integral part of a theory of society, see L. Robbins, *The Theory of Economic Policy in English Classical Political Economy* (London, 1952).

There are several things to notice about this way of placing rules within the utilitarian theory.[1]

[1] This footnote should be read after sec. 3 and presupposes what I have said there. It provides a few references to statements by leading utilitarians of the summary conception. In general it appears that when they discussed the logical features of rules the summary conception prevailed and that it was typical of the way they talked about moral rules. I cite a rather lengthy group of passages from Austin as a full illustration.

John Austin in his *Lectures on Jurisprudence* meets the objection that deciding in accordance with the utilitarian principle case by case is impractical by saying that this is a misinterpretation of utilitarianism. According to the utilitarian view '. . . our conduct would conform to *rules* inferred from the tendencies of actions, but would not be determined by a direct resort to the principle of general utility. Utility would be the test of our conduct, ultimately, but not immediately: the immediate test of the rules to which our conduct would conform, but not the immediate test of specific or individual actions. Our rules would be fashioned on utility; our conduct, on our rules' (vol. 1, p. 116). As to how one decides on the tendency of an action he says: 'If we would try the tendency of a specific or individual act, we must not contemplate the act as if it were single and insulated, but must look at the class of acts to which it belongs. We must suppose that acts of the class were generally done or omitted, and consider the probable effect upon the general happiness or good. We must guess the consequences which would follow, if the class of acts were general; and also the consequences which would follow, if they were generally omitted. We must then compare the consequences on the positive and negative sides, and determine on which of the two the *balance* of advantage lies . . . . If we truly try the tendency of a specific or individual act, we try the tendency of the class to which that act belongs. The *particular* conclusion which we draw, with regard to the single act, implies a *general* conclusion embracing all similar acts. . . . To the rules thus inferred, and lodged in the memory, our conduct would conform *immediately* if it were truly adjusted to utility' (ibid., p. 117). One might think that Austin meets the objection by stating the practice conception of rules; and perhaps he did intend to. But it is not clear that he has stated this conception. Is the generality he refers to of the statistical sort? This is suggested by the notion of tendency. Or does he refer to the utility of setting up a practice? I don't know; but what suggests the summary view is his subsequent remarks. He says: 'To consider the specific consequences of single or individual acts, would *seldom* [my italics] consist with that ultimate principle' (ibid., p. 117). But would one ever do this? He continues: '. . . this being admitted, the necessity of pausing and calculating, which the objection in question supposes, is an imagined necessity. To preface each act or forbearance by a conjecture and comparison of consequences, were clearly *superfluous* [my italics] and mischievous. It were clearly superfluous, inasmuch as the *result of that process* [my italics] would be embodied in a known *rule*. It were clearly mischievous, inasmuch as the *true* result would be expressed by that rule, whilst the process would probably be faulty, if it were done on the spur of the occasion' (ibid., pp. 117–118). He goes on: 'If our experience and observation of particulars were not *generalized*, our experience and observation of particulars would seldom avail us in *practice* . . . The inferences suggested to our minds by repeated experience and observation are, therefore, drawn into *principles*, or compressed into *maxims*. These we carry about us ready for use, and apply to individual cases promptly . . . without reverting to the process by which they were obtained; or without recalling, and arraying before our minds, the numerous and intricate considerations of which they are *handy abridgments* [my italics] . . . . True theory is a *compendium* of particular truths. . . . Speaking then, generally, human conduct is inevitably *guided* [my italics] by *rules*, or by *principles* or *maxims* (ibid., pp. 117–118). I need not trouble to show

1. The point of having rules derives from the fact that similar cases tend to recur and that one can decide cases more quickly if one records past decisions in the form of rules. If similar cases didn't recur, one would be required to apply the utilitarian principle directly, case by case, and rules reporting past decisions would be of no use.

2. The decisions made on particular cases are logically prior to rules. Since rules gain their point from the need to apply the utilitarian principle to many similar cases, it follows that a particular case (or several cases similar to it) may exist whether or not there is a rule covering that case. We are pictured as recognizing particular cases prior to there being a rule which covers them, for it is only if we meet with a number of cases of a certain sort that we formulate a rule. Thus we are able to describe a particular case as a particular case of the requisite sort whether there is a rule regarding *that* sort of case or not. Put another way: what the A's and the B's refer to in rules of the form 'Whenever A do B' may be described as A's and B's whether or not there is the rule 'Whenever A do B', or whether or not there is any body of rules which makes up a practice of which that rule is a part.

how all these remarks incline to the summary view. Further, when Austin comes to deal with cases 'of comparatively rare occurrence' he holds that specific considerations may outweigh the general. 'Looking at the reasons from which we had inferred the rule, it were absurd to think it inflexible. We should therefore dismiss the *rule*; resort directly to the *principle* upon which our rules were fashioned; and calculate *specific* consequences to the best of our knowledge and ability' (ibid., pp. 120–121). Austin's view is interesting because it shows how one may come close to the practice conception and then slide away from it.

In *A System of Logic*, Bk. VI, ch. xii, par. 2, Mill distinguishes clearly between the position of judge and legislator and in doing so suggests the distinction between the two concepts of rules. However, he distinguishes the two positions to illustrate the difference between cases where one is to apply a rule already established and cases where one must formulate a rule to govern subsequent conduct. It's the latter case that interests him and he takes the 'maxim of policy' of a legislator as typical of rules. In par. 3 the summary conception is very clearly stated. For example, he says of rules of conduct that they should be taken provisionally, as they are made for the most numerous cases. He says that they 'point out' the manner in which it is least perilous to act; they serve as an 'admonition' that a certain mode of conduct has been found suited to the most common occurrences. In *Utilitarianism*, ch. ii, par. 24, the summary conception appears in Mill's answer to the same objection Austin considered. Here he speaks of rules as 'corollaries' from the principle of utility; these 'secondary' rules are compared to 'landmarks' and 'direction-posts'. They are based on long experience and so make it unnecessary to apply the utilitarian principle to each case. In par. 25 Mill refers to the task of the utilitarian principle in adjudicating between competing moral rules. He talks here as if one then applies the utilitarian principle directly to the particular case. On the practice view one would rather use the principle to decide which of the ways that make the practice consistent is the best. It should be noted that while in par. 10 Mill's definition of utilitarianism makes the utilitarian principle apply to morality, i.e., to the rules

To illustrate this consider a rule, or maxim, which could arise in this way: suppose that a person is trying to decide whether to tell someone who is fatally ill what his illness is when he has been asked to do so. Suppose the person to reflect and then decide, on utilitarian grounds, that he should not answer truthfully; and suppose that on the basis of this and other like occasions he formulates a rule to the effect that when asked by someone fatally ill what his illness is, one should not tell him. The point to notice is that someone's being fatally ill and asking what his illness is, and someone's telling him, are things that can be described as such whether or not there is this rule. The performance of the action to which the rule refers doesn't require the stage-setting of a practice of which this rule is a part. This is what is meant by saying that on the summary view particular cases are logically prior to rules.

3. Each person is in principle always entitled to reconsider the correctness of a rule and to question whether or not it is proper to follow it in a particular case. As rules are guides and aids, one may ask whether in past decisions there might not have been a mistake in applying the utilitarian principle to get the rule in question, and wonder whether or not it is best in this case. The reason for rules is that people are not able to apply the utilitarian principle effortlessly and flawlessly; there is need to save time and to post a guide. On this view a society of rational utilitarians would be a society without rules

and precepts of human conduct, the definition in par. 2 uses the phrase 'actions are right in *proportion* as they *tend* to promote happiness' [my italics] and this inclines towards the summary view. In the last paragraph of the essay 'On the Definition of Political Economy', *Westminister Review* (October, 1836), Mill says that it is only in art, as distinguished from science, that one can properly speak of exceptions. In a question of practice, if something is fit to be done 'in the majority of cases' then it is made the rule. 'We may ... in talking of art *unobjectionably* speak of the *rule* and the *exception*, meaning by the rule the cases in which there exists a preponderance ... of inducements for acting in a particular way; and by the exception, the cases in which the preponderance is on the contrary side.' These remarks, too, suggest the summary view.

In Moore's *Principia Ethica*, ch. v, there is a complicated and difficult discussion of moral rules. I will not examine it here except to express my suspicion that the summary conception prevails. To be sure, Moore speaks frequently of the utility of rules as generally followed, and of actions as generally practised, but it is possible that these passages fit the statistical notion of generality which the summary conception allows. This conception is suggested by Moore's taking the utilitarian principle as applying directly to particular actions (pp. 147–148) and by his notion of a rule as something indicating which of the few alternatives likely to occur to anyone will generally produce a greater total good in the immediate future (p. 154). He talks of an 'ethical law' as a prediction, and as a generalization (pp. 146, 155). The summary conception is also suggested by his discussion of exceptions (pp. 162–163) and of the force of examples of breaching a rule (pp. 163–164).

in which each person applied the utilitarian principle directly and smoothly, and without error, case by case. On the other hand, ours is a society in which rules are formulated to serve as aids in reaching these ideally rational decisons on particular cases, guides which have been built up and tested by the experience of generations. If one applies this view to rules, one is interpreting them as maxims, as 'rules of thumb'; and it is doubtful that anything to which the summary conception did apply would be called a *rule*. Arguing as if one regarded rules in this way is a mistake one makes while doing philosophy.

4. The concept of a *general* rule takes the following form. One is pictured as estimating on what percentage of the cases likely to arise a given rule may be relied upon to express the correct decision, that is, the decision that would be arrived at if one were to correctly apply the utilitarian principle case by case. If one estimates that by and large the rule will give the correct decision, or if one estimates that the likelihood of making a mistake by applying the utilitarian principle directly on one's own is greater than the likelihood of making a mistake by following the rule, and if these considerations held of persons generally, then one would be justified in urging its adoption as a general rule. In this way *general* rules might be accounted for on the summary view. It will still make sense, however, to speak of applying the utilitarian principle case by case, for it was by trying to foresee the results of doing this that one got the initial estimates upon which acceptance of the rule depends. That one is taking a rule in accordance with the summary conception will show itself in the naturalness with which one speaks of the rule as a guide, or as a maxim, or as a generalization from experience, and as something to be laid aside in extraordinary cases where there is no assurance that the generalization will hold and the case must therefore be treated on its merits. Thus there goes with this conception the notion of a particular exception which renders a rule suspect on a particular occasion.

The other conception of rules I will call the practice conception. On this view rules are pictured as defining a practice. Practices are set up for various reasons, but one of them is that in many areas of conduct each person's deciding what to do on utilitarian grounds case by case leads to confusion, and that the attempt to coordinate behaviour by trying to foresee how others will act is bound to fail. As an alternative one realizes that what is required is the establishment of a practice, the specification of a new form of activity; and from this one sees that a practice necessarily involves the abdication of full liberty to act on utilitarian and prudential grounds. It is the mark of a practice that being taught how to engage in it involves being instructed in the rules which define it, and that appeal is made to those rules to correct the behaviour of those engaged in it. Those engaged in a practice recognize the rules as defining it. The rules cannot be taken as simply describing how those engaged in the practice in fact behave: it is not simply that they act as if they were obeying the rules. Thus it is essential to the notion of a practice that the rules are publicly known and understood as definitive; and it is essential also that the rules of a practice can be taught and can be acted upon to yield a coherent practice. On this conception, then, rules are not generalizations from the decisions of individuals applying the utilitarian principle directly and independently to recurrent particular cases. On the contrary, rules define a practice and are themselves the subject of the utilitarian principle.

To show the important differences between this way of fitting rules into the utilitarian theory and the previous way, I shall consider the differences between the two conceptions on the points previously discussed.

1. In contrast with the summary view, the rules of practices are logically prior to particular cases. This is so because there cannot be a particular case of an action falling under a rule of a practice unless there is the practice. This can be made clearer as follows: in a practice there are rules setting up offices, specifying certain forms of action appropriate to various offices, establishing penalties for the breach of rules, and so on. We may think of the rules of a practice as defining offices, moves, and offences. Now what is meant by saying that the practice is logically prior to particular cases is this: given any rule which specifies a form of action (a move), a particular action which would be taken as falling under this rule given that there is the practice would not be *described as* that sort of action unless there was the practice. In the case of actions specified by practices it is logically impossible to perform them outside the stage-setting provided by those practices, for unless there is the practice, and unless the requisite proprieties are fulfilled, whatever one does, whatever movements one makes, will fail to count as a form of action which the practice specifies. What one does will be described in some *other* way.

One may illustrate this point from the game of baseball. Many of the actions one performs in a game of baseball one can do by oneself or with others whether there is the game or not. For example, one can throw a ball, run, or swing a peculiarly shaped piece of wood. But one cannot steal base, or strike out, or draw a walk, or make an error, or balk; although one can do certian things which appear to resemble these actions such as sliding into a bag, missing a grounder and so on. Striking out, stealing a base, balking, etc., are all actions which can only happen in a game. No matter what a person did, what he did would not be described as stealing a base or striking out or drawing a walk unless he could also be described as playing baseball, and for him to be doing this presupposes the rule-like practice which constitutes the game. The practice is logically prior to particular cases: unless there is the practice the terms referring to actions specified by it lack a sense.[1]

2. The practice view leads to an entirely different conception of the authority which each person has to decide on the propriety of following a rule in particular cases. To engage in a practice, to perform those actions specified by a practice, means to follow the appropriate rules. If one wants to do an action which a certain practice specifies then there is no way to do it except to follow the rules which define it. Therefore, it doesn't make sense for a person to raise the question whether or not a rule of a practice correctly applies to *his* case where the action he contemplates is a form of action defined by a practice. If someone were to raise such a question, he would simply show that he didn't understand the situation in which he was acting. If one wants to perform an action specified by a practice, the only legitimate question concerns the nature of the practice itself ('How do I go about making a will?').

This point is illustrated by the behaviour expected of a player in games. If one wants to play a game, one doesn't treat the rules of the game as guides as to what is best in particular cases. In a game of baseball if a batter were to ask 'Can I have four strikes?' it would be assumed that he was asking what the rule was; and if, when told what the rule was, he were to say that he meant that on this occasion he thought it would be best on the whole for him to have four strikes rather than three, this would be most kindly taken as a joke. One might contend that baseball would be a better game if four strikes

---

[1] One might feel that it is a mistake to say that a practice is logically prior to the forms of action it specifies on the grounds that if there were never any instances of actions falling under a practice then we should be strongly inclined to say that there wasn't the practice either. Blue-prints for a practice do not make a practice. That there is a practice entails that there are instances of people having been engaged and now being engaged in it (with suitable qualifications). This is correct, but it doesn't hurt the claim that any given particular instance of a form of action specified by a practice presupposes the practice. This isn't so on the summary picture, as each instance must be 'there' prior to the rules, so to speak, as something from which one gets the rule by applying the utilitarian principle to it directly.

were allowed instead of three; but one cannot picture the rules as guides to what is best on the whole in particular cases, and question their applicability to particular cases as particular cases.

3 and 4. To complete the four points of comparison with the summary conception, it is clear from what has been said that rules of practices are not guides to help one decide particular cases correctly as judged by some higher ethical principle. And neither the quasi-statistical notion of generality, nor the notion of a particular exception, can apply to the rules of practices. A more or less general rule of a practice must be a rule which according to the structure of the practice applies to more or fewer of the kinds of cases arising under it; or it must be a rule which is more or less basic to the understanding of the practice. Again, a particular case cannot be an exception to a rule of a practice. An exception is rather a qualification or a further specification of the rule.

It follows from what we have said about the practice conception of rules that if a person is engaged in a practice, and if he is asked why *he* does what *he* does, or if he is asked to defend what he does, then his explanation, or defence, lies in referring the questioner to the practice. He cannot say of *his* action, if it is an action specified by a practice, that he does it rather than some other because he thinks it is best on the whole.[1] When a man engaged in a practice is queried about his action he must assume that the questioner either doesn't know that he is engaged in it ('Why are you in a hurry to pay him?' 'I promised to pay him today') or doesn't know what the practice is. One doesn't so much justify one's particular action as explain, or show, that it is in accordance with the practice. The reason for this is that it is only against the stage-setting of the practice that one's particular action is described as it is. Only by reference to the practice can one *say* what one is doing. To explain or to defend one's own action, as a particular action, one fits it into the practice which defines it. If this is not accepted it's a sign that a different question is being raised as to whether one is justified in accepting the practice, or in tolerating it. When the challenge is to the practice, citing the rules (saying what the practice is) is naturally to no avail. But when the challenge is to the particular action defined by the practice, there is nothing one can do but refer to the rules. Concerning particular actions there is only a question for one who isn't clear as to what the practice is, or who doesn't know that it is being engaged in. This is to be contrasted with

[1] A philosophical joke (in the mouth of Jeremy Bentham): 'When I run to the other wicket after my partner has struck a good ball I do so because it is best on the whole'.

the case of a maxim which may be taken as pointing to the correct decision on the case as decided on *other* grounds, and so giving a challenge on the case a sense by having it question whether these other grounds really support the decision on this case.

If one compares the two conceptions of rules I have discussed, one can see how the summary conception misses the significance of the distinction between justifying a practice and justifying actions falling under it. On this view rules are regarded as guides whose purpose it is to indicate the ideally rational decision on the given particular case which the flawless application of the utilitarian principle would yield. One has, in principle, full option to use the guides or to discard them as the situation warrants without one's moral office being altered in any way: whether one discards the rules or not, one always holds the office of a rational person seeking case by case to realize the best on the whole. But on the practice conception, if one holds an office defined by a practice then questions regarding one's actions in this office are settled by reference to the rules which define the practice. If one seeks to question these rules, then one's office undergoes a fundamental change: one then assumes the office of one empowered to change and criticize the rules, or the office of a reformer, and so on. The summary conception does away with the distinction of offices and the various forms of argument appropriate to each. On that conception there is one office and so no offices at all. It therefore obscures the fact that the utilitarian principle must, in the case of actions and offices defined by a practice, apply to the practice, so that general utilitarian arguments are not available to those who act in offices so defined.[1]

Some qualifications are necessary in what I have said. First, I may have talked of the summary and the practice conceptions of rules as if only one of them could be true of rules, and if true of any rules, then necessarily true of *all* rules. I do not, of course, mean this. (It is the

---

[1] How do these remarks apply to the case of the promise known only to father and son? Well, at first sight the son certainly holds the office of promisor, and so he isn't allowed by the practice to weigh the particular case on general utilitarian grounds. Suppose instead that he wishes to consider himself in the office of one empowered to criticize and change the practice, leaving aside the question as to his right to move from his previously assumed office to another. Then he may consider utilitarian arguments as applied to the practice; but once he does this he will see that there are such arguments for not allowing a general utilitarian defence in the practice for this sort of case. For to do so would make it impossible to ask for and to give a kind of promise which one often wants to be able to ask for and to give. Therefore he will not want to change the practice, and so as a promisor he has no option but to keep his promise.

critics of utilitarianism who make this mistake insofar as their arguments against utilitarianism presuppose a summary conception of the rules of practices.) Some rules will fit one conception, some rules the other; and so there are rules of practices (rules in the strict sense), and maxims and 'rules of thumb'.

Secondly, there are further distinctions that can be made in classifying rules, distinctions which should be made if one were considering other questions. The distinctions which I have drawn are those most relevant for the rather special matter I have discussed, and are not intended to be exhaustive.

Finally, there will be many border-line cases about which it will be difficult, if not impossible, to decide which conception of rules is applicable. One expects border-line cases with any concept, and they are especially likely in connexion with such involved concepts as those of a practice, institution, game, rule, and so on. Wittgenstein has shown how fluid these notions are.[1] What I have done is to emphasize and sharpen two conceptions for the limited purpose of this paper.

IV

What I have tried to show by distinguishing between two conceptions of rules is that there is a way of regarding rules which allows the option to consider particular cases on general utilitarian grounds; whereas there is another conception which does not admit of such discretion except insofar as the rules themselves authorize it. I want to suggest that the tendency while doing philosophy to picture rules in accordance with the summary conception is what may have blinded moral philosophers to the significance of the distinction between justifying a practice and justifying a particular action falling under it; and it does so by misrepresenting the logical force of the reference to the rules in the case of a challenge to a particular action falling under a practice, and by obscuring the fact that where there is a practice, it is the practice itself that must be the subject of the utilitarian principle.

It is surely no accident that two of the traditional test cases of utilitarianism, punishment and promises, are clear cases of practices. Under the influence of the summary conception it is natural to suppose that the officials of a penal system, and one who has made a

[1] *Philosophical Investigations* (Oxford, 1953), i, pars. 65–71, for example.

promise, may decide what to do in particular cases on utilitarian grounds. One fails to see that a general discretion to decide particular cases on utilitarian grounds is incompatible with the concept of a practice; and that what discretion one does have is itself defined by the practice (e.g., a judge may have discretion to determine the penalty within certain limits). The traditional objections to utilitarianism which I have discussed presuppose the attribution to judges, and to those who have made promises, of a plenitude of moral authority to decide particular cases on utilitarian grounds. But once one fits utilitarianism together with the notion of a practice, and notes that punishment and promising are practices, then one sees that this attribution is logically precluded.

That punishment and promising are practices is beyond question. In the case of promising this is shown by the fact that the form of words 'I promise' is a performative utterance which presupposes the stage-setting of the practice and the proprieties defined by it. Saying the words 'I promise' will only be promising given the existence of the practice. It would be absurd to interpret the rules about promising in accordance with the summary conception. It is absurd to say, for example, that the rule that promises should be kept could have arisen from its being found in past cases to be best on the whole to keep one's promise; for unless there were already the understanding that one keeps one's promises as part of the practice itself there couldn't have been any cases of promising.

It must, of course, be granted that the rules defining promising are not codified, and that one's conception of what they are necessarily depends on one's moral training. Therefore it is likely that there is considerable variation in the way people understand the practice, and room for argument as to how it is best set up. For example, differences as to how strictly various defences are to be taken, or just what defences are available, are likely to arise amongst persons with different backgrounds. But irrespective of these variations it belongs to the concept of the practice of promising that the general utilitarian defence is not available to the promisor. That this is so accounts for the force of the traditional objection which I have discussed. And the point I wish to make is that when one fits the utilitarian view together with the practice conception of rules, as one must in the appropriate cases, then there is nothing in that view which entails that there must be such a defence, either in the practice of promising, or in any other practice.

Punishment is also a clear case. There are many actions in the sequence of events which constitute someone's being punished which presuppose a practice. One can see this by considering the definition of punishment which I gave when discussing Carritt's criticism of utilitarianism. The definition there stated refers to such things as the normal rights of a citizen, rules of law, due process of law, trials and courts of law, statutes, etc., none of which can exist outside the elaborate stage-setting of a legal system. It is also the case that many of the actions for which people are punished presuppose practices. For example, one is punished for stealing, for trespassing and the like, which presuppose the institution of property. It is impossible to say what punishment is, or to describe a particular instance of it, without referring to offices, actions, and offences specified by practices. Punishment is a move in an elaborate legal game and presupposes the complex of practices which make up the legal order. The same thing is true of the less formal sorts of punishment: a parent or guardian or someone in proper authority may punish a child, but no one else can.

There is one mistaken interpretation of what I have been saying which it is worthwhile to warn against. One might think that the use I am making of the distinction between justifying a practice and justifying the particular actions falling under it involves one in a definite social and political attitude in that it leads to a kind of conservatism. It might seem that I am saying that for each person the social practices of his society provide the standard of justification for his actions; therefore let each person abide by them and his conduct will be justified.

This interpretation is entirely wrong. The point I have been making is rather a logical point. To be sure, it has consequences in matters of ethical theory; but in itself it leads to no particular social or political attitude. It is simply that where a form of action is specified by a practice there is no justification possible of the particular action of a particular person save by reference to the practice. In such cases then action is what it is in virtue of the practice and to explain it is to refer to the practice. There is no inference whatsoever to be drawn with respect to whether or not one should accept the practices of one's society. One can be as radical as one likes but in the case of actions specified by practices the objects of one's radicalism must be the social practices and people's acceptance of them.

I have tried to show that when we fit the utilitarian view together with the practice conception of rules, where this conception is appropriate,[1] we can formulate it in a way which saves it from several traditional objections. I have further tried to show how the logical force of the distinction between justifying a practice and justifying an action falling under it is connected with the practice conception of rules and cannot be understood as long as one regards the rules of practices in accordance with the summary view. Why, when doing philosophy, one may be inclined to so regard them, I have not discussed. The reasons for this are evidently very deep and would require another paper.

[1] As I have already stated, it is not always easy to say where the conception is appropriate. Nor do I care to discuss at this point the general sorts of cases to which it does apply except to say that one should not take it for granted that it applies to many so-called 'moral rules'. It is my feeling that relatively few actions of the moral life are defined by practices and that the practice conception is more relevant to understanding legal and legal-like arguments than it is to the more complex sort of moral arguments. Utilitarianism must be fitted to different conceptions of rules depending on the case, and no doubt the failure to do this has been one source of difficulty in interpreting it correctly.

XII

EXTREME AND RESTRICTED UTILITARIANISM[1]

J. J. C. SMART

I

UTILITARIANISM is the doctrine that the rightness of actions is to be judged by their consequences. What do we mean by 'actions' here? Do we mean particular actions or do we mean classes of actions? According to which way we interpret the word 'actions' we get two different theories, both of which merit the appellation 'utilitarian'.

(1) If by 'actions' we mean particular individual actions we get the sort of doctrine held by Bentham, Sidgwick, and Moore. According to this doctrine we test individual actions by their consequences, and general rules, like 'keep promises', are mere rules of thumb which we use only to avoid the necessity of estimating the probable consequences of our actions at every step. The rightness or wrongness of keeping a promise on a particular occasion depends only on the goodness or badness of the consequences of keeping or of breaking the promise on that particular occasion. Of course part of the consequences of breaking the promise, and a part to which we will normally ascribe decisive importance, will be the weakening of faith in the institution of promising. However, if the goodness of the consequences of breaking the rule is *in toto* greater than the goodness of the consequences of keeping it, then we must break the rule, irrespective of whether the goodness of the consequences of *everybody's* obeying the rule is or is not greater than the consequences of *everybody's* breaking it. To put it shortly, rules do not matter, save *per accidens* as rules of thumb and as *de facto* social institutions with which the utilitarian has to reckon when estimating consequences. I shall call this doctrine 'extreme utilitarianism'.

(2) A more modest form of utilitarianism has recently become

From *Philosophical Quarterly*, Vol. 6 (1956), pp. 344–54. Reprinted, with emendation, by permission of the author and the *Philosophical Quarterly*.

[1]Based on a paper read to the Victorian Branch of the Australasian Association of Psychology and Philosophy, October 1955. [The article is discussed in H. J. McCloskey, 'An Examination of Restricted Utilitarianism' *Philosophical Review* (1957); also by D. Lyons, *Forms and Limits of Utilitarianism* (Clarendon Press, Oxford, 1965). Ed.]

fashionable. The doctrine is to be found in Toulmin's book *The Place of Reason in Ethics*, in Nowell-Smith's *Ethics* (though I think Nowell-Smith has qualms), in John Austin's *Lectures on Jurisprudence* (Lecture II), and even in J. S. Mill, if Urmson's interpretation of him is correct (*Philosophical Quarterly*, Vol. 3, pp. 33-39, 1953). Part of its charm is that it appears to resolve the dispute in moral philosophy between intuitionists and utilitarians in a way which is very neat. The above philosophers hold, or seem to hold, that moral rules are more than rules of thumb. In general the rightness of an action is *not* to be tested by evaluating its consequences but only by considering whether or not it falls under a certain rule. Whether the rule is to be considered an acceptable moral rule, is, however, to be decided by considering the consequences of adopting the rule. Broadly, then, actions are to be tested by rules and rules by consequences. The only cases in which we must test an individual action directly by its consequences are (*a*) when the action comes under two different rules, one of which enjoins it and one of which forbids it, and (*b*) when there is no rule whatever that governs the given case. I shall call this doctrine 'restricted utilitarianism'.

It should be noticed that the distinction I am making cuts across, and is quite different from, the distinction commonly made between hedonistic and ideal utilitarianism. Bentham was an extreme hedonistic utilitarian and Moore an extreme ideal utilitarian, and Toulmin (perhaps) could be classified as a restricted ideal utilitarian. A hedonistic utilitarian holds that the goodness of the consequences of an action is a function only of their pleasurableness and an ideal utilitarian, like Moore, holds that pleasurableness is not even a necessary condition of goodness. Mill seems, if we are to take his remarks about higher and lower pleasures seriously, to be neither a pure hedonistic nor a pure ideal utilitarian. He seems to hold that pleasurableness is a necessary condition for goodness, but that goodness is a function of other qualities of mind as well. Perhaps we can call him a quasi-ideal utilitarian. When we say that a state of mind is good I take it that we are expressing some sort of *rational preference*. When we say that it is pleasurable I take it that we are saying that it is enjoyable, and when we say that something is a higher pleasure I take it that we are saying that it is more truly, or more deeply, enjoyable. I am doubtful whether 'more deeply enjoyable' does not just mean 'more enjoyable, even though not more enjoyable on a first look', and so I am doubtful whether quasi-ideal utilitarianism, and possibly ideal utilitarianism too, would not collapse into hedonistic utilitarianism on a closer scrutiny of the logic of words like 'preference', 'pleasure', 'enjoy', 'deeply enjoy', and so on. However, it is beside the point of the present paper to go into these questions. I am here concerned only with the issue between extreme and restricted utilitarianism and am ready to concede that both forms of utilitarianism can be either hedonistic or non-hedonistic.

The issue between extreme and restricted utilitarianism can be illustrated by considering the remark 'But suppose everyone did the same'. (Cf. A. K. Stout's article in *The Australasian Journal of Philosophy*, Vol. 32, pp. 1–29) Stout distinguishes two forms of the universalization principle, the causal forms and the hypothetical form. To say that you ought not to do an action A because it would have bad results if everyone (or many people) did action A may be merely to point out that while the action A would otherwise be the optimific one, nevertheless when you take into account that doing A will probably cause other people to do A too, you can see that A is not, on a broad view, really optimific. If this causal influence could be avoided (as may happen in the case of a secret desert island promise) then we would disregard the universalization principle. This is the causal form of the principle. A person who accepted the universalization principle in its hypothetical form would be one who was concerned only with what would happen *if* everyone did the action A: he would be totally unconcerned with the question of whether in fact everyone would do the action A. That is, he might say that it would be wrong not to vote because it would have bad results if everyone took this attitude, and he would be totally unmoved by arguments purporting to show that my refusing to vote has no effect whatever on other people's propensity to vote. Making use of Stout's distinction, we can say that an extreme utilitarian would apply the universalization principle in the causal form, while a restricted utilitarian would apply it in the hypothetical form.

How are we to decide the issue between extreme and restricted utilitarianism? I wish to repudiate at the outset that milk and water approach which describes itself sometimes as 'investigating what is implicit in the common moral consciousness' and sometimes as 'investigating how people ordinarily talk about morality'. We have only to read the newspaper correspondence about capital punishment or about what should be done with Formosa to realize that the common moral consciousness is in part made up of superstitious elements, of morally bad elements, and of logically confused elements. I address myself to good hearted and benevolent people and so I hope

that if we rid ourselves of the logical confusion the superstitious
and morally bad elements will largely fall away. For even among good
hearted and benevolent people it is possible to find superstitious
and morally bad reasons for moral beliefs. These superstitious and
morally bad reasons hide behind the protective screen of logical confusion. With people who are not logically confused but who are openly
superstitious or morally bad I can of course do nothing. That is,
our ultimate pro-attitudes may be different. Nevertheless I propose
to rely on *my own* moral consciousness and to appeal to *your* moral
consciousness and to forget about what people ordinarily say. 'The
obligation to obey a rule', says Nowell-Smith (*Ethics*, p. 239), 'does
not, *in the opinion of ordinary men*', (my italics), 'rest on the beneficial
consequences of obeying it in a particular case'. What does this prove?
Surely it is more than likely that ordinary men are confused here.
Philosophers should be able to examine the question more rationally.

II

For an extreme utilitarian moral rules are rules of thumb. In
practice the extreme utilitarian will mostly guide his conduct by
appealing to the rules ('do not lie', 'do not break promises', etc.)
of common sense morality. This is not because there is anything
sacrosanct in the rules themselves but because he can argue that probably he will most often act in an extreme utilitarian way if he does
not think as a utilitarian. For one thing, actions have frequently to
be done in a hurry. Imagine a man seeing a person drowning. He
jumps in and rescues him. There is no time to reason the matter out,
but usually this will be the course of action which an extreme utilitarian would recommend if he did reason the matter out. If, however,
the man drowning had been drowning in a river near Berchtesgaden
in 1938, and if he had had the well known black forelock and mous-
tache of Adolf Hitler, an extreme utilitarian would, if he had time,
work out the probability of the man's being the villainous dictator,
and if the probability were high enough he would, on extreme utilitarian grounds, leave him to drown. The rescuer, however, has not
time. He trusts to his instincts and dives in and rescues the man.
And this trusting to instincts and to moral rules can be justified on
extreme utilitarian grounds. Furthermore, an extreme utilitarian who
knew that the drowning man was Hitler would nevertheless praise the
rescuer, not condemn him. For by praising the man he is strengthening
a courageous and benevolent disposition of mind, and in general this
disposition has great positive utility. (Next time, perhaps, it will be

Winston Churchill that the man saves!) We must never forget that an extreme utilitarian may praise actions which he knows to be wrong. Saving Hitler was wrong, but it was a member of a class of actions which are generally right, and the motive to do actions of this class is in general an optimific one. In considering questions of praise and blame it is not the expediency of the praised or blamed action that is at issue, but the expediency of the praise. It can be expedient to praise an inexpedient action and inexpedient to praise an expedient one.

Lack of time is not the only reason why an extreme utilitarian may, on extreme utilitarian principles, trust to rules of common sense morality. He knows that in particular cases where his own interests are involved his calculations are likely to be biased in his own favour. Suppose that he is unhappily married and is deciding whether to get divorced. He will in all probability greatly exaggerate his own unhappiness (and possibly his wife's) and greatly underestimate the harm done to his children by the break up of the family. He will probably also underestimate the likely harm done by the weakening of the general faith in marriage vows. So probably he will come to the correct extreme utilitarian conclusion if he does not in this instance think as an extreme utilitarian but trusts to common sense morality.

There are many more and subtle points that could be made in connexion with the relation between extreme utilitarianism and the morality of common sense. All those that I have just made and many more will be found in Book IV Chapters 3–5 of Sidgwick's *Methods of Ethics*. I think that this book is the best book ever written on ethics, and that these chapters are the best chapters of the book. As they occur so near the end of a very long book they are unduly neglected. I refer the reader, then, to Sidgwick for the classical exposition of the relation between (extreme) utilitarianism and the morality of common sense. One further point raised by Sidgwick in this connexion is whether an (extreme) utilitarian ought on (extreme) utilitarian principles to propagate (extreme) utilitarianism among the public. As most people are not very philosophical and not good at empirical calculations, it is probable that they will most often act in an extreme utilitarian way if they do not try to think as extreme utilitarians. We have seen how easy it would be to misapply the extreme utilitarian criterion in the case of divorce. Sidgwick seems to think it quite probable that an extreme utilitarian should not propagate his doctrine too widely. However, the great danger to humanity comes nowadays on the plane of public morality—not private morality. There is a greater danger to humanity from the hydrogen bomb than from an increase of the divorce rate, regrettable though that might be, and there seems no doubt that extreme utilitarianism makes for good sense in international relations. When France walked out of the United Nations because she did not wish Morocco discussed, she said that she was within her rights because Morocco and Algiers are part of her metropolitan territory and nothing to do with U.N. This was clearly a legalistic if not superstitious argument. We should not be concerned with the so-called 'rights' of France or any other country but with whether the cause of humanity would best be served by discussing Morocco in U.N. (I am not saying that the answer to this is 'Yes'. There are good grounds for supposing that more harm than good would come by such a discussion.) I myself have no hesitation in saying that on extreme utilitarian principles we ought to propagate extreme utilitarianism as widely as possible. But Sidgwick had respectable reasons for suspecting the opposite.

The extreme utilitarian, then, regards moral rules as rules of thumb and as sociological facts that have to be taken into account when deciding what to do, just as facts of any other sort have to be taken into account. But in themselves they do not justify any action.

III

The restricted utilitarian regards moral rules as more than rules of thumb for short-circuiting calculations of consequences. Generally, he argues, consequences are not relevant at all when we are deciding what to do in a particular case. In general, they are relevant only to deciding what rules are good reasons for acting in a certain way in particular cases. This doctrine is possibly a good account of how the modern unreflective twentieth century Englishman often thinks about morality, but surely it is monstrous as an account of how it is most rational to think about morality. Suppose that there is a rule R and that in 99% of cases the best possible results are obtained by acting in accordance with R. Then clearly R is a useful rule of thumb; if we have not time or are not impartial enough to assess the consequences of an action it is an extremely good bet that the thing to do is to act in accordance with R. But is it not monstrous to suppose that if we *have* worked out the consequences and if we have perfect faith in the impartiality of our calculations, and if we *know* that in this instance to break R will have better results than to keep it, we should nevertheless obey the rule? Is it not to erect R into a sort of idol if we keep it when breaking it will prevent, say, some avoidable misery? Is not this a form of superstitious rule-worship (easily explicable psychologically) and not the rational thought of a philosopher?

The point may be made more clearly if we consider Mill's comparison of moral rules to the tables in the nautical almanack. (*Utilitarianism*, Everyman Edition, pp. 22-23). This comparison of Mill's is adduced by Urmson as evidence that Mill was a restricted utilitarian, but I do not think that it will bear this interpretation at all. (Though I quite agree with Urmson that many other things said by Mill are in harmony with restricted rather than extreme utilitarianism. Probably Mill had never thought very much about the distinction and was arguing for utilitarianism, restricted or extreme, against other and quite non-utilitarian forms of moral argument.) Mill says: 'Nobody argues that the art of navigation is not founded on astronomy, because sailors cannot wait to calculate the Nautical Almanack. Being rational creatures, they go out upon the sea of life with their minds made up on the common questions of right and wrong, as well as on many of the far more difficult questions of wise and foolish . . . . Whatever we adopt as the fundamental principle of morality, we require subordinate principles to apply it by'. Notice that this is, as it stands, only an argument for subordinate principles as rules of thumb. The example of the nautical almanack is misleading because the information given in the almanack is in all cases the same as the information one would get if one made a long and laborious calculation from the original astronomical data on which the almanack is founded. Suppose, however, that astronomy were different. Suppose that the behaviour of the sun, moon and planets was very nearly as it is now, but that on rare occasions there were peculiar irregularities and discontinuities, so that the almanack gave us rules of the form 'in 99% of cases where the observations are such and such you can deduce that your position is so and so'. Furthermore, let us suppose that there were methods which enabled us, by direct and laborious calculation from the original astronomical data, not using the rough and ready tables of the almanack, to get our correct position in 100% of cases. Seafarers might use the almanack because they never had time for the long calculations and they were content with a 99% chance of success in calculating their positions. Would it not be absurd, however, if they *did* make the direct calculation, and finding that it disagreed with the almanack calculation, nevertheless they ignored it and stuck to the almanack conclusion? Of course the case would be altered if there were a high enough probability of making slips in the direct calculation: then we might stick to the almanack result, liable to error though we knew it to be, simply because the direct calculation would be open to error for a different reason, the fallibility of the computer. This would be analogous to the case of the extreme utilitarian who abides by the conventional rule against the dictates of his utilitarian calculations simply because he thinks that his calculations are probably affected by personal bias. But if the navigator were sure of his direct calculations would he not be foolish to abide by his almanack? I conclude, then, that if we change our suppositions about astronomy and the almanack (to which there are no exceptions) to bring the case into line with that of morality (to whose rules there are exceptions), Mill's example loses its appearance of supporting the restricted form of utilitarianism. Let me say once more that I am not here concerned with how ordinary men think about morality but with how they ought to think. We could quite well imagine a race of sailors who acquired a superstitious reverence for their almanack, even though it was only right in 99% of cases, and who indignantly threw overboard any man who mentioned the possibility of a direct calculation. But would this behaviour of the sailors be rational?

Let us consider a much discussed sort of case in which the extreme utilitarian might go against the conventional moral rule. I have promised to a friend, dying on a desert island from which I am subsequently rescued, that I will see that his fortune (over which I have control) is given to a jockey club. However, when I am rescued I decide that it would be better to give the money to a hospital, which can do more good with it. It may be argued that I am wrong to give the money to the hospital. But why? (a) The hospital can do more good with the money than the jockey club can. (b) The present case is unlike most cases of promising in that no one except me knows about the promise. In breaking the promise I am doing so with complete secrecy and am doing nothing to weaken the general faith in promises. That is, a factor, which would normally keep the extreme utilitarian from promise breaking even in otherwise unoptimific cases, does not at present operate. (c) There is no doubt a slight weakening in my own character as an habitual promise keeper, and moreover psychological tensions will be set up in me every time I am asked what the man made me promise him to do. For clearly I shall have to say that he made me promise to give the money to the hospital, and, since I am an habitual truth teller, this will go very much against the grain with me. Indeed I am pretty sure that in practice I myself would keep the promise. But we are not discussing what my moral habits would probably make me do; we are discussing what I ought to do. Moreover, we must not forget that even if it would be most rational of me to give the money to the hospital it would also be most rational of you to punish or condemn me if you did, most improbably, find out the truth (e.g. by finding a note washed ashore in a bottle). Furthermore, I would agree that though it was most rational of me to give the money to the hospital it would be most rational of you to condemn me for it. We revert again to Sidgwick's distinction between the utility of the action and the utility of the praise of it.

Many such issues are discussed by A. K. Stout in the article to which I have already referred. I do not wish to go over the same ground again, especially as I think that Stout's arguments support my own point of view. It will be useful, however, to consider one other example that he gives. Suppose that during hot weather there is an edict that no water must be used for watering gardens. I have a garden and I reason that most people are sure to obey the edict, and that as the amount of water that I use will be by itself negligible no harm will be done if I use the water secretly. So I do use the water, thus producing some lovely flowers which give happiness to various people. Still, you may say, though the action was perhaps optimific, it was unfair and wrong.

There are several matters to consider. Certainly my action should be condemned. We revert once more to Sidgwick's distinction. A right action may be rationally condemned. Furthermore, this sort of offence is normally found out. If I have a wonderful garden when everybody else's is dry and brown there is only one explanation. So if I water my garden I am weakening my respect for law and order, and as this leads to bad results an extreme utilitarian would agree that I was wrong to water the garden. Suppose now that the case is altered and that I can keep the thing secret: there is a secluded part of the garden where I grow flowers which I give away anonymously to a home for old ladies. Are you still so sure that I did the wrong thing by watering my garden? However, this is still a weaker case than that of the hospital and the jockey club. There will be tensions set up within myself: my secret knowledge that I have broken the rule will make it hard for me to exhort others to keep the rule. These psychological ill effects in myself may be not inconsiderable: directly and indirectly they may lead to harm which is at least of the same order as the happiness that the old ladies get from the flowers. You can see that on an extreme utilitarian view there are two sides to the question.

So far I have been considering the duty of an extreme utilitarian in a predominantly non-utilitarian society. The case is altered if we consider the extreme utilitarian who lives in a society every member, or most members, of which can be expected to reason as he does. Should he water his flowers now? (Granting, what is doubtful, that in the case already considered he would have been right to water his flowers.) As a first approximation, the answer is that he should not do so. For since the situation is a completely symmetrical one, what is rational for him is rational for others. Hence, by a *reductio ad absurdum* argument, it would seem that watering his garden would be rational for none. Nevertheless, a more refined analysis shows that the above argument is not quite correct, though it is correct enough for practical purposes. The argument considers each person as confronted with the choice either of watering his garden or of not watering it. However there is a third possibility, which is that each person should, with the aid of a suitable randomizing device, such as throwing dice, give himself a certain probability of watering his garden. This would be to adopt what in the theory of games is called 'a mixed strategy'. If we could give numerical values to the private benefit of garden watering and to the public harm done by 1, 2, 3, etc., persons using the water in this way, we could work out a value of the probability of watering his garden that each extreme utilitarian should give himself. Let a be the value which each extreme utilitarian gets from watering his garden, and let $f(1)$, $f(2)$, $f(3)$, etc., be the public harm done by exactly 1, 2, 3, etc., persons respectively watering their gardens. Suppose that p is the probability that each person gives himself of watering his garden. Then we can easily calculate, as functions of p, the probabilities that exactly 1, 2, 3, etc., persons will water their gardens. Let these probabilities be $p_1, p_2, \ldots p_n$. Then the total net probable benefit can be expressed as

$$V = p_1\,(a - f(1)) + p_2\,(2a - f(2)) + \ldots p_n\,(na - f(n))$$

Then if we know the function $f(x)$ we can calculate the value of p for which $(dV/dp) = 0$. This gives the value of p which it would be rational for each extreme utilitarian to adopt. The present argument does not of course depend on a perhaps unjustified assumption that the values in question are measurable, and in a practical case such as that of the garden watering we can doubtless assume that p will be so small that we can take it near enough as equal to zero. However the argument is of interest for the theoretical underpinning of extreme utilitarianism, since the possibility of a mixed strategy is usually neglected by critics of utilitarianism, who wrongly assume that the only relevant and symmetrical alternatives are of the form 'everybody does X' and 'nobody does X'.[1]

I now pass on to a type of case which may be thought to be the trump card of restricted utilitarianism. Consider the rule of the road. It may be said that since all that matters is that everyone should do the same it is indifferent which rule we have, 'go on the left hand side' or 'go on the right hand side'. Hence the only *reason* for going on the left hand side in British countries is that this is the rule. Here the rule does seem to be a reason, in itself, for acting in a certain way. I wish to argue against this. The rule in itself is not a reason for our actions. We would be perfectly justified in going on the right hand side if (a) we knew that the rule was to go on the left hand side, and (b) we were in a country peopled by super-anarchists who always on principle did the opposite of what they were told. This shows that the rule does not give us a reason for acting so much as an indication of the probable actions of others, which helps us to find out what would be our own most rational course of action. If we are in a country not peopled by anarchists, but by non-anarchist extreme Utilitarians, we expect, other things being equal, that they will keep rules laid down for them. Knowledge of the rule enables us to predict their behaviour and to harmonize our own actions with theirs. The rule 'keep to the left hand side', then, is not a logical *reason* for action but an anthropological *datum* for planning actions.

I conclude that in every case if there is a rule R the keeping of which is in general optimific, but such that in a special sort of circumstances the optimific behaviour is to break R, then in these circumstances we should break R. Of course we must consider all the less obvious effects of breaking R, such as reducing people's faith in the moral order, before coming to the conclusion that to break R is right: in fact we shall rarely come to such a conclusion. Moral rules, on the extreme utilitarian view, are rules of thumb only, but they are not bad rules of thumb. But if we *do* come to the conclusion that we should break the rule and if we have weighed in the balance our own fallibility and liability to personal bias, what good reason remains for keeping the rule? I can understand 'it is optimific' as a reason for action, but why should 'it is a member of a class of actions which are usually optimific' or 'it is a member of a class of actions which as a class are more optimific than any alternative general class' be a good reason? You might as well say that a person ought to be picked to play

---

[1][This paragraph has been substantially emended by the author. Ed.]

for Australia just because all his brothers have been, or that the Australian team should be composed entirely of the Harvey family because this would be better than composing it entirely of any other family. The extreme utilitarian does not appeal to artificial feelings, but only to our feelings of benevolence, and what better feelings can there be to appeal to? Admittedly we can have a pro-attitude to anything, even to rules, but such artificially begotten pro-attitudes smack of superstition. Let us get down to realities, human happiness and misery, and make these the objects of our pro-attitudes and anti-attitudes.

The restricted utilitarian might say that he is talking only of *morality*, not of such things as rules of the road. I am not sure how far this objection, if valid, would affect my argument, but in any case I would reply that as a philosopher I conceive of ethics as the study of how it would be *most rational* to act. If my opponent wishes to restrict the word 'morality' to a narrower use he can have the word. The fundamental question is the question of rationality of action *in general*. Similarly if the restricted utilitarian were to appeal to ordinary usage and say 'it might be most rational to leave Hitler to drown but it would surely not be *wrong* to rescue him', I should again let him have the words 'right' and 'wrong' and should stick to 'rational' and 'irrational'. We already saw that it would be rational to praise Hitler's rescuer, even though it would have been most rational not to have rescued Hitler. In ordinary language, no doubt, 'right' and 'wrong' have not only the meaning 'most rational to do' and 'not most rational to do' but also have the meaning 'praiseworthy' and 'not praiseworthy'. Usually to the utility of an action corresponds utility of praise of it, but as we saw, this is not always so. Moral language could thus do with tidying up, for example by reserving 'right' for 'most rational' and 'good' as an epithet of praise for the motive from which the action sprang. It would be more becoming in a philosopher to try to iron out illogicalities in moral language and to make suggestions for its reform than to use it as a court of appeal whereby to perpetuate confusions.

One last defence of restricted utilitarianism might be as follows. 'Act optimifically' might be regarded as itself one of the rules of our system (though it would be odd to say that this rule was justified by its optimificality). According to Toulmin (*The Place of Reason in Ethics*, pp. 146–8) if 'keep promises', say, conflicts with another rule we are allowed to argue the case on its merits, as if we were extreme utilitarians. If 'act optimifically' is itself one of our rules then there will always be a conflict of rules whenever to keep a rule is not itself optimific. If this is so, restricted utilitarianism collapses into extreme utilitarianism. And no one could read Toulmin's book or Urmson's article on Mill without thinking that Toulmin and Urmson are of the opinion that they have thought of a doctrine which does *not* collapse into extreme utilitarianism, but which is, on the contrary, an improvement on it.

NOTES ON THE CONTRIBUTORS

C. L. STEVENSON is a Professor of Philosophy at the University of Michigan. His very influential book *Ethics and Language* was published in 1945, and he has written many articles, mostly on ethics, in philosophical periodicals.

G. E. MOORE, who died in 1958, was Professor of Philosophy at Cambridge from 1925 to 1939, and taught during the last war at many universities in America. His writings, among the most influential of the present century, include *Principia Ethica* (1903), *Some Main Problems of Philosophy* (1953), *Philosophical Papers* (1959), and *Philosophical Studies* (2nd. edn., 1960).

W. K. FRANKENA is a Professor of Philosophy at the University of Michigan. His book *Ethics* was published in 1963.

P. T. GEACH, who taught for some years at the University of Birmingham, is now Professor of Philosophy at the University of Leeds. Among his publications are *Mental Acts* (1960), and *Reference and Generality* (1962).

R. M. HARE, now White's Professor of Moral Philosophy at Oxford, was formerly a Fellow of Balliol College. His books *The Language of Morals* (1952) and *Freedom and Reason* (1963) have been an important influence on recent developments in ethical theory.

PHILIPPA FOOT, the editor of this volume, is Senior Research Fellow of Somerville College, Oxford, and has taught at universities in America.

JOHN R. SEARLE is a Professor of Philosophy in the University of California at Berkeley. His book *Speech Acts* appeared in 1969, and he is editing *The Philosophy of Language* in the present series.

J. O. URMSON is a Fellow of Corpus Christi College, Oxford, and was formerly Professor of Philosophy at Dundee. His book *Philosophical Analysis* was published in 1956, and he edited the late J. L. Austin's William James lectures, *How to Do Things with Words* (1962).

J. D. MABBOTT was President of St. John's College, Oxford, from 1963 to 1969 and was formerly a Fellow of that College. His publications include *The State and the Citizen* (2nd edn., 1952), and *Introduction to Ethics* (1966).

JOHN RAWLS, until recently Professor of Philosophy at the Massachusetts Institute of Technology, is now at Harvard. His writings on ethical theory have been very influential.

J. J. C. SMART is Hughes Professor of Philosophy at the University of Adelaide. His book *Philosophy and Scientific Realism* was published in 1963.

BIBLIOGRAPHY

(not including material in this volume)

I. BOOKS

AUSTIN, J. L., *How to do Things with Words* (Clarendon Press, Oxford, 1962).

AYER, A. J., *Language, Truth and Logic* (Gollancz, London, 1936. Second Edition 1946).

BAIER, K., *The Moral Point of View: A Rational Basis of Ethics* (Cornell University Press, Ithaca, N.Y., 1958).

HARE. R. M., *The Language of Morals* (Clarendon Press, Oxford, 1952).

HARE, R. M., *Freedom and Reason* (Clarendon Press, Oxford, 1963).

LYONS, D., *Forms and Limits of Utilitarianism* (Clarendon Press, Oxford, 1965).

MOORE, G. E., *Principia Ethica* (Cambridge University Press, Cambridge, 1903).

MOORE, G. E., *Ethics* (Home University Library, Williams and Norgate, London, 1912).

NOWELL-SMITH, P. H., *Ethics* (Penguin Books, 1954. Blackwells, Oxford, 1957).

OGDEN, C. K. and RICHARDS, I. A., *The Meaning of Meaning* (Kegan Paul, London, 1923).

PRICHARD, H. A., *Moral Obligation: Essays and Lectures* (Clarendon Press, Oxford, 1949).

ROSS, W. D., *The Right and the Good* (Clarendon Press, Oxford, 1930).

ROSS, W. D., *Foundations of Ethics* (Clarendon Press, Oxford, 1939).

SCHILPP, P. A., (ed.), *The Philosophy of G. E. Moore* (Northwestern University Press, Evanston, 1942. Second Edition 1952, Tudor Publishing Company, New York).

SCHLICK, M., *The Problems of Ethics* (Prentice Hall, New York, 1938).

SINGER, M. G., *Generalisation in Ethics* (Eyre and Spottiswoode, London, 1963).

STEVENSON, C. L., *Ethics and Language* (Yale University Press, New Haven, 1945).

STEVENSON, C. L., *Facts and Values: Studies in Ethical Analysis* (Yale

University Press, New Haven, 1963).

WARNOCK, M., *Ethics Since 1900* (Clarendon Press, Oxford, 1960).

WILLIAMS, B. and MONTEFIORE, A., *British Analytic Philosophy* (Routledge and Kegan Paul, London, 1966).

ZIFF, P., *Semantic Analysis* (Cornell University Press, Ithaca, N.Y., 1960).

II. ARTICLES

(1) *Relevant to Numbers I–VIII in this volume.*

ANSCOMBE, G. E. M. A., 'On Brute Facts', *Analysis* (1958).

BAIER, K., and TOULMIN, S. E., 'On Describing', *Mind* (1952).

BARNES, W., 'Ethics Without Propositions', *Proceedings of the Aristotelian Society* (1948–9).

BLACK, M., 'Some Questions about Emotive Meaning', *Philosophical Review* (1964).

BLACK, M., 'The Gap Between "Is" and "Should"', *Philosophical Review* (1964).

BRANDT, R. B., 'The Emotive Theory of Ethics', *Philosophical Review* (1950).

COHEN, M. F., '"Is and Should": An Unbridged Gap', *Philosophical Review* (1965).

DIGGS, B. J., 'A Technical Ought', *Mind* (1960).

DUNCAN-JONES, 'Good Things and Good Thieves', *Analysis* (1966).

FLEW, A. 'On not deriving "ought" from "is"', *Analysis* (1964).

FINDLAY, J. N., 'Morality by Convention', *Mind* (1944).

FOOT, P. R., 'Moral Arguments', *Mind* (1958).

FOOT, P. R., 'Goodness and Choice', *Aristotelian Society Supplementary Volume*, XXXV (1961).

GARDINER, P. L., 'On Assenting to a Moral Principle', *Proceedings of the Aristotelian Society* (1954–5).

GEWIRTH, A., 'Meanings and Criteria in Ethics', *Philosophy* (1963).

HARE, R. M., 'Universalisability', *Proceedings of the Aristotelian Society* (1954–5).

HARE, R. M., 'Descriptivism', *Annual Philosophical Lecture, Henrietta Hertz Trust, British Academy* (1963).

MACINTYRE, A., 'Hume on "Is" and "Ought"' *Philosophical Review* (1959).

MONTEFIORE, A., 'Goodness and Choice', *Aristotelian Society Supplementary Volume*, XXXV (1961).